A TOTAL PROGRAM
TO STRENGTHEN AND
EXPAND YOUR MOST
IMPORTANT RESOURCE

BOOST YOUR BRAIN POWER

By Ellen Michaud,
Russell Wild, and
the Editors of
Prevention
Magazine

MJF BOOKS

NEW YORK

Published by MJF Books
Fine Communications
Two Lincoln Square
60 West 66th Street
New York, NY 10023

Library of Congress Catalog Card Number 93-77372
ISBN 1-56731-026-5

This edition published by arrangement with Rodale Press, Inc.

Manufactured in the United States of America

MJF Books and the MJF colophon are trademarks of Fine Creative
Media, Inc.

10   9   8   7   6   5   4

Credits

The quiz in "You're Only as Young as You Score on This Test" on pages 16–19 is reprinted by permission of the Maharishi Ayur-Veda Foundation. For a detailed discussion of aging risk factors, please refer to *Perfect Health*, by Deepak Chopra, M.D. (Harmony Books, 1990).

The quiz in "What Turns Your Memory On?" on page 82 is reprinted by permission of Rodale Press, Inc. from *Total Recall*, by Joan Minninger. Copyright © 1984 by Joan Minninger.

Portions of chapter 5 are reprinted by permission of Harcourt Brace Jovanovich, Inc., from *Intelligence Applied: Understanding and Increasing Your Intellectual Skills*, by Robert J. Sternberg, copyright © 1986 by Harcourt Brace Jovanovich, Inc., and by permission of Viking Penguin, Inc., from *The Triarchic Mind*, by Robert J. Sternberg, copyright © 1988 by Viking Penguin, Inc.

The suggestions in "Write for a Specific Period of Time" on pages 162–63 are reprinted by arrangement with Shambhala Publications, Inc. from *Writing Down the Bones*, by Natalie Goldberg. Copyright © 1986.

The dialogue on pages 265–66 is reprinted by permission of Vintage Books from *Knots*, by R. D. Laing. Copyright © 1970 by The R. D. Laing Trust.

The quotation on page 284 is reprinted by permission of John Wiley & Sons from *Do's and Taboos around the World*, by Roger Axtell. Copyright © 1988 by the Parker Pen Co.

Some quotes in "The Art of Being Vague" on pages 264–65 are reprinted by permission of Meadowbrook Press from *Lexicon of Intentionally Ambiguous Recommendations (LIAR)*, by Robert Thornton. Copyright © 1988 by Robert Thornton.

The quiz in "How Good Is Your Intuition?" on pages 292–94 is reprinted by permission of Sage Publications, Inc., from *Intuition in Organizations*, by Weston Agor. Copyright © 1989 by Sage Publications, Inc.

Some of the material in the tables on pages 30 and 236 was adapted from *The Essential Guide to Prescription Drugs*, by John W. Long, M.D. (New York: Harper & Row, 1990).

The puzzles on pages 60, 114, 145, 183, 245, 285, 305, 327, 355, 379, 403, 433, and 453, are reprinted by permission of Addison-Wesley Publishing Co., Inc., from *Mensa Genius Quiz-a-Day Book*, by Abbie F. Salny and the Members of Mensa. Copyright © 1989 by Abbie F. Salny.

Editor: **Debora Tkac**

Writers: **Ellen Michaud: Chapters 1, 2, 3, 4, 5, 7, and 13
Russell Wild: Chapters 6, 8, 10, 11, 12, 14, 15, 16, and 17**

Contributing Writers: **Don Barone, Sid Kirchheimer (Chapter 9), William LeGro, Judith Lin, Porter Shimer**

Research Chief: **Ann Gossy**

Researchers and Fact-Checkers: **Anne Castaldo, Christine Dreisbach, Paris Mihely-Muchanic, Cynthia Nickerson**

Production Editor: **Jane Sherman**

Copy Editor: **Laura Stevens**

Indexer: **Ed Yeager**

Cover and Interior Designer: **Denise M. Shade**

Illustrator: **Kathi Ember**

Office Personnel: **Karen Earl-Braymer, Roberta Mulliner**

Contents

CONTENTS

An Essential Mind-Building Skill ▪ Jane, Meet Dick ▪ Keeping
Friendship in Repair ▪ Communicating beyond Words ▪ Intimates and
Other Strangers ▪ Communication in Special Relationships ▪ All in the
Family ▪ The Business Side of Communication ▪ Crossing Cultural
Borders ▪ The Universal Signal

Chapter 11
Intuition
Tools That Tap Your Inner Voice ....
Two Schools of Thought ▪ You're Only As Intuitive As You Feel
▪ Fertile Surroundings, Fertile Thoughts ▪ Intuition Comes to Some
Easier Than Others ▪ It Has Changed the Course of History ▪ It's a
Little Like Swimming ▪ Into the Deepness of Your Mind ▪ An Intuition
You Can Trust ▪ What's the Big Deal?

Chapter 12
Mental Energy
Feel the Flow of Enthusiasm ....
The Brain in the Energetic Lane ▪ Energy Is a State of Mind ▪ A
Deeper Sense of Self ▪ Sh-h-h-h-h. Mind at Work ▪ The Will to Succeed
▪ Of Body and of Mind

Chapter 13
The Tranquil Mind
Mental Renewal through Personal Peace ....
The Tranquillity Zone ▪ The Quick Fix ▪ Muscle-Mind Therapy ▪ The
Word on Meditation ▪ "Purr-fect" Solutions

Chapter 14
Dreams
Improve Your Mind While You Sleep ....
Using Dreams to Build Your Mind ▪ The Wonderful World of Lucid
Dreaming ▪ You Can Be a World-Class Sleeper

CONTENTS

The Brain

A Master Mind at Work

The score is 40-all and your sister, who is determined to beat your skirt off at tennis, gets set for her next serve. She's going to smash the ball right through your forecourt, but you know that you can save the set—and turn the match around—if you can just return her serve.

She bounces the ball once, twice, throws it up in the air, stretches, and—THWACK!—comes down on top of that fuzzy green globe of compressed air with 50 years' worth of power. The ball blurs through the hot, dry air straight toward your sweating face. Your entire body springs into action. The strings vibrate with your concentration.

Can you repel the attack? Can you break her serve? Can you hit the ball, send it spinning back over the net, and show her, once and for all, who's the better tennis player?

Well, that depends on your brain.

Brain!?! That's right. Good tennis may be a display of superior strength, natural talent, eagle-eye vision, and good reflexes. But what really defines these qualities—what drives the body—is the brain.

Why Each Mind Is Unique

How well and how fast your brain works, says Leif Finkel, M.D., Ph.D., a neuroscientist at the University of Pennsylvania, depends on the genetic structure of your brain and the experiences you've exposed it to over your own 40, 50, or 60 years.

Everyone's brain starts out a little differently.

"Everybody's brain starts off just a little bit differently," explains Dr. Finkel, "because genetic programming influences how your nervous system gets set up in the first place. If you have a hundred antelopes, for example, they're not all equally fast at running and they don't have the same visual capability. So when the lion comes to chase them, certain ones are going to get away and certain ones aren't."

Billions of brain cells account for our individual talents.

The same difference in ability is true in people, he adds. All of us have billions of densely interconnected brain cells that continually fire electrochemical messages back and forth. But the difference in the way these cells connect is the reason that some of us can do complicated math in our head, others can write novels, and some can ace a tennis serve.

One reason for these different capabilities lies in the visual cortex, an area in the back of the brain that processes images. "There are about two dozen different areas in the visual cortex," says Dr. Finkel, and each has a slightly different task. There's one area that handles color vision, one that handles motion, one that handles depth, one that handles texture, and so on.

Everybody has these same areas, says Dr. Finkel, but in one person the color area is larger while in another it's the texture area that's superior. And each area is so different from one person to another that, in essence, our brains are as individual as our fingerprints.

Your brain is as individual as your fingerprints.

Experience Counts

If you could actually look at your brain, you'd see that it is constantly changing. How this change progresses is directly influenced by the experiences you feed it each and every day of your life. The brain is so malleable in response to what you experience and how you think that it continually reorganizes itself into what amounts to a new structure.

Your brain is in a constant state of change.

Michael Merzenich, Ph.D., a scientist at the University of California at San Francisco, first demonstrated this with monkeys in his lab. Dr. Merzenich figured out which areas of the brain a monkey uses to reach for food, and then, like some ancient cartographer scoping the geography of China, he drew a map of the areas involved. When the map was complete, he trained the monkey to use only one particular finger to get the food, then redrew the map.

The result? When Dr. Merzenich compared the two maps of the monkey's brain—

4

one in which the monkey used his entire hand,
the other in which he used only one finger—
he found that the areas involved in processing
signals from the monkey's overused finger had
grown by 600 percent. Using one particular
part of the monkey's brain over and over had
literally increased that part of the brain sixfold.

Does this happen to people? Yes. The
brain alters its basic structure as though it's in
a constant state of evolution, says Dr. Finkel,
who has observed similar changes in computer
simulations of the human brain. That's why no
two brains act and react exactly alike. Not even
those of identical twins—and especially not
those of rival tennis players.

Brain Hard at Work

To see just how your brain works, let's take
a look at a scenario that tests the mind's ability
to see, think, feel, and react with emotion-
packed, split-second timing.

Imagine that you're driving down a dark,
winding road, listening to the snap of twigs and
the crunch of leaves under your tires. The only
movement you've seen for miles is moonbeams
flickering through bare branches and across a
frost-covered meadow. It's just you alone on
the road.

Or so you thought. Suddenly, without a
sound—without a hint of movement or a moment of warning—a pair of mountain bikes
bursts from the autumn darkness of a side road
and into the halogen glare of your headlights.
They pause, seemingly suspended in the center of your windshield, and then—Scr-e-e-e-ch!

Whump-bhump!—hit a camouflaged pothole and spill over, one right after the other.

Two small boys turn frightened faces toward you, their dark eyes drawn like startled deer to your headlights. You gape back as, in an infinitesimal moment of time, the knowledge of danger begins to surge through your body. Are you going to be able to think and react fast enough to avoid hitting them? In other words, is your brain going to be able to see the danger, feel the fear, analyze your options, and get your body to respond—all in the space of a few heartbeats?

The speed of your brain can mean life or death.

■ *See the Danger*

The basic processes involved in how the brain "sees" is pretty much the same from driver to driver. Dr. Finkel explains it this way: When you're driving down that road, all the automatic functions of your brain are keeping your body going. Your heart's beating, you're breathing at a certain rate, your body temperature's being controlled.

Your brain can compute and relay a series of responses in a split second.

Your cerebellum—a section of the brain located at the base of your skull—is maintaining your posture and keeping you from falling to one side. The parietal cortex—a layer of brain cells extending roughly from ear to ear over the top of your head—is constantly computing what's moving and making minute postural adjustments to keep you and the car in alignment. Still other parts of your brain are making sure your hands make minor adjustments to keep the car on the road. Meanwhile, your eyes are scanning the field around you, drawing

6

your attention to different objects as they come up and then disappear from your field of vision.

Then, all of a sudden, the boys fall off their bikes in front of you. "What happens first," says Dr. Finkel, "is that a very sensitive motion-detection system in the cortex picks up that motion. You don't know what it is, so the next thing that happens is that the signal gets fed into the brain's ocular motor system, which causes your eyes to move so that you have whatever's moving centered on your retina. Once your retina has a good view of what's moving—which takes about 200 milliseconds—it sends the image to the temporal cortex, the part of your brain near your temples which analyzes shape."

No one knows exactly where the identification is made, adds Dr. Finkel, but it involves sections of the brain known as the temporal cortex and the prefrontal cortex—both of which are located around the forehead and both of which are involved in complex behavior. The identification may also involve structures deep inside your brain, the hippocampus and the amygdala, which are involved in long-term memory storage.

In a split second, you get the message: "Danger." And the danger spells fear.

It takes 200 milliseconds for your brain and eyes to communicate.

■ Feel the Fear

Your brain triggers the feeling of fear that washes over you at almost the same instant you recognize the danger. This feeling is actually a chemical reaction—and a very crucial one. It enables your brain to accelerate and

Fear is a chemical reaction.

process visual images in much more detail than usual.

"Fear is simply the word we humans have given to the combination of internal feelings that we are experiencing at the time," says Floyd Bloom, M.D., chairman of neuropharmacology at the Scripps Clinic and Research Foundation in La Jolla, California. "It's your heart racing, your palms sweating, and your blood pressure going up under conditions of unexpected and severe stress."

It's your body's reaction to a group of nerve cells in the part of the brain called the pons—the bridge between the lower brain and the upper brain—which is firing a burst of chemical signals wildly in the brain.

"This allows the brain to 'come to attention,' so to speak," says Dr. Bloom, "and to process the events that are happening at that moment with a more effective signal. This gives us a way of paying special attention to momentary events."

Fear makes you pay special attention to momentary events.

These brain chemicals also give us that sense of unreality that seemingly hovers like slow motion over the experience of impending danger. "Time seems to pass much more slowly because under these conditions your locus ceruleus—a section of the brain that produces chemical bulletins—is processing those events with greater detail and precision" than it normally would, according to Dr. Bloom.

Things seem to happen in slow motion when we're frightened.

■ *Analyze Your Options*

But what part of your brain tells your foot that it's time to hit the brake? Your brain makes decisions in two ways, explains John Duncan, Ph.D., a research scientist at the Medical Research Council in Cambridge, England, where a significant amount of study has been done on driving and the brain.

One way involves processing information through the brain, retrieving it, and matching it up with the particular situation that requires some action. That's how the brain "thinks." But the brain also seems to be able to take a short-cut when it needs to. And it's apparently somewhere along this second, shorter route that the almost-instantaneous decision to brake is made.

The brain may know how to take short-cuts.

■ *Hit the Brake*

Once your brain has decided how to react, its next task is to get that decision from brain to foot. And, fortunately for the children on the road, says Dr. Finkel, your brain has a file of fixed motor programs that it keeps on hand for just this type of emergency.

Your brain has a file of fixed motor programs to respond to various situations.

"There are connections that go from higher-order visual areas over to the motor cortex, where fixed motor programs tell you how to generate a particular action," explains Dr. Finkel. "Actions involve large populations of cells, so the whole motor cortex is going to get activated. But somehow your brain manages to pick out the program that's going to cause your foot to step on the brake."

The motor program sends a signal down through the pyramidal tracts to your spinal cord, where it goes out to peripheral nerves that travel to your leg muscles. The signal causes one set of muscles to contract and others to relax so that your leg extends and your foot pushes the brake to the floor.

At the same time, a signal travels to the nerves that control your hands so you can swerve the wheel away from the kids. And just so you don't end up on the floor when you push the brake or against the door when you wrench the wheel, your brain—now on full alert—fires a volley of chemical signals that keep you upright, in your seat, and ready to take any further evasive action that may be necessary.

Are you going to avert disaster? Yes, you are. Because the brain we just described is providing tip-top performance.

Your brain is like a symphony conductor—directing many things at once.

You Can Boost Your Brainpower

All of the things that went into that split-second performance—the clear thinking, the emotional control, the total recall, even the ability to see out of the corner of your eye—are, to a great degree, qualities you can control. Qualities you can hone and improve. That's because they are all activated by the electrical fibers, cells, fluids, nerves, and hormones that make up the brain. *Your* brain.

Thinking, emotional control, recall, even the ability to see out of the corner of your eye, can be honed.

A brain working in peak condition—as in the scenario above—is able to perform magnificently. But when it's ignored through lack of interest or abused through mental stress, it just muddles along. Or even deteriorates. You get forgetful, make bad decisions, and feel moody.

A brain in peak condition will perform magnificently.

10

Performance starts to slip. You feel tired, fragmented, unfulfilled—a relic in a modern age.

But none of this has to happen. Science has proven that you can improve your mind. You can keep on learning, have a memory like a computer, become a better thinker and decision-maker, even boost your IQ—no matter what your age.

The following pages will show you how.

———————■

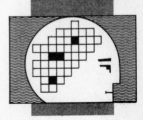

Aging

You Can Prevent Mental Slowdown

When Gene Shirk's tenure as a city mayor to 85,000 Pennsylvania residents was up at the age of 76, he saw it as an opportunity for a career change. By age 90, he had coached the Albright College cross-country running team to seven straight winning seasons while also playing host to a local TV call-in show for high school students. In between he still finds time to keep on top of what he is *really* noted for: his winning tennis game.

W. Edwards Deming first came into the spotlight in post-World War II days when he went to Japan and taught managers, engineers, and scientists how to manufacture quality products. "The Japanese adopted it straight away, and the whole world knows the result," says Deming, now in his early nineties. Deming works 6½ days a week as a consultant, advising corporations

11

nationwide how to improve quality and profitability.

Alyce Michaud is neither corporate giant, athlete, nor Ivy League scholar. She is a suburban-Philadelphia homemaker. But those who know her say she can match wits with the best of them, especially when it comes to arguing politics. In her early eighties, Alyce is a lifelong devotee of world affairs, spending hours each day with her daily newspapers and magazines and tuning in to news broadcasts from around the globe.

Although totally diverse in their backgrounds and interests, these three "seniors" have one thing in common: They're proof that you're only as old as you think—that senility is *not* a natural part of aging.

You're only as old as you think.

The Myth of Senility

Conventional thinking has it that senility is as inevitable in old age as hair loss and wrinkles. But it doesn't have to be that way.

"People age differently," explains Robin Barr, Ph.D., the administrator in charge of cognitive research at the National Institute on Aging. You may be able to say that everyone who reaches age 70 is going to lose some hair. But you cannot say that everyone who reaches age 70 is going to lose his or her ability to think and remember. The idea that everyone is going to grow up, grow old, and grow senile is a myth. And there are plenty of studies to prove it.

Senility is not a natural part of the aging process.

At Pennsylvania State University, for example, researchers tested a group of elderly people to measure the impact of their age on five different mental abilities. "The majority of people showed a decline in one ability by age 80," says Dr. Barr. "But nobody showed a decline in all of them, and some people showed no decline in any.

"It's clear that some older adults do indeed become senile," he adds. "But it's also clear that the majority of older adults do not. It's possible to retain substantial—and *good*—mental functioning until the day you die, even if you live to your eighties or nineties."

Gene Shirk, Edwards Deming, and Alyce Michaud are all proof of that!

In a Penn State study of 80-year-olds, the majority showed a decline in only one of five mental abilities.

The Aging Brain

That doesn't mean that the brain doesn't change as we age. It does—but not as much as most people seem to think, says Michael J. Kushner, M.D., a neurologist at the Wilson Clinic in North Carolina.

"In general, I think there are probably natural changes in the aging brain just as there are natural changes in the muscles, the joints, and the heart as they age," he explains. "It shrinks a little bit, it occupies less volume, the cells have less fluid."

Yet, says Dr. Kushner, these changes are considered relatively minor. For example, once you reach adulthood, you start to lose cells in the area of the brain that processes memory. But given that you have almost five *million* of these cells, losing what amounts to 20 or even 30 percent by the time you're 70 or 80

The brain goes through natural changes as we age.

14

isn't going to have a whole lot of effect on your memory.

But it does have *some* effect. Long-term memory—the mechanism you use to store memoirs of that vacation to Tahiti ten years ago—declines to a degree as you age. So, too, does your ability to solve problems, and the speed at which your brain works. But all this means is that by the time you hit your seventies, you may forget a phone number you don't use very often, hesitate before you recall a name, make decisions a few seconds more slowly, or find it more difficult to grapple with complex issues such as an amended federal income tax form.

But short-term memory—the kind you use to absorb new information when you read a book or watch the news—is apparently not impaired nearly as much. What your short-term memory usually can't handle in later years is overload: You lose your ability to pay attention to more than one thing at a time.

If you were sitting in a classroom at the age of 16 and your best friend leaned over to tell you a secret while the teacher was reading aloud, for example, chances are you'd absorb what the teacher *and* your friend were saying. But if you were sitting in a classroom at the age of 76 and the same thing happened, your diminished ability to divide your attention would mean that you would remember what was said by *either* the teacher *or* your friend.

Why, then, are there so many people shuffling through their seventies and eighties in a state of confusion, forgetfulness, and impaired thinking?

"Disease," says Dr. Kushner succinctly.

Preventable disease—like stroke, high blood pressure, diabetes, and heart disease. They're the demons that get a stranglehold on the brain. It's not aging that wears out the brain; it's the diseases that often go along with aging. The hardening and clogging of arteries caused by these diseases over the years eventually take their toll. Blood flow to the brain diminishes, and with it the nourishing flow of oxygen and food. And without an adequate supply of either, brain cells begin to die in quantities far in excess of the number caused by normal aging.

"Around age 70, people who are in good health are going to remain good neurologically," says Dr. Kushner. But people who have these diseases will begin to feel mental decline.

> Older people who are in good physical health will remain in good mental health.

High-Risk Brain Drain

Mental decline can also come about from a disease of a different sort. It's called disinterest. Disinterest in life.

At particular risk are women without a career who have been recently widowed, says K. Warner Schaie, Ph.D., director of the Pennsylvania State University's gerontology center and past president of the American Psychological Association's division on adult development and aging. When a spouse dies, he says, the tendency is to withdraw from the world and spend a lot of time sitting passively in front of the television instead of going out and interacting with people. Without stimulation, the mind stalls.

(continued on page 20)

You're Only as Young as You Score on This Test

How well are you aging—in body, mind, and spirit? Your answers to the following questions should give you an idea.

The questionnaire was developed by Deepak Chopra, M.D., and is based on lifestyle factors that have been identified to be related to aging. Although it takes only a few minutes to answer, it will give you an estimate of whether you can expect to age successfully—both in years and in mental ability. If you feel you fulfill the criteria of each question, circle the value next to the item. Add up the circled items to get your aging risk profile.

Happiness
1 pt.　　I am generally happy.

Bodily Comfort
1 pt.　　I am comfortable with my body. I like it the way it is. I experience no sensation of dis-ease in any part of it.

Psychological Age
Irrespective of how old I am:
1 pt.　　I have a zest for life.
1 pt.　　I feel youthful.
1 pt.　　I do not allow consideration about my age to get in the way of enjoying myself.

Exercise
1 pt.　　I exercise moderately at least 20 to 30 minutes at least three times per week (preferred exercise is walking, swimming, yoga).

Nutrition
1 pt.　　I feel good about what I eat.
1 pt.　　I enjoy eating.
1 pt.　　I feel energetic after eating.
1 pt.　　I am within 10 percent of my ideal weight.

16

Fear

1 pt.   I don't have any major fears in my life.

1 pt.   Fear of aging does not dominate my awareness.

Drinking and Drug Habits

1 pt.   I drink less than two cups of coffee or tea per day.

1 pt.   I don't drink alcohol.

1 pt.   I don't use recreational drugs or tranquilizers.

Relationships

1 pt.   I have a happy family life.

1 pt.   I get along with peers in the workplace.

1 pt.   I enjoy friendships.

Sleep

1 pt.   I can usually sleep at night for more than 6 hours without resorting to tranquilizers, sleeping pills, or alcohol.

1 pt.   My sleep is restful and I wake up refreshed.

Stress

I do not feel threatened and get tense about:

1 pt.   My physical well-being.

1 pt.   My emotional and psychological well-being.

1 pt.   My financial well-being.

1 pt.   Minor hassles of life, such as getting caught in traffic jams, someone being rude to me, missing an appointment, deadlines, etc.

Life Values

1 pt.   My self-conversation (the chatter that goes on in my head) is dominated by the theme "How can I help?," rather than " Me, Me, Me." In other words, I think of others more often than my own selfish interests.

1 pt.   I like to get involved in community or civic activities.

3 pts.   I like to get involved in global issues.

(continued)

You're Only as Young as You Score—*Continued*

Optimism

1 pt.   I usually see the bright side of things.

1 pt.   I usually perceive problems as potential opportunities.

Humor

1 pt.   I find occasion to laugh every day.

1 pt.   I am able to laugh at myself.

Perception of Time

1 pt.   I am not often in a hurry.

1 pt.   I have a sense of control over my time rather than
allowing time to control me.

1 pt.   I am rarely hassled by time urgency.

Purpose in Life

Define your purpose in life:

_____

_____

5 pts.   If it was easy to fill this out, give yourself 5 points.

Mental Activity

1 pt.   I am mentally active (I enjoy reading, writing, solving problems, keeping up with the news, what is happening in my environment and in the world.)

Experience of Pure Joy

5 pts.   I have moments of pure joy (bliss) without a reason.

Adjustment to Change

1 pt.   I am flexible and can adjust to change easily.

1 pt.   I am not rigidly attached to an idea about how things
have to be.

Challenge

1 pt.   I enjoy challenges.

Commitment

1 pt.   I am able to commit myself to a specific task, project, or job.

1 pt.   I am able to commit myself to a relationship.

Creativity

1 pt.   I seek out opportunities for creative expression.

Inner Silence

5 pts.   I am able to enjoy inner silence (transcendence) regularly on a daily basis.

Job Satisfaction

5 pts.   I love my job.

Scoring

Add up your total points.

46 to 64 points: Exceptional potential to maximize life span.

41 to 45 points: Excellent potential to maximize life span.

30 to 40 points: Good. But you need to pay attention to the missing factors revealed in this quiz. Remember, quality of life translates into quantity of life.

Below 30 points: You should seriously consider rethinking and restructuring your priorities in life as soon as possible.

20

Also at particular risk, says Dr. Schaie, are executives who retire. A busy, stimulating life—full of problems to solve, people to see, and crises to handle—is exchanged for days spent in a chaise lounge beside the pool wondering why life is suddenly dull.

Then one day it happens. They stand in front of the refrigerator and wonder why it's open. Or they'll go to the hardware store and stand by the door trying to remember what it was that they came to buy. Or maybe they won't be able to understand the directions that came with a new lawn mower.

But senility doesn't have to be *your* sentence. Even if it seems that your brain has already reached the point of diminishing returns, it still hasn't reached the point of no return. You can slow mental aging.

The "Use It or Lose It" Syndrome

The prescription for a long-lasting mind is simple: activity.

"The key to avoiding mental decline is to keep your mind active," says Dr. Schaie. You need to work your mind daily. To exercise and tone it the same way you would exercise and tone any muscle that has a tendency to get weaker as you get older.

In fact, it appears that the harder you make your brain work, the better off you will be. In a study conducted several years ago at Harvard University, two groups of men between the ages of 75 and 80 were taken to a ten-acre retreat for a five-day experiment that would mentally take them back in time to 1959. One group was to literally pretend it *was* 1959—to think, talk, write, and act like the people they were back then. They listened to old radio programs, played "The Price Is Right," heard a recorded speech by President Eisenhower, and watched movies such as *Anatomy of a Murder*. The other group was asked to simply reminisce and talk about the year.

The results of this mental time-machine experiment were intriguing. After just one week, the men who were instructed to act out the year—to work their minds the hardest— actually showed *improvement* in their scores on tests of intelligence and reaction time. The other group remained the same or declined in almost every area.

One experiment that physically put a group of men back in time actually resulted in improvement in their brainpower.

Does this mean the brain can actually regain some of the mental abilities it has lost over the years? Quite possibly, especially when you consider the results of a study conducted by Dr. Schaie, which followed hundreds of men and women in the Seattle area for more than 30 years. He found that rigorous mental activity helped improve the minds of those who had already started to show mental deterioration.

In the experiment, he and his colleagues asked those who showed a drop in mental function to undergo five comprehensive 1-hour sessions that focused on abstract reasoning abilities and mental speed. In most cases, says Dr. Schaie, those who went through his program— the majority of whom were between the ages of 64 and 95—were able to bring thinking and reaction time back to where it had been *14 years earlier*. And in some cases, he adds, they boosted it even more.

Although Dr. Schaie's program was quite intensive and required professional guidance, he says it followed a principle you'll be seeing a lot in this book: Use it or lose it.

Here are some of the best ways to keep your mind mentally active.

■ Lift Mental Weights

Giving your mind a problem that makes it perceive, sort, and analyze is similar to an aerobic workout.

Problem solving is to the brain what aerobic exercise is to the body. It's the best way to keep your brain in peak condition. Give your brain a problem to solve and it goes to work. It perceives, it sorts, it remembers, it compares, it analyzes. It thinks and decides.

If you could actually see your brain go through the "exercise" of solving a problem, you would see an explosion of activity as every neural circuit flashed into action. You'd see neurotransmitters zipping back and forth. Capillaries expanding. Blood flow increasing— more oxygen going in, more carbon dioxide going out.

Studies show that your brain will stay younger longer if you exercise.

The result of all this activity? Studies indicate that your brain will stay younger longer, says Nancy Wadsworth Denney, Ph.D., a professor of psychology at the University of Wisconsin at Madison. And your ability to handle complex issues—things that involve both reasoning and remembering—will remain strong five or ten years longer than those of other people your age who don't routinely lift such mental weights.

You'll find specific problem-solving techniques in chapter 5. Here are some other ideas you might enjoy.

■ Take a Mental Mystery Tour

Detective and mystery books do more than keep you entertained. They can also keep you mentally young. But the idea isn't just to read the books, says Dr. Denney. You should also use your own mental muscle to try to solve the mystery before the author makes it obvious.

Television can also be a great medium for exercising this mental task. A good example of a modern mystery that lets you enjoy the challenge is "Columbo." Producers of "Columbo" usually let you know the who-done-it part in the opening scene of the show. The intrigue comes in watching how Columbo is going to solve the mystery. The crime always looks perfect—except that there's always one tiny, seemingly insignificant piece of evidence that will give Columbo what he needs to solve it. Can you find what it is before Columbo?

If you like games, Clue is a great way to play detective—and you get to solve the murder yourself. Not only do you have to figure out who committed the murder, you have to figure out how and where the crime took place. Was it Mrs. Peacock in the ballroom? Colonel Mustard in the study? Professor Plum in the conservatory? And what did they use? A lead pipe? A candlestick? A rope? The only way you can win at Clue is to consider a multitude of options

Use TV, books, and games in ways that will keep your mind young.

(continued on page 28)

Diseases That Age Your Brain

Alzheimer's disease, alcoholism, stroke, and Parkinson's disease attack by killing brain cells, meaning they can make you old before your time. Here's a rundown on each.

Alzheimer's Disease

A diagnosis of Alzheimer's is a grim one. Today, the cause and cure of this all-too-common disorder are unknown, but its outcome is certain. Alzheimer's is usually fatal within 3 to 20 years of onset, and it is now the fourth-ranking killer of adults in the United States, exceeded only by heart disease, cancer, and stroke. About four million Americans have this deadly degenerative brain disease; if you're over 80, there's a better than one-in-five chance of getting it.

"Many years ago, when people lost their memory and became senile as they aged, it was thought that was a natural effect of getting older," says Mark Alberts, M.D., a neurologist at the Alzheimer's Disease Research Center at Duke University Hospital. "But we know now that senility is *not* a normal function of aging. It's not normal to get to be 70 or 80 and not be able to understand and remember things. That's clearly *abnormal*."

Alzheimer's can strike people in their forties or fifties. But it's much more common in people in their eighties.

Autopsies of Alzheimer's victims reveal structural changes. "An Alzheimer's brain shows atrophy. It's much smaller than a normal brain should be." Millions of cells die in the cortex and the hippocampus—in other words, in the thinking, feeling, doing, remembering brain. "In some people it just progresses inexorably. In others it progresses, stabilizes, and then progresses again," Dr. Alberts says.

Generally, there's an early stage of three or four years when memory, judgment, and intellectual abilities begin to fail and emotional imbalance appears. Later, the victim has

24

trouble walking or talking. He may not recognize family members or even know himself when he looks in a mirror. Daily activities like eating, bathing, and grooming become difficult, and incontinence, insomnia, and behavior problems appear. The victim becomes a shell of his former self.

Alcoholism

"About 75 percent of alcoholics develop brain disease," says Ralph Tarter, Ph.D., professor of psychiatry at the University of Pittsburgh School of Medicine. "Alcohol changes the structure of the brain." It destroys both neurons and glial cells, supporting cells involved in nutrition and energy storage that allow the neurons to do their work.

By shrinking and killing neurons, alcohol weakens the brain, frequently causing a kind of dementia that means a permanent loss of intellectual abilities. And the thiamine (vitamin B_1) deficiencies many alcoholics get can cause memory loss, psychosis, and an unsteady gait.

Alcohol's devastating effects can add ten years of premature aging to the brain of those who drink too much. A study of 40 alcoholics, ranging in age from the thirties to the sixties, showed that their performance on neuropsychological tests was closer to that of normal people ten years older than it was to that of their own age group. Reporting on the somber findings, the researchers said, "In a manner of speaking, alcoholism appears to cost the individual about a decade in terms of level of cognitive ability."

Parkinson's Disease

By the time the first symptoms of Parkinson's disease appear, the part of the brain it attacks is 80 percent destroyed. The symptoms are insidiously gradual and progressive: trembling, slowing of movement, stiffness, weakness, loss of bal-
(continued)

Diseases That Age Your Brain—*Continued*

ance. The facial muscles lose their ability to smile or frown; from the inside out the face crystallizes into an empty mask. The mind remains intact but imprisoned. Unfortunately, Parkinson's is all too common: It affects 1 in every 100 Americans over age 60.

Doctors know what happens to the brain in Parkinson's, but they don't know why or how to stop it, says Juan Sanchez-Ramos, M.D., Ph.D., assistant professor of neurology at the University of Miami and a research associate for the National Parkinson's Foundation.

Parkinson's destroys a tiny but uniquely important area deep in the midbrain called the substantia nigra. Many of its neurons contain the neurotransmitter dopamine, a crucial link in a metabolic chain that enables us to move our body. Neurons need both dopamine and another neurotransmitter, acetylcholine, to communicate. Normally these two are in balance, but Parkinson's somehow kills the dopamine cells. Your muscles no longer can do what you tell them because they aren't getting the message.

Mild cases of Parkinson's can be treated with drugs that inhibit acetylcholine. When Parkinson's becomes more severe and disabling, the drug levodopa (L-dopa) is given so neurons can make their own dopamine.

Stroke

A stroke may seem like a bolt from the blue, but for most people it's actually a long time coming. Doctors know what causes more than half a million Americans each year to suffer a stroke. (More than 150,000 of these strokes are fatal.) They know that by the age of 30, one-fourth of all Americans have had the kinds of changes in their brain arteries that set them up for a stroke at any time.

There are two major types of stroke—ischemic and hemorrhagic. In an ischemic stroke, the type that accounts for 70 to 80 percent of strokes, a clot of blood sticks in the artery feeding your brain and starves the cells. In a hemorrhagic stroke, a defective artery bursts in the brain.

In either case, stroke deprives the affected brain cells of food and oxygen, causing them to die.

Unfortunately, treating a stroke is a bit like closing the barn door after the horse gets out. "Prevention is strongly advised," says neurologist John Marler, M.D., of the Division of Stroke and Trauma at the National Institutes of Neurological Disorders and Stroke. "The risk factors to be concerned about are the same as those for heart attack—especially high blood pressure." ———■

and then ask your opponents some hard questions. Even Columbo might find it a mind-building exercise!

■ Get the Story behind the Story

Alyce Michaud starts each day with a cup of coffee—and two hours of news from National Public Radio. While she exercises, does her chores, and putters around the house, she listens to her shortwave radio, which scans for news broadcasts from Moscow to China and other foreign shores. In between she makes sure to fit in the *New York Times* and *Philadelphia Inquirer,* as well as a stack of popular and political magazines. She reads and analyzes them, marking their margins with questions, observations, and objections.

Some might say Alyce is a news junkie, but she'll tell you she's not. It's just her way of staying informed. And, says Dr. Denney, it's also an ideal way of staying mentally active.

"The 5:30 evening news can only give you a superficial account of what's happening," says Dr. Denney. It can't make you an informed individual. And it's not enough to keep you mentally active.

On the other hand, news shows, like "Nightline" or "The MacNeil-Lehrer Report" can give you a more in-depth view of world events. "These shows take a problem and really deal with it, really see what people are thinking about or what's being done to correct it," says Dr. Denney.

It takes more effort than simply watching the evening news to become an informed individual.

The same goes for newspapers. *USA Today* may be popular, but it can only give you a glimpse of the news.

Can the quality of television programming or the difference between, say, the *New York Times* and *USA Today* really make such a difference? "Yes," says Dr. Denney emphatically, it can.

What you watch and what you read can make a difference.

■ *Get Involved in Issues That Keep You Mentally on the Move*

For Gertrude Fox, age 74, staying mentally active means being the environmental watchdog for the Monocacy Creek near Bethlehem, Pennsylvania—the only stream, she says, that supports both wild trout and an industrial city of 70,000 people.

Every week, Fox reads the *Pennsylvania Bulletin,* a state publication that lists any requests for building permits, to see if any developers are planning to work near the Monocacy and its environs. If there are, she works with the developers to protect the environment and attends township meetings to raise questions and issues with the engineers and township supervisors.

A variety of interests in life will help you grow mentally.

As a result of her environmental efforts, she has become one of the early recipients of the Theodore Roosevelt Conservation Award from President Bush.

But you don't have to be an environmental activist—or an activist of any kind—to get your mind working. Whether it's doing volunteer

(continued on page 32)

Drugs Can Cause Pseudo-Senility

An older person who seems to be confused, disoriented, or even delirious is frequently thought to be senile. Yet in many instances, these symptoms may really be the side effects of a drug prescribed for a heart condition, high blood pressure, depression, or Parkinson's disease.

Most drugs your doctor prescribes will do exactly what they're intended to do. But here are a few that are known to occasionally cause confusion, disorientation, or delirium. In some cases, entire classes of drugs carry the potential side effects. If you are taking any of these drugs and are experiencing any of the symptoms mentioned, you should see your doctor.

Drug or Drug Class	Used For/As
Acetazolamide	Glaucoma
Aminophylline	Asthma
Antidepressants	Depression
Antihistamines	Allergies
Atropinelike drugs	Muscle spasms
Barbiturates	Sedatives
Benzodiazepines	Tranquilizers
Bromides	Convulsions
Carbamazepine	Convulsions, nerve pain

Drug or Drug Class	Used For/As
Chloroquine	Malaria/anti-amoebic
Cimetidine	Ulcer
Cortisonelike drugs	Inflammation
Cycloserine	Tuberculosis
Digitalis	Cardiovascular disorders
Digitoxin	Cardiovascular disorder
Digoxin	Cardiovascular disorders
Disulfiram	Alcoholism
Ethchlorvynol	Sedative, hypnotic
Ethinamate	Sedative, hypnotic
Fenfluramine	Obesity
Glutethimide	Sedative, hypnotic
Isoniazid	Tuberculosis
Levodopa	Parkinson's disease
Meprobamate	Anxiety, convulsions
Phenelzine	Antidepressant
Phenothiazines	Psychotherapeutics
Phenytoin	Convulsions
Piperazine	Roundworm, pinworm
Primidone	Convulsions
Propranolol	Cardiovascular disorders
Reserpine	High blood pressure
Scopolamine	Muscle spasms

32

work, serving on the town council, or playing the stock market, say experts, it's important to spread your interests and stay involved in them.

■ *Take Your Mind Back to the Classroom*

One way to stay involved is to resume your education. Going back to school—no matter how long an absence it's been—can be mentally exhilarating.

And it can be particularly beneficial to folks who live alone, because it puts them in a position to meet and interact with other people.

Whether it's a cooking or language class at your local community college or an economics course at your state university, learning something new is one of the best ways there is to keep your mind from getting limp. In fact, say the experts, learning can actually be easier as an adult than it was as a child. (Chapter 7 is filled with ideas on how to make learning a mind-boosting experience.)

■ *Keep in Touch with the Minds of the Young*

When Gene Shirk hosts his TV call-in show for teenagers, he says the discussions range from teenage pregnancies to the latest Middle East crisis. No subject is taboo.

The talk show, he says, is the light of his life because it keeps him in touch with the young, and that in turn keeps him thinking young.

The interaction in a classroom is particularly beneficial to those who live alone.

Being around young people will keep you thinking young.

"Being with young people keeps you young in your thinking," says Shirk. "I think the young people today will straighten the world out—like *we* were supposed to do!"

Fit Body, Fit Mind

There are those who'd say it's not just teenage minds that help keep Gene Shirk mentally young. They'd say it's the track team. And his tennis—the game he's played several times every week as far back as he can remember.

That's because a body that is fit has a mind that is fit.

"Remember that the brain is a physical organ," says Dr. Kushner, "and its fitness is dependent upon the fitness of the body in which it resides." There are studies that support this.

One study at Scripps College in Claremont, California, for example, found that people who exercise routinely actually think better, remember more, and react more quickly than people who don't exercise at all.

One study found that people who routinely exercise actually think better, remember more, and react more quickly than people who don't.

Researchers divided 124 men and women between the ages of 55 and 88 into two groups based upon their level of exercise. The exercise group reported that they spent a minimum of 1 hour and 15 minutes each week at a variety of strenuous activities, including athletics, heavy housework, gardening, walking, and climbing stairs. The nonexercise group reported that they spent no more than 10 minutes each week at such activities.

Then the researchers spent 3 hours in two separate sessions testing the memory, ability to reason, and reaction time of each person. Their findings? The exercisers scored significantly higher on working-memory tests and reasoning tests than did the couch potatoes. And their reaction time was a lot better, too.

The reason that physical exercise can help prevent mental aging is still up for grabs. One theory is that the cardiovascular effects of exercise—the lower blood pressure, lower heart rate, and increased blood flow—actually prevent the degenerative changes in the brain that are associated with natural aging.

■ Free Your Mind of Stress

Another nice side effect of exercise is that it is a proven stress release. And that's good because scientists have found that chronic stress may cause your body to secrete chemicals that can actually destroy brain cells.

Stress can cause your body to secrete chemicals that can destroy brain cells.

Animal studies indicate that chemicals naturally produced in the body are released into the bloodstream when the body is under chronic stress. The chemicals travel to the brain, where they slow the formation of cells that transmit information between other brain cells, then actually kill the brain cells themselves. The result is extensive damage to the area of the brain primarily responsible for processing memory. In fact, a comparison between young laboratory rats that were subjected to high levels of stress chemicals for four months—that's like you being under chronic stress at the office for a couple of years—revealed that the parts of their brains that process memory were so damaged that they resembled the brains of elderly, senile rats.

■ Pick an Exercise That Jogs the Brain

So, what exercise is good for the brain? Rhythmic, continuous exercises like walking, jogging, and swimming, says Bonnie Berger, Ed.D., director of the sports psychology laboratory at the City University of New York's Brooklyn College.

Exercise hard enough to work up a sweat and get the heart pumping for 20 minutes at least three times a week, says Dr. Berger. And if you're elderly or are under medical care for any reason, make sure to get your doctor's okay before starting out.

Exercising three times a week is good for the brain.

Not only might it help prevent mental aging, but you might even notice some mental improvement, especially if you're the forgetful sort. At least that's what Salt Lake City psychologist Robert Dustman, Ph.D., found when he spent four months studying the exercise habits of a group of senior citizens.

Dr. Dustman divided the group, whose members ranged in age from 55 to 70, into three categories: vigorous aerobic exercisers who accelerated their heart rate during a workout, nonaerobic exercisers whose workouts were less vigorous, and those who did no exercise at all.

"The aerobic exercisers showed an improvement in short-term memory, had faster reaction times, and were more creative than nonaerobic exercisers," says Dr. Dustman. And while the nonaerobic exercisers did show

Senior citizens put on an aerobic exercise program showed an improvement in short-term memory skills.

36

small improvement, "the nonexercisers showed absolutely no change in mental ability."

Aging Is All in Your Head

Age is a state of mind, says Deepak Chopra, M.D., a Massachusetts endocrinologist and expert on mind/body interaction. How old you feel has a lot to do with your attitude about how old you are.

Anthropologists studying world populations have found people in such places as the the Andes and south Georgia in the Soviet Union who have lived to be up to 115 and are in excellent physical and mental health. The most important factor in the longevity and mental acuity of these cultures, studies reveal, is that each has a very different concept of what it means to get old.

"To get old in these societies," says Dr. Chopra, "means to get better, to get wise. To run farther and faster."

But the American culture is structured with the expectation that you will grow old between 55 and 65, then die between 80 and 85. "We're caught up in a collective thinking that hypnotizes us into progressing through old age," says Dr. Chopra. By thinking you're old, you're actually programming yourself to be so, he says. But it shouldn't be that way.

In some societies, to grow older means to grow wiser and stronger.

■ *Pick Any Age You Want to Be*

Think back on an age you really liked and enjoyed, suggests Dr. Chopra. Not only an age in which you felt great physically, but also one in which you felt on top of it all mentally.

Was it 40? 50? Maybe 30? Whatever it was pick it—and *be* it. If you liked being 40, there's no reason why you can't think like your 40-year-old self for the rest of your life.

"It's really just that simple," says Dr. Chopra. ————■

It's possible to pick the mental age you want to be and stay there.

PUZZLE POWER

Afraid of growing old and losing your mental edge? Don't be. Studies show no deterioration in various mental skills among those over 60 who keep mentally active. What better time to put your brain on an exercise program than right now! Try this challenging crossword puzzle.

ACROSS

1 Legal guarantees: abbr.
4 Onetime Russian ruler
8 People who don't do this will age more slowly
13 People who eat less red _____ will age more slowly
14 Telegram
15 Kitchen tool
16 This kind of person will retain mental skills in later years: 2 words
19 Musical preface
20 Persuade
21 Summit
22 Right away
24 Deviate from a course
26 Cat's foot
29 Have a chat
32 Kind of exercise that will enhance intellectual skills
37 "_____'s Irish Rose"
39 One way to stay mentally sharp
41 Yogi of baseball
42 Mental ability that improves with age: 2 words
45 Ceramic repair person
46 Reach across
47 Most August babies, astrologically

48 Novel that Michener wrote in his eighties
50 Gets better, they say
52 Sign of Broadway success: abbr.
53 Letters after R
55 Remained inactive
57 Sphere
60 Largest continent
63 People who have more of this in their diets may age more slowly

67 This seems to short-circuit in older people: 2 words
70 Musical sounds
71 Not genuine: abbr.
72 Run in neutral
73 People who keep mentally active stay _____
74 Little bits
75 Recolor

DOWN

1 Jockey's strap
2 President before Wilson
3 Violinist Isaac _____
4 Bill that Jefferson is on
5 Mineral deficiency linked to senility
6 Jason's mythical ship
7 Kind of race
8 Fitness center
9 Shopping center
10 "Yes _____—make up your mind!": 2 words
11 Hold onto
12 Make a mistake
13 1051 in Roman numerals
17 Ill-gotten gains
18 Final or midterm
23 Advise of danger

25 Jack of "Dragnet"
26 Italian food specialty
27 Seething
28 Author Cather
30 Table supports
31 Phi Beta _____
33 Singer/actress Carter
34 Joyce Kilmer poem
35 Knight wear
36 Cowboy's rope
38 December 24 and 31
40 Haul
43 Annoys
44 Unspecified people
49 Rat- _____ (rapping sound)
51 Place for valuables
54 "_____ or lose it": 2 words

56 Shy
57 Expression of dread: 2 words
58 Hollywood reporter Barrett
59 Rabbit or Fox of fiction
61 _____ La Douce
62 In the center of
64 Main part of a letter
65 Author _____ Stanley Gardner
66 Deli bread
67 Urban thoroughfares: abbr.
68 Recipe measure: abbr.
69 The Rockies, for instance: abbr.

To find the answers, see Solution #1 on page 454.

CHAPTER

3

Nutrition

Eat Right, Eat Smart

Your brain is always hungry. Second by second, minute by minute, hour by hour, it voraciously devours the protein, carbohydrates, fats, vitamins, and minerals you eat, then turns them into the membranes and chemicals your brain uses to learn, think, feel, and remember.

How does the brain get its nourishment? Well, let's say you had a steak, baked potato, and salad for dinner last night. The protein from your steak went straight through your stomach to your intestines, where it was broken down into amino acids. The amino acids were absorbed into your bloodstream, then circulated throughout your body to power your muscles and organs. When they got to your brain, however, not all of these amino acids were

41

welcome. No, the brain is as selective as a New York nightclub. When the doors open, only those at the head of the line are permitted in. And if a particular amino acid isn't up front and noticed, chances are it will be ignored and left standing at the door. And just like the nightclub scene, who gains entrance will help set the mood for the night.

Why Amino Acids Are Amazing

In the brain there are two amino acids that compete with one another to enter. One is tyrosine, which your brain uses to make the neurotransmitters dopamine and norepinephrine, two electrically charged chemical messengers that are cruicial to quick thinking, fast reactions, long-term memory, and a feeling of being alert and in control. The other is tryptophan, which your brain uses to make the neurotransmitter serotonin, a chemical messenger that slows your reaction time, impairs concentration, makes you sleepy, and reduces the need to be in control. On the nightclub circuit, tyrosine would be the life of the party and tryptophan the party pooper.

How do these two amino acids affect the activity going on in the brain? If tyrosine gets to your brain first, it will stimulate production of the neurotransmitters that spark mental performance—you'll be ready to function at peak intellectual levels all night long. But if tryptophan gets in ahead of tyrosine, serotonin will steal the show—mental performance will wane and your brain will prepare to shut down early.

Tyrosine will rev you up and tryptophan will relax you.

■ To Stay Alert, Reach for the Protein First

Many scientists believe that you can control the activity level of your mind with the food that you eat. One scientist on the forefront of this theory is Judith Wurtman, Ph.D., a researcher at the Massachusetts Institute of Technology (MIT) and author of *Managing Your Mind and Mood through Food*.

If you want the stimulating effects of tyrosine, she advises, eat the protein portion of a meal (such as meat) before you take a single bite of anything that contains carbohydrates. If you're eating a normal-sized meal, this would be about 3 ounces of meat.

Protein is loaded with tyrosine but only modest amounts of tryptophan, which means tyrosine wins out when it comes to getting to the brain first. It takes carbohydrates to get the tryptophan to the brain, she explains. Just 3 or 4 ounces of protein—meat, fish, or poultry—will send tyrosine zipping off to your brain while the tryptophan lies in wait for the carbohydrates—such as breads, pastas, and potatoes—still sitting on your plate.

If you ate half of last night's steak before you started on the potato, for example, tyrosine would have "made it past the door" and your mind would have been ready for action. If you ate only the potato, ten to one you'd wish you had never left home.

Some scientists believe you can control the activity level of your brain with food.

Choose protein without carbohydrates for a mental lift.

■ Tyrosine Can Clear a Muddled Mind

Tyrosine's ability to boost mental performance is so powerful it may even be able to

Don't Give Your Accountant a Cup of Coffee

A cup of caffeinated coffee in the morning, scientists can vouch, can actually shift your brain into gear and keep it working—for up to 6 hours. But give it too much, they've also proven, and caffeine can backfire.

How much is too much? A lot depends on individual tolerance, but up to two cups is considered mind-boggle-free.

That is, unless you're working with numbers.

In a study at the University of Leicester in Britain, 32 male students were given beverages containing either no caffeine, 125 milligrams of caffeine (about 1 mug of coffee), or 250 milligrams of caffeine (about 2 mugs).

Then the students were subjected to a battery of tests that evaulated how their brain worked. There wasn't much difference in their ability to perform until they got to a numerical test that demanded quick thinking in the midst of confusing or ambiguous information—kind of like what your accountant does when he prepares your taxes. The students who didn't drink any coffee did just fine on the test. But the students who drank the most caffeine had the worst scores. In fact, they had *twice* as many errors as those who had no caffeine. Those who drank just one cup didn't measure up to the nondrinkers either, but they fared a bit better than the two-cup students.

The message in this story? If you have to get up and count, count the coffee out. ———■

overcome the mind-muddling effects of stress.

In a study conducted at the U.S. Army Research Institute of Environmental Medicine in Massachusetts, researchers found that tyrosine countered the effects of stress on the mental performance of soldiers.

Twenty-three soldiers between the ages of 18 and 20 participated in the study, which simulated suddenly airlifting them to 15,500 feet (roughly equivalent to a fast trip up the side of Pike's Peak in the Colorado Rockies) under chilly conditions.

The simulation was done twice, once after half the soldiers had been given a tyrosine capsule and half had been given a placebo (inert pill), then once again so that those who had received the tyrosine now got a placebo and those who had received the placebo got tyrosine.

On the morning of each simulation, the soldiers, given either tyrosine—equal to about 80 percent of a day's normal intake of protein—or a placebo, were left in the test situation for 4½ hours. During each simulation they were given a battery of tests that determined their ability to translate messages into code, chart coordinates on a map, think clearly, and make decisions.

The result? Soldiers who normally experienced stress—headaches, fatigue, muddled thinking, poor performance, depression, and tension—under these conditions found that tyrosine diminished that stress. Soldiers who normally did not find these conditions stressful, however, found that the tyrosine did not affect them one way or the other. But researchers were not surprised.

"You have to be sick or ill or showing the effects of the [stress] condition before tyrosine can be of benefit," explains Louis Banderet, Ph.D., the research psychologist who led the study. "But that shouldn't be too surprising. If

Soldiers who reacted poorly to stressful situations were better able to cope when given tyrosine.

you were testing a treatment for cancer, you would not expect it to benefit people unless they were showing the effects of cancer."

■ Protein Is the Real Power Lunch

Find it hard to believe that you can turn your brain on and off so simply? Scientists have had their doubts as well, particularly regarding the effects of carbohydrates. But in a study conducted at MIT (which has since been duplicated), scientists feel they have finally established a strong case in favor of the theory.

MIT researchers found that a meal high in carbohydrates can impair mental performance.

In one study, researchers gave 40 men between the ages of 18 and 28 a large portion of turkey breast for lunch, then asked them to do some complicated mental tasks. On another day, they gave the same men an equivalent number of calories in the form of wheat starch—almost pure carbohydrate—then gave them another set of mental tasks. The result? Mental performance was "significantly impaired" after the carbohydrate meal. But it was fine after the protein lunch.

■ Carbos Cause Double Trouble after 40

Another study, conducted at Harvard University, indicates that the effects of carbohydrates on the brain are even more dramatic in those over the age of 40. In that study 184 men and women were fed either the same protein-rich turkey used in the other studies or sherbet, which, like the wheat starch, is almost pure carbohydrate. The result of this particular experiment? Much the same as the others, except that scientists also discovered that people over the age of 40 who ate the sherbet had up to twice the difficulty concentrating, remembering, and performing mental tasks as those who had eaten the turkey. People under the age of 40 were less likely to be affected.

What and when you eat can have a bigger impact on mental performance after age 40.

■ *Eat Carbohydrates to Unwind*

Carbohydrates, of course, aren't all bad. In fact, in some situations they can be all good. Remember, scientists say that carbohydrates can slow down your brain. If you've had a long, stressful day and all you want to do is go home, stretch out on the couch, and watch the news, carbohydrates can actually help you unwind.

According to Dr. Wurtman, just 1½ ounces of a carbohydrate is sufficient to relieve the anxiety and frustration of a stressful day.

Just 1½ ounces of a carbohydrate is enough to relieve stress.

In a study jointly conducted by the Chicago Medical School, Temple University, and Texas Tech University, seven healthy women between the ages of 18 and 29 were fed either high protein, high carbohydrate, or a combination of the two for lunch on different days. Blood samples were drawn several times after each lunch, and the women were given tests that measured several factors, including their fatigue and activity levels.

Drowsiness among women who ate the high-carbohydrate lunch was almost *twice* that of women who ate the other lunches, reported the researchers. And their activity levels were cut by 46.7 percent.

One study found the drowsiness level doubled in women when they ate a high-carbohydrate meal.

48

■ *Carbohydrates Stimulate SAD People*

Interestingly, however, eating carbohydrates has the *opposite* effect on someone who suffers from seasonal affective disorder (SAD), a mental disorder characterized by lethargy and depression during the fall and winter seasons. The disorder is linked to shortened daylight hours.

In a study conducted at the National Institute of Mental Health, for example, 16 depressed adults with SAD and 16 healthy adults were each given a high-protein lunch of turkey salad one day and a high-carbohydrate lunch of specially prepared cookies on another. After each lunch, study participants were given blood tests to measure the amount of tryptophan and tyrosine in their blood and another series of tests that indicated mental function and mood.

The results were nothing short of astounding to the researchers, who had come to expect the calming effect of carbohydrates: Not only did the adults with SAD *not* become fatigued after eating the carbohydrate-loaded cookies, they actually became *invigorated*. As a result, scientists are now beginning to suspect that some biochemical abnormality in the brains of people with SAD is what causes the disorder—and that the abnormality may be corrected by eating carbohydrates.

Eating carbohydrates gave a mental lift to people suffering from winter-related depression.

The Tryptophan Problem

Notice that, in all this talk of carbohydrates, researchers are discussing the effects of tryptophan as it occurs naturally. Nobody is talking about tryptophan supplements, which were linked in 1989 and 1990 to a number of deaths from a blood disorder known as eosinophilia-myalgia syndrome (EMS). As a result, manufacturers were asked by the federal Food and Drug Administration to withdraw the supplements from the market.

Although an investigation uncovered the possibility of tainted supplements, there appears to be another good reason to avoid tryptophan supplements. Taking supplemental tryptophan to induce sleep may actually carry side effects similar to those of sleeping pills. "I think that tryptophan has the potential to be addictive," says Joe Tecce, Ph.D., a neuropsychologist at Boston College who has been studying tryptophan for more than five years. He told how he and his staff took moderate amounts of the supplements while conducting nutrition and sleep studies at the Human Nutrition Research Center on Aging at Tufts University. "We found that the morning after we felt like we had hangovers. We all agreed—independently—that we needed that second cup of coffee right away to get started in the morning." And, he adds, "It seems that some of my students at Boston College got hooked on tryptophan to go to sleep."

Interestingly, a full year before the tryptophan-related deaths were reported, Dr. Tecce presented a paper to the American College of Neuropsychopharmacology which indicated that supplemental tryptophan does not seem to be the innocuous substance it was first thought to be.

Tryptophan supplements may have an addictive nature.

■ *It Takes B₆ to Work*

Aside from rousing his suspicion that supplemental tryptophan's effect is both druglike and addictive, Dr. Tecce's work has also revealed a lot about how tryptophan works in the brain. Not only has he confirmed that it can make you sleepy, but he also discovered that it has little if any effect unless it's teamed up with vitamin B_6.

What does this mean to you? It means that you can eat all the carbohydrates in the world to unwind, but it won't do your brain much good unless your diet contains good sources of B_6, such as avocados, bananas, kidney beans, turkey, fish, and most vegetables.

Foods containing carbohydrates and B₆ can help you unwind.

Vitamins for Your Brain

Dr. Tecce's finding that tryptophan needs a boost from B_6 to do its work comes as no surprise to Vernon Mark, M.D., a retired Boston City Hospital neurosurgeon who is president of Boston's Center for Memory Impairment and Neuro-Behavior Disorders. Dr. Mark believes not only that certain vitamins, particularly B_6, can boost your brainpower, but that if you follow the present Recommended Dietary Allowances (RDA) you will not be eating nearly enough to do the job.

Tryptophan needs help from vitamin B₆ in order to work.

■ *You Need More Vitamins to Power Your Brain than to Prevent Disease*

The RDA is a minimum guideline for good nutrition. But what's sufficient for good nutrition is not necessarily sufficient for the development of optimal intellect.

"I'm not suggesting that vitamins or anything else will give you any more intellectual abilities than your genetic capabilities have endowed you with," cautions Dr. Mark. "What I'm saying is that when analyzing vitamin need, particularly for B_6, B_{12}, folate, niacin, and thiamine, nutritionists look at disease states, not mental function."

The brain depends on good nutrition to keep you thinking clearly.

■ Go for B_6—the Best of the B's

For example, your brain's requirement of B_6—important for optimal development and function—is more likely to be around 20 milligrams a day than the RDA of 1.6 milligrams for women and 2 milligrams for men, says Dr. Mark. But there is a catch-22. Vitamin B_6 is toxic in high doses, although 20 milligrams is believed to be within safe limits. It's still best to get your daily allotment from food. Fish, chicken, kidney, liver, pork, and eggs, as well as unmilled rice, soybeans, oats, whole wheat breads and cereals, peanuts, and sweet potatoes, are all good sources of B_6. Liberally include these foods in your diet, says Dr. Mark. And don't take B_6, or any vitamin, as a supplement without approval from your doctor.

Fish, chicken, oats, and wheat are good sources of important vitamin B_6.

■ It Pays to "B" Wise

Although vitamin B_6 is an important B vitamin, says Dr. Mark, the other B's also play very significant roles in brain function. Thia-

B vitamins convert
protein and carbohy-
drates into mental
energy.

mine, riboflavin, and niacin—vitamins B_1, B_2, and B_3 respectively—are used to convert carbohydrates and protein into mental energy, and vitamin B_{12} actually helps in the manufacture and repair of brain tissues. Folate and biotin help your brain manufacture proteins or fats, while pantothenate helps your brain use them.

As with vitamin B_6, the amount Dr. Mark feels you need for healthy brain function is higher than the RDA, although the doses are believed to be within safe limits. Nevertheless, you should not go on this or any supplement program without the consent of your doctor. Below is a table that, according to Dr. Mark, reflects the minimum and optimum amount of each B vitamin necessary for brain function.

■ *Keep Your B's in Balance*

If you eat a well-balanced diet, getting your share of B vitamins should not be a problem. Three-quarters of a cup of cooked oatmeal, for example, will provide at least the minimum amount of thiamine your brain requires, and any kind of meat will give you more than a

Vitamin	Daily Minimum	Daily Optimum
B_6 (pyridoxine)	2 mg	20 mg
B_{12}	6 mcg	100 mcg
Biotin	—	200 mcg
Folate	400 mcg	1 mg
Niacin (B_3)	20 mg	250 mg
Pantothenate	10 mg	20 mg
Riboflavin (B_2)	1.7 mg	10 mg
Thiamine (B_1)	1.5 mg	20 mg

day's supply of B_{12}. Asparagus, spinach, and broccoli are rich sources of folate, while chicken and fish (particularly fresh salmon or tuna) will take care of your need for niacin. You get the idea. Check your diet. If you feel you may not be getting an adequate amount of brain-boosting B's, talk to your doctor about taking a B-complex supplement.

Any kind of meat will give you more than a day's supply of vitamin B_{12}.

■ Vitamin C May Help You Get an A

Another vitamin that helps keep the brain in good working condition is vitamin C, says Dr. Mark. It helps your brain use protein to make the neurotransmitters that keep your brain thinking and remembering, a process that cannot be overestimated—especially in older folks.

Vitamin C can help the thinking process.

In a landmark study at the University of New Mexico Medical School, scientists checked the blood levels of several nutrients—including vitamin C—in 260 well-educated and affluent men and women over the age of 60, then tested the memory and thinking abilities of each.

The tests were not far removed from the kinds of mental skills people use every day. In the memory test, a researcher read a one-paragraph story to each individual, then asked him or her to repeat the story immediately afterward and again 30 minutes later. In the thinking test, they were asked to make various calculations and decisions that tested their ability to solve problems.

After comparing blood levels of vitamin C with test results, the researchers found that the

(continued on page 56)

Think Yourself Thin

For some of us, undernutrition—not getting enough vitamins, minerals, fats, and protein to power the brain—is a major problem. But for others, *over*nutrition—too much of just about everything—is creating a whole new class of fatheads.

Yet overeating is something that starts in your head. It starts, says endocrinologist Deepak Chopra, M.D., when your mind doesn't listen to your body. When it doesn't hear the internal message that says, "No, thank you." Or the ones that say, "Enough."

How can you tune in to those messages? Here are eight tips from Dr. Chopra that will help you listen in on the hotline between body and mind. If you really pay attention to what your body is saying, he promises, within six weeks you'll normalize your eating. And that means that excess pounds will begin to evaporate effortlessly into the cosmos.

Get in touch with the physical sensation of hunger. Most of us aren't forced to experience what it really feels like to be hungry, so we don't really know what it's like. Yet it's one of the ways the body talks to the mind. So go hungry once in a while just so you can tune into the body/mind conversation.

Put your hands on your stomach when you're thinking of eating and close your eyes. Then promise yourself you won't feel foolish when you ask your stomach flat out: "Are you hungry?" Put the answer—and yes, there will be an answer—on a scale of one to ten. One means your tummy is totally empty, five means it feels good, and ten means it's so stuffed you feel sick. You should eat at one or two on the scale, says Dr. Chopra, and stop at five.

Eat only when you feel hungry. Don't let a clock dictate when you eat. Instead, listen to your stomach.

Eat no more than the equivalent of two handfuls of food. That's really all your stomach can comfortably hold. Any more is totally unnecessary.

Do not put any food in your mouth until the previous bite has gone to your stomach. Too many people rush through their meals without realizing what or how much they've eaten. By savoring each bite and eating slowly, you'll find you can get by on much less.

Keep a log of when you eat. Include both the time you started and the time you stopped.

Don't fight natural cravings. If you still have the urge to eat after a meal, wait 5 minutes and then ask your stomach once again if it's hungry. Eighty percent of all cravings will disappear within that time, says Dr. Chopra. If they don't, go ahead and eat a little more. Otherwise you'll start to feel stressed, and that can play havoc with your overall health.

Experience the six different tastes. If you constantly crave more food than your stomach tells you it needs, your body is yammering at you not because it needs more food but because it needs more variety. Your body needs a variety of foods that are reflected in these six different tastes, says Dr. Chopra: sweet, sour, salty, pungent, bitter, and astringent.

Dr. Chopra defines these tastes in an unusual way. Sweet foods, he says, include sugar, rice, milk, poultry, and fish. Sour foods include cheese and lemons, grapes, and other sour fruits. Salty foods, of course, are anything with salt. Pungent foods are mostly spiced with such flavors as pepper, cumin, ginger, onion, and garlic, while bitter foods include spinach and other green-leaved vegetables. Astringent foods include beans, lentils, and foods flavored with turmeric.

If you're trying to lose weight, adds Dr. Chopra, you're less likely to have satisfied your body's need for a sweet food. So begin your meal with dessert and get that particular taste taken care of first. ———■

56

One study found those who had the most trouble thinking and remembering also had low levels of vitamin C.

lower the blood levels of vitamin C, the lower the scores on both tests. And vitamin C was the only nutrient measured that simultaneously affected both thinking and remembering.

Want to keep *your* scores from sinking? It may help to keep up on your vitamin C, says Dr. Mark. Fruits and vegetables, most notably broccoli, bell peppers, collards, oranges, and grapefruit, are abundant in vitamin C. Much of the vitamin C content of fruits and vegetables is lost in cooking, so eat them raw whenever possible.

■ Consider a Multivitamin an Insurance Policy

Now you know what your brain needs to thrive. But what happens when it's not getting it? Deficiencies can be so subtle, warn researchers, that they can easily go undetected.

Children given a multivitamin increased nonverbal IQ by 10 points.

In a British study of 90 apparently healthy, well-fed schoolchildren between the ages of 12 and 13, for example, scientists found that giving a simple multivitamin to one group of children over an eight-month period increased nonverbal IQ by nearly 10 points. Children who did not receive the supplement did not increase their IQ's. Apparently, concluded the researchers, the students must have had undetected vitamin or mineral deficiencies that had significantly impaired their mental performance—even though they appeared to be in otherwise perfect condition.

If you want to take a multivitamin as an insurance policy, check with your doctor first.

The Mineral Message

Scientists have barely begun to study the effects of various minerals on the brain. But if their early studies are any indication, minerals are as important to your brain as vitamins. Scientists believe they are necessary for an enzyme function that acts as the stimulus or catalyst for the various chemical messengers—neurotransmitters—that enable you to remember, think, and feel emotion.

Minerals are just as important as vitamins when it comes to mental performance.

■ Get Your Share of the Mind Minerals

James Penland, Ph.D., a research psychologist at the United States Department of Agriculture's Grand Forks Human Nutrition Research Center in North Dakota, heads the research team that is charting new territory in this area. In a series of studies covering certain minerals and trace minerals, Dr. Penland and his colleagues have discovered that less-than-adequate intakes of boron, copper, iron, and manganese can impair memory, thought, and mood.

When boron, a trace mineral generally found in apples and raisins, was reduced in the diet of older men and women, they seemed to experience some loss of short-term memory, the kind used in learning. They also showed a reduction in mental alertness. When intake of copper, a trace mineral found in seafood, fresh vegetables, and fruits, was reduced in the diet of young men, they too noticed some memory

Less-than-adequate levels of certain trace minerals can impair memory, thought, and mood.

loss, and they experienced some degree of confusion, depression, and anxiety. In another study, reducing the iron intake of young women also impaired mental alertness. Meat is your best source of iron.

Dr. Penland found one exception in his minerals-for-the-brain studies: Higher levels of zinc, abundant in oysters and organ meats, led to "poorer mood"—depression and anxiety—in study participants. Zinc and copper are basically competitive with one another, explains Dr. Penland, and it's copper that seems to be responsible for more positive moods. What probably happened in the study, he adds, was that the higher level of zinc interfered with absorption of enough copper to maintain a positive mood.

Zinc and copper compete with each other.

"What these studies demonstrate collectively," says Dr. Penland, "is that trace elements have some function in maintaining cognitive skills like attention, perception, memory, and even spatial and motor performance. But we are not to the point where we can say, 'If you take more iron, you'll greatly improve your memory or math skills.' " So until there's more research, he adds, the best advice is simply to eat a balanced diet.

The Fat Factor

Here's a fact you may find surprising: When balancing your diet, don't ignore fats. Fats literally provide much of the raw material of which our minds are made. In other words, you really are a fathead.

The type of fat you eat can affect mental performance.

Brain cells are actually made up of fats, explains Carol E. Greenwood, Ph.D., an associate professor of nutrition at the University of Toronto. It takes 24 days for the fat in the diet to alter the physical composition of your brain, but get there it does. And, although researchers don't quite understand how, it affects your thinking when it arrives.

■ Run Your Brain on Quality Oil

Not all fats are created equal, and it's the kind of fat you eat—and don't eat—that makes the difference. Studies indicate that diets rich in saturated fats—the kind found in tropical oils and fatty meats—seem to decrease your ability to think, while diets rich in polyunsaturated fats—safflower, sunflower, or soybean oils—tend to help thinking.

In one study conducted at the University of Toronto by Dr. Greenwood and her colleagues, laboratory rats were divided into three groups and placed on three different diets. One group received a diet high in polyunsaturated fats from soybean oil, the second group received a diet high in saturated fats from lard, and the third group received its regular chow.

Days later the researchers tested the animals' ability to learn. They placed each animal in a tub of water with a submerged platform that the animal couldn't see, then timed how long it took each to find the platform.

Those with diets rich in polyunsaturated fats learned about 20 percent faster than animals on the other diets. And they were less likely to forget what they had learned.

Animals fed polyunsaturated fats learned 20 percent faster than those put on a diet of saturated fat.

PUZZLE POWER

After a nutritious meal, you might want to take a pleasant walk to help you digest your food. On the other hand, particularly if it's a rainy day, you may prefer a little postprandial mental exercise. Here are some brain teasers to test your wit.

Mix and Match

The names of three foods are mixed up on each of the following lines. The words are given with their letters in correct order, but each word is "interlettered" with the others. See if you can pick out the foods.

C F H R M E U E E I A S E T T

A P E P P A R L E P L S S U M S

Say "Cheese"

The names of three well-known cheeses are interlettered in the following line. Once again, all the letters are in the correct order. See if you can unscramble the three cheeses.

R L C O I M H Q B E U U D E R D F O G E R R A T R

To find the answers, see Solution #2 on page 454.

Luckily, the saturated fats which researchers tell us are bad for the brain are the same ones that heart researchers tell us are bad for the heart. And what's good for the heart is also good for the brain.

Now that's food for thought. ■

4

Memory

From the Ordinary to the Extraordinary

Every Sunday morning, the Reverend David Misenheimer, frocked in the flowing white robes of the Lutheran ministry, stands on the steps of Christ Lutheran Church in Charlotte, North Carolina, and greets every single man, woman, and child by name. All 1,800 of them.

"I really don't know how I do it," chuckles the good-natured pastor when asked how he can remember so many names. "It's a marvelous gift that constantly amazes me. I can even remember a vistor's name if he comes again six months later."

Amazing? Sure, especially when you consider that most of us have trouble remembering a new telephone number long enough to dial it. It's hard to believe that anyone—even someone with a Friend at the Top—can remember 1,800 names and faces along with the life histories that go with them. But it's really not so amazing, maintains Douglas J. Herrmann, Ph.D., a memory expert

It's possible to remember 1,800 names and the faces that go with them.

and author of *Supermemory*. Excellent recall—even remembering 1,800 names—is a marvelous gift, he adds, but it's a marvelous gift we all can share. Given the motivation, time, and practice, every one of us can be just as quick on the recall.

Memories That Amaze

Being good at remembering names, even *that* many names, really isn't all that extraordinary, especially considering the Rev. Misenheimer's line of work, notes Dr. Herrmann. He cites current scientific studies to prove his point. "Most of these studies indicate that you can take people of relatively normal memory ability and give them the same task day in and day out—learning names, learning faces, learning information—and after several years they'll be very good at those tasks."

In a study at Carnegie Mellon University, for instance, a student learned to memorize strings of random digits. Although he could learn only six digits at a time in his first tries, after a couple of weeks of practice, he could learn more numbers. And after 18 months of practice he could listen to an 84-digit list and repeat it back to the researcher. The student, who was a runner, found he could learn the digits by taking the numbers in groups of three or four and associating them with his racing times. His other memory skills, however, stayed the same.

One student could listen to a series of 84 digits and repeat it back.

Like ministers, schoolteachers are an example of a professional group known for excellent recall. Teachers invariably know the names, faces, and family histories of several hundred children at any given time. Professional coaches frequently know the names, faces, team affiliation, statistical standings, and contract status of every player in a particular sport—plus every play in every championship game they've ever coached.

Schoolteachers and waitresses are known for their remarkable memory.

Waitresses, in particular, fascinate memory researchers. "If you watch waitresses, their performance on memory tasks is really phenomenal," says Dr. Herrmann. "They have to be able to remember what someone ordered, who ordered it, where they're sitting, and—since everybody is beginning and ending courses at different times—who's ready for what."

It's not an easy job. "If researchers tried to set up a task like that in a laboratory," says Dr. Herrmann, "people would freak out. The memory tasks of being a waitress are harder than any scientific memory test we currently have."

Think about it and watch what goes on next time you go into a restaurant. Experienced waitresses and waiters do write things down when taking an order (mostly for the convenience of the chef), but they often don't refer to anything when they're serving the food. And they almost always get it right.

Whom Can You Trust?

Or at least they get it right *then and there*. Ask the same waitress what those people ordered from her *last* week and you'll likely find

Is It Déjà Vu?

You're walking down a tiny cobblestone street when you get the eerie feeling that you've been here before. And even though you know that you've never been in this city, somehow you have this feeling that you've walked down this street before, smelling the geraniums and touching the rough, sunwarmed brick of the houses.

It's *déjà vu,* and most of us have experienced it many times. But what causes it? What causes us to "know" something that we cannot know, "remember" something of which we can have no memory?

That question has intrigued scientists as much as it has everyone else. And the answer is just as fleeting as the feeling itself. One theory holds that, although a particular situation is new, enough of its components have been previously experienced that the current situation seems like a repetition of the past. You may not have walked down this particular eighteenth-century street, but eighteenth-century streets have enough in common—cobblestones, geraniums, and rowhouses—that you feel you've been here when you've actually been somewhere similar.

that her recall is not so accurate. Better yet, ask two servers who waited on the same table the same questions about an evening's events and you'll likely get somewhat varied stories.

Memories are not carbon copies of events.

That's because memories aren't always carbon copies of an event, says Elizabeth Loftus, Ph.D., a researcher at the University of Washington who has studied eyewitness accounts of everything from murder to revolution.

Another idea is that déjà vu is the feeling you get when you encounter something that stimulates a suppressed memory. If you had previously walked down this same street while arguing with someone you loved and then lost, you may very well have suppressed the memory of that argument and its environs because it recalls a great deal of personal pain.

A third idea is based on the theory that memory is not the recalling of fixed forms or images but a dynamic *reconstruction* of the past. But since any reconstruction is subject to error—omissions, abbreviations, elaborations, and distortions—the memory that's reconstructed may not exactly match the reality of what you're seeing now. In this case, scientists say, déjà vu may simply be the feeling that results from a discrepancy between memory and reality. You feel as though you've experienced something before because you have. It's just not exactly the way you remembered it, so it feels familiar and unfamiliar at the same time.

Many people feel that their memory of an event is like a film and will never change. But the always-active brain, taking more recent information into account, can go back and edit the original memory so that it reflects the newly acquired facts.

This process helps to explain why memories seem to change over time and why one person's view of a particular incident may be quite different from someone else's, says Dr.

Eyewitness accounts can be changed by those who know how.

Loftus. And it doesn't just happen with events that took place long ago. Your recall of something that happened just a few moments ago can be distorted.

Dr. Loftus demonstrated this in a study in which she had a group of people observe a simulated traffic accident. After watching the accident, the "eyewitnesses" were given a written report describing what took place. One group received an accurate description while the other group received information that erroneously referred to a stop sign as a yield sign.

The result? When asked whether they originally saw a stop sign or a yield sign, those who were given the phony information said they had seen a yield sign. And they had no idea that they weren't telling the truth.

Other studies, she says, show similar examples of memory distortion. "People have recalled nonexistent broken glass and tape recorders, a clean-shaven man as having a mustache, straight hair as curly, and even something as large and conspicuous as a barn in a bucolic scene that contained no buildings at all," she reports. "Misleading post-event information can alter a person's recollection in a powerful, even predictable, manner."

Memory distortion is a normal, predictable part of how your brain handles information, notes Dr. Loftus. It means that your memory isn't always as reliable as you might think.

How to Say "I'm Right" and Be Right

A little disturbing isn't it, especially when you consider how often you must depend on your own or someone else's memory. But it sure explains why your recollection of a certain event can sometimes differ from someone else's—while both of you stubbornly insist that you are correct!

So how can you have a rock-solid memory for detail? How can you fight your mind's natural tendency to distort memories? When you know you have to rely on your memory for accurate recall, Dr. Loftus recommends this two-pronged approach.

There are ways to train your mind to become more dependable.

■ Inscribe a Memory in Indelible Ink

This suggestion may sound obvious, but if you want to remember something *exactly* as it happened, write it down *in detail* immediately afterward, says Dr. Loftus. Then review it—aloud, if necessary.

Bank tellers, for example, are trained to write down the details of a robbery immediately afterward—before they even talk to police. Otherwise a police officer's questions could easily alter the teller's memory. A simple "Did he wear a stocking mask?" might cause your mind to edit the memory, slipping a mask right over the robber's head.

Bank tellers are trained to write down details of a robbery immediately after it happens.

Writing down what happened serves several purposes, explains Dr. Loftus. "It records the memory while it's still fresh, it reinforces the memory by freezing it in place, and it provides you with an opportunity to review what really happened so that the original memory doesn't fade or get distorted as easily." Using this technique can really pay off when you need an accurate recollection of business meetings or the negotiating terms of a major purchase.

■ *Watch Out for the Master Manipulator*

People have been manipulating minds for as long as there have been minds to manipulate. Take, for example, the butcher who insists you ordered 15 pounds of steak when you know it was only 5. The cashier who claims you handed him $10 when you're sure you gave him $20. The politician who claims he never promised to cut taxes when you know darn well he made that pledge—the same day you promised to give him your vote.

You don't want to let your memory get caught off-guard. When you order 5 pounds, get the butcher to repeat it. When the cashier challenges you, be ready to say, "I left the house with four 20s and two 10s. Let's take a look and see what I have left." Be prepared to say to your local representative, "It says right here in the newspaper . . ."

Courtrooms are well known for being stages for mind play, says Dr. Loftus. "Many people will eventually serve on a jury," she reminds, "and they'll be asked to decide someone's fate when, frequently, the only evidence is someone else's memory."

How dependable would your eyewitness account be?

Courtrooms are well known for being stages of mind play.

I Left It on the, Uh . . . Er . . .

So you say your concern isn't about how well you can remember—it's about how easily you can forget! That's not surprising, say memory experts. Given the frantic life many of us lead, it's a miracle we remember anything.

There are lots of logical explanations for why we tend to be forgetful, says Dr. Herrmann. Sometimes our mind is simply just too busy. We're dividing our attention among so many things that we don't really make a solid memory. Sickness, even a cold or the flu, also can affect how well we make memories, says Dr. Herrmann. And, of course, alcohol and even certain drugs not only affect the making of memories but also interfere with their recall.

Dividing your attention among too many things may be why you're so forgetful.

In addition, we can sometimes suppress certain memories because they're painful, he says. If you said something really mean to your daughter one day, for example, the memory carries with it an awareness of just how rotten you can really be. And that's a trait that you would just as soon forget. And so you do.

For most of us, however, forgetting is an inconvenient and sometimes embarrassing aggravation.

Tricks to improve memory have been around for, well, as long as anyone can remember. Yet too many of us, it seems, are still forgetting. So what's not working—besides our memory? Monica E. Gregory, Ph.D., a cognitive psychologist at the Hazleton campus of Pennsylvania State University, thinks she has the answer. Instead of trying to improve your memory in general, you should concentrate on the particular things you're most likely to forget. Chances are it's not your memory as a whole that's slipping—it's your memory for certain things. Like where you put your keys.

It's not your memory as a whole, it's your memory for certain things that is slipping.

72

Misplaced keys are the universal memory slip.

■ *The Key Clue: A Place for Everything*

Come to think of it, where *are* your keys? Misplaced keys are a universally vexing memory slip, says Dr. Herrmann. If you have an object that you consistently misplace—whether it's keys, the bottle opener, or the remote control for your TV—find a spot for that object and put it there each time it leaves your hand. If it's your keys, they should have a special place at home—a key rack or a bowl by the door—and a special place when you're not at home—like your left front pocket. Just make sure that every time you open the door to your home, your keys go immediately to their special place.

■ *Retrace Your Steps*

If one day something is not where it's supposed to be, picture the last time you saw or used the missing object, then visualize your actions from that moment on. Chances are, as you mentally retrace your steps, something will trigger your recollection. If visualization doesn't work, check all the places where, in your previously disorganized past, you might have put it.

Visualization can help jog your memory.

■ *Say It Out Loud*

If you frequently forget whether or not you've done something, try talking out loud to yourself while you're doing it, suggests Dr. Herrmann.

Remembering whether you took your medicine or not, for example, can be a problem for some people. You don't want to risk taking a double dose, but you also don't want to risk going without your medication. Dr. Herrmann suggests you say something like this to help you remember: "I am now picking up the pill bottle to take my pill. I am now taking the cap off the pill bottle to take my pill. I am now putting the pill in my hand to pop in my mouth."

Making your mind consciously aware of where you're putting something will help your recall later on.

■ Turn Numbers into Words

Think of how many numbers you must deal with in your daily life. You have a Social Security number, employee identification number, voter registration number, supermarket check-cashing–privilege number. Numbers for your bank accounts, charge accounts, driver's license, license plate, auto registration. You get called on to furnish purchase order numbers, confirmation numbers, frequent flyer numbers, delivery numbers. Then there are zip codes for your home and office, plus any number of very important phone numbers.

You can help yourself to remember these random digits by translating them into letters, some experts suggest. This technique is similar to the one many companies now use to make their phone numbers more memorable: Dial 1-LUV-MILK for the dairy. Another way to better remember a number is to group the digits. For example, a confirmation number of 30004021 becomes "three thousand, forty, twenty-one." Or affix signficant events to parts of it: 3,000, your age (40), the legal drinking age (21).

Translate digits into letters to remember phone numbers.

74

Numbers become easy to remember when you make them relevant to something meaningful in your life.

The idea behind remembering numbers, says Dr. Herrmann, is to relate them to something else that's more meaningful to you personally.

■ Use Visualization to Remember What You've Read

Say you've just read a terrific article in today's newspaper that intelligently analyzes both sides of a hot community issue. You want to remember the salient points on each side and who was quoted so you're well armed when you go to the public meeting that addresses the issue.

Reduce an article to about six important signposts.

How do you begin? Reduce the article to about six key terms, suggests Dr. Herrmann, then draw a diagram of the article. Include all important "signposts"—names, places, dates.

Now look at what you've drawn and analyze the relationships among the key terms on your paper. Then use visualization to keep them straight in your mind. Suppose that land development, for example, is the issue at hand. Think of some synonyms for the terms—dirt for landfill, a groundhog for the developer.

If you want to remember that the developers have bribed county officials to let them put a landfill on the site of a proposed community park, picture a groundhog tunneling under a playground and popping up in a garbage heap with a pile of money in his mouth.

You might also want to read the article aloud, emphasizing important points, says Dr. Herrmann, then write a short summary. Or ask yourself questions about what's in the article.

In any case, if anyone asks *you* a question about the issue, you'll be well prepared with both an answer and an argument. If you have trouble remembering any of it, just bring the image to mind and go from there.

■ *Play Around with Names*

Names are one of the hardest things to remember, especially if you're shy. A friend introduces you to someone and you're so busy trying to keep your chin from hitting the ground that the name literally breezes right by you—it never enters your conscious mind.

The key to remembering the name is to concentrate on the person you're meeting and not yourself, says Michael L. Epstein, Ph.D., chairman of the Psychology Department at Rider College in Lawrenceville, New Jersey. It also helps to play around with the name in your mind. If you've just met Emily, for example, and her prominent widow's peak gives her hairline the shape of an "M," use the "M" to remember "Em—Emily."

Rhyming is another name saver: Frank broke the bank. Mark's like a shark. Jerry rides a ferry. If you can rhyme a name, you can embed it in your memory.

If no rhyme comes to mind, use the person's name to invent an unforgettable image. Harris is an easy name to remember if Harris happens to be someone with a lot of hair.

For a name like Yastrzemski, try another tack. Imagine your neighbor doing something that sounds like his name. Yastrzemski? You strum a ski. It's a silly image, all right—silly enough to be memorable.

Names are one of the hardest things to remember, especially if you're shy.

Using imagery is the easiest way to remember names.

You can also use imagery to associate your neighbor's name with what it means. If the name is Farmer, picture her driving a combine through a field of wheat in her front yard.

Use these techniques in any way that works for you. The only limitation is your imagination. "The last syllable of my name is -*stein*," says Dr. Epstein. "To remember it, think of drinking beer out of a stein."

Better yet, since the most prominent feature on his face happens to be his nose, picture an upside-down stein on his face instead of a nose. Then think about turning it right side up. "Then you've got 'up stein,' which is close to Epstein," he says.

■ Roll It off the Tip of Your Tongue

Visualization works. You know it for a fact! After all, how many times have you said to yourself, "I can *see* it, I can *see* it. . . ," but you just can't *say* it.

Pry something loose from the tip of your tongue by throwing letters around in your mind.

You can usually help pry something from the tip of your tongue by throwing some letters around in your mind, says Dr. Herrmann. Say you're trying to recall the name of someone who just walked into the room. Start with the letter *A*—"Alan, Alvin, Andy?" Nope. Was it *B*? "Bill, Bob, Barry, Benedict?" Nope. How about *C*? "Let's see: Carl, Calvin, Carson. That's it! Carson!"

Frequently, just hearing the first letter is enough to jog your memory, says Dr. Herrmann.

If the simple alphabet trick doesn't work, you'll have to probe a little deeper. Recall everything you can that might be associated with the information you're trying to dig up, suggests Dr. Herrmann.

Recall everything you can that might be associated with what you are trying to remember.

If you're still trying to remember someone's name, for example, think about the last time you talked to this person. Where were you? What were you doing right before you met? What did he say? What did you talk about?

How did you feel when you last met? Were you happy? Tired? Angry? Try to recapture that mood. Probing your memory should shake something loose that will help you recall the name, says Dr. Herrmann.

Wanted: Foolproof Memory

Does your memory have a bad reputation? If the ol' gray matter just ain't what it used to be, a look in the mirror might be able to tell you why.

Research indicates that overall memory performance can range from good to bad depending on your physical and emotional state. In fact, their importance cannot be overstated, says Dr. Herrmann. "If you're kind of tired or bummed out, you can't pay attention well enough to remember things," he says.

Memory performance can range from good to bad depending on your physical and emotional state.

If your aim is to improve your memory, says Dr. Herrmann, you have to take care of yourself, both physically and mentally.

78

■ Sleep Is Essential

The importance of sleep to memory is overwhelming. Dr. Herrmann reports that cutting your normal night's sleep by as little as 2 hours may impair your ability to remember things the next day.

This is especially true of complicated things. Research at the University de Lille in France indicates that the mind actually depends on sleep to retain difficult memory tasks. It doesn't, however, seem to affect simple things you want to remember.

Other scientists suggest that sleep is important because your brain may use dreams to clean extraneous debris out of your memory circuits.

Some scientists believe that sleep gives your memory circuits time to unload extraneous debris.

It's as though you were typing merrily along on a computer keyboard, hit the wrong command key to store information, and found yourself with a screen full of hieroglyphics. You can't use the information on the screen, nor can you continue with your work. Dreaming may be the key that gets rid of any hieroglyphics your brain has created while processing information. And the fact that you have trouble remembering the details of a dream may be an indication of just how effective dream dumping is.

■ Exercise Your Body to Improve Your Mind

Researchers in California found that people between the ages of 55 and 89 who exercised regularly were far better at remembering than their peers who didn't exercise. (Other studies have found similar results.) The researchers speculate that aerobic exercise improves mental functioning because it increases the amount of oxygen reaching the brain.

Aerobic exercise increases the amount of oxygen that goes to the brain.

How much exercise will keep your memory in peak condition? A minimum of a 20-minute walk every day is probably enough, says Dr. Herrmann. "The thing is to get out, move your body around, get your blood circulating, and shake up those old and new memories."

■ Paint Yourself a Rainbow

How does mood affect memory? Scientists really aren't sure. But it may be that good feelings help us to remember good memories, says Alice M. Isen, Ph.D., a psychology professor at Cornell University and a professor at Cornell's Johnson Graduate School of Management.

Her own work indicates that feeling good improves your memory for recalling positive things. The feeling seems to act as a retrieval cue—a way for you to access an abundance of pleasurable memories. This is why, she claims, positive and happy people are also more creative.

Feeling good improves your ability to recall happy and positive memories.

Fortunately, the same isn't true of bad memories, says Dr. Isen. You can't use your bad moods to improve your memory.

■ Forget the Booze and Cigarettes

Alcohol and tobacco can play games with your head—and that means with your ability to remember.

Even low doses of alcohol reduce the ability of various brain cells involved in memory to do their job, according to researchers at the National Institute on Alcohol Abuse and Alcoholism.

Smoking also impairs memory, because it constricts arteries and reduces blood flow to the brain, says Dr. Herrmann. In one study, nonsmokers were able to recall a list of numbers more quickly than smokers, and nonsmokers also scored higher on standard memory tests.

Smoking constricts arteries and reduces blood flow to the brain.

■ *Reach for the Decaf*

A cup of coffee may be just as memory zapping as either alcohol or nicotine. In a study at the University of North Carolina at Charlotte, reseachers discovered that the amount of caffeine in a single cup of coffee can reduce your recall of newly learned material.

Researchers divided 32 students into two groups. One group received a glass of Gatorade in which a 100-milligram tablet of caffeine had been dissolved. The second group received a glass of Gatorade in which a placebo (inert pill) had been dissolved.

In one study, caffeine reduced students' ability to recall a 15-word list.

Immediately after the students finished their drinks—and before the caffeine could have an effect—the researchers tested the students' memory abilities by asking them to recall a 15-word list of common nouns they had just learned. Forty minutes later—when they could be sure that the caffeine had kicked in—they asked the students to recall words from a new list. The researchers repeated their test five more times. Each time, the students who had *not* received any caffeine remembered more than the students who had.

■ Learn to Relax

One of the most effective ways to improve your memory may be to consciously relax all of your muscles right before you try to learn something, report researchers at Stanford University School of Medicine. It seems that muscle relaxation reduces the amount of anxiety people frequently feel when they're trying to learn something new. Somehow, the easier the memory goes in, the easier it comes out.

Relaxation reduces the anxiety of learning.

A group of 39 men and women between the ages of 62 and 83, for example, volunteered for a memory-improvement program conducted by the researchers. The volunteers were divided into two groups. Members of one group were taught to relax every muscle in their body from head to toe, while the other group was simply given a lecture about how to improve their attitude toward aging. Then each group underwent a 3-hour memory-training course.

Later the researchers tested the volunteers' ability to learn and then recall a series of names and faces. The group that had practiced consciously relaxing their body before learning names and faces was able to remember 25 percent more than the group that had not relaxed.

Those who used relaxation techniques were able to recall more.

At-ten-tion!

How many times have you gotten into your car to drive to the grocery store and then driven
(continued on page 84)

What Turns Your Memory On?

Some people remember their shopping lists like a series of picture postcards. That's visual memory. Some people's feet automatically launch into the latest dance steps whenever the music begins. That's kinesthetic memory. And some people never forget a name after they've been introduced to someone. That's verbal memory.

Which is your memory strong point?

Rate yourself with this test. If your answer is "true" or "yes," check the box to the right of the question. If the answer is "false" or "no," leave the box blank. Then add up the check marks in each of the three vertical columns.

Verbal   Visual   Kinesthetic

Think about what you had for dinner last night.

1. Do you have a vivid visual picture of it? ☐
2. Did you just reexperience the tastes and smells? ☐
3. Can you list everything you ate? ☐
4. Can you recall the brand names of the different foods you ate? ☐
5. Can you remember the color of the plate and cup? The tablecloth? ☐
6. Can you recall where you ate? How you sat? The position of the food on your plate? ☐

Verbal Visual Kinesthetic

Now imagine you are standing in front of the first house you can remember living in as a child.

7. Do you see the color clearly? Do you have a strong image of how many windows there are? The kind of steps? How many steps? □

8. Do you remember the address and phone number? □

9. Can you remember whether the doorknob is on the left or right? Do you know if you step up to go inside? □

Now answer these general questions.

10. I am usually very aware of the furniture arrangement in a room. □

11. If friends painted their living room a new color I would definitely notice. □

12. I know whether the numbers on my watch are Arabic or Roman numerals. □

13. I know my Social Security number. □

(continued)

83

What Turns Your Memory On?—*Continued*

		Verbal	Visual	Kinesthetic
14.	I'm good at sports and/or dancing.			☐
15.	I respond to the colors around me.		☐	
16.	I always got good grades in English.	☐		
17.	I didn't have much trouble learning to ride a bike.			☐
18.	I love to do crossword puzzles.	☐		

If your scores are about the same in each category, you are good at all three ways of encoding and filing each new memory. To reinforce a new memory, you should use all three methods. For example, if you're playing cards and want to remember the two of diamonds using kinesthetic memory, hold the card second from the left in your hand. Prompt your visual memory by looking at the card. Then fix the verbal memory by mentally saying "two of diamonds."

If you scored best in visual memory, you can reinforce your verbal or kinesthetic memory with a visual image. Write

right past it? Or how many times have you driven to the store, gone inside, and then stood in the middle of an aisle trying to remember what you'd come for?

It happens to everybody. The reason we don't remember is that we simply don't pay enough attention to what we're doing. If we're thinking about how to pay our income tax on

out names, addresses, and phone numbers and look at them. Imprint that image with a memory picture. See new acquaintances with their names written on their chests. If you learn a physical skill, watch yourself doing it.

If your score is highest in verbal memory, you can help yourself remember things if you name them. When you meet new people, for instance, say their names and add a verbal description. Also, make mental lists to back up your visual and kinesthetic memory. If you want to remember where your car is parked in the shopping center lot, tell yourself the name of the store it is nearest and repeat the aisle letter or number.

If you scored best in kinesthetic memory, you probably never misplace your car keys, but you might have problems remembering what you were supposed to pick up at the drugstore on your way home. Your best bet is to add a kinesthetic memory to other information so you can remember more easily. Shake hands when you meet a person and notice the texture of the person's hand while you repeat the name. Is the skin soft or calloused? Is the grip strong or light? Learn a new telephone number by dialing it a couple of times. Feel the rhythm as you punch the number onto the keypad.

the way to the supermarket, it's not really surprising that we'll forget about needing cat food.

■ Learn How to Really Look at the World

To increase attentiveness, you have to observe your world more closely, says Robin

West, Ph.D., a psychologist at the University of Florida. The more you notice and the more vivid your observations, the more ways your mind will have of searching for and recalling what it needs.

When you drive to the grocery store, for example, observe the first gas station you pass by noticing distinct features—its sign, the soda machine out front, the flowers along the side, the constantly changing prices.

Or, as Dr. Herrmann suggests, stand outside your home late at night and—without doing anything that might alarm your neighbors—practice listening for faint, unpredictable sounds or looking for dim lights. You might try watching a plane cross the sky, listening for a mouse to scurry across the driveway, or guessing what your neighbor is dropping in the trash just by the sound it makes.

Improving your senses of sight and sound will help you improve your memory.

Anything you can do to both increase your ability to sustain your attention and increase your ability to notice details is going to help you improve your memory.

■ *Watch Two TV's at Once*

Many of us forget important things when we try to divide our attention between too many things at once. The pot boils over on the stove while you're simultaneously talking on the phone and signing a package receipt at the door. Or you miss a turn while driving because you're listening to the radio and talking to a passenger.

Things that are important enough to remember should get your undivided attention.

But it is possible to do two things (or more than two things) at once without dividing your attention.

One of the easiest ways to learn how to do this, says Dr. Herrmann, is to put two TV's next to each other, tune them to different channels, and try to listen to both at once. See how much information you can absorb from each and try not to miss a thing.

You can also use both TV's to learn how to resist distractions. Turn them on as before and flip them to different channels, but this time, instead of trying to absorb everything, concentrate on one program and ignore the other. It'll be hard at first, but stay with it. When you can consistently pay attention to only one TV, says Dr. Herrmann, make the exercise even harder by lowering the volume on the set you're watching and raising it on the one you're not. If it doesn't drive you crazy first, this technique is guaranteed to teach you how to pay attention effectively.

Memorization Made Easy

Experts say you can improve your memory 100 percent by simply learning a few basic tricks.

When researchers test memory skills, they generally use a 30-item list as a gauge to judge how well someone can remember. Studies conducted at various universities around the country have found similar results: Those who are asked to memorize the items randomly, that is, without implementing any learning strategies, usually are able to recall around 10 items. Those who use a few memorization skills can recall about 20 items. And those who use as many strategies as possible are frequently able to memorize all 30 items.

By implementing certain memory tricks, you can score 100 percent on a memory test.

There are a variety of memorization tricks, and most will take some time to master, says Janet Fogler, a clinical social worker who has conducted memory workshops for the University of Michigan Medical Center's Turner Geriatric Services. Also, what works great for someone else may not work at all for you. Try them all, she advises, then pick those that feel right and practice them over and over until they become second nature.

To get started, suggests Dr. Herrmann, you might want to try to match the tricks to your personality. If you like to live simply, for example, choose simple tricks. If you like intricate stories and explanations, choose complex ones. If you like crossword puzzles, try tricks that involve verbal manipulations. If you're visually oriented—you have a penchant for art, for example—imagery-based tricks would probably work best for you.

Choose memory tricks that complement your personality.

■ *Take a Mental Snapshot*

Let's say you're asked to observe a scene—a group of people on a trip in Portugal—for later recall. The group (you've already counted ten women and four men) is laughing it up on a tour of a Portuguese castle. Look at the tour bus parked in the castle courtyard, then scan the area systematically for details. What's on top of the courtyard walls? What are the flag's colors? Is the stone under your feet dark or light? How far down the walls does the sun shine?

Now watch as the group gets back on the bus, one by one. What are they wearing? Who doesn't have a camera? Which one limps from too much walking? Who is first on the bus? Who is last?

Close your eyes and ask yourself the same questions, then open your eyes to check the answers. Keep opening and closing, asking and checking until you feel the scene is indelibly recorded in your memory.

By purposely seeking out details, asking yourself questions, and rechecking the answers, you are helping to embed that image in your mind, says Dr. Herrmann. This technique can help you recall the scene down to the tiniest details.

Purposely seek out details. Close your eyes and ask yourself questions.

■ Smell and Touch Your Memories

All your senses come into play when imprinting a memory. The more senses you use in trying to record a memory, any memory, the more likely you are to remember it, says Dr. Herrmann.

Can you smell any flowers in the courtyard at the castle? Anyone's perfume? A pipe?

Now run your fingers across a stone in one of the walls. Is it rough or smooth? Is it cold? Does it feel as though the history of a thousand years is pulsing through your fingers?

The sense of touch is also important when it comes to total recall.

The more attuned your senses are, the better will be your ability to recall, say the experts. To find out more about your senses and how to hone them, see chapter 15.

■ Put Some Rhythm in Your Thinking

If you think memorizing the scene at the castle was a trick, think of the tour guide who had to memorize the names to go with 14 faces!

You've already learned how to use association to recall someone's name. But let's say you want to remember the names of all the people on the tour. One way to do it is to repeat each name as you meet the person. Saying a name aloud is another way to stamp the names on your memory. Then you might simply repeat each name over and over to yourself after you've left the group.

But a better way, says Dr. Herrmann, might be to put those names to a beat. After all, just think how hard it is to forget the words to a song you like. Try repeating the names in a rhythmic pattern, either in syllables—Kar-en, Da-vid, Jer-ry—or to a certain beat—Kar' en-en, Da' vid-vid, Jer' ry-ry. You can even insert their names into a familiar song—"Happy Birthday to Karen, Happy Birthday to David, Happy Birthday dear Jer-ry, Happy Birthday to you."

Songs are so easy to remember because of the beat.

■ *Reflection Makes for Deeper Roots*

It's been a wonderful trip, something you want to remember for the rest of your life. But considering the way your memory's been working lately, how *well* will you remember it? It depends a lot on how meaningful you make it.

Reflecting on something and thinking about what it means to you is an excellent way to enhance later recall, says Dr. Herrmann. If you want to recall the exquisite details of the castle, for example, mentally reconstruct your visit and think about the differences between your life and the life of someone who lived there hundreds of years ago. Think about how this visit might affect your life. Has it made you think about how pampered your life is compared to the brutal struggle for survival that people experienced in the Middle Ages? Has it made you appreciate the conveniences of elevators, central heating, hot showers, and flush toilets? Or has it made you crave a simpler world?

Roll the answers to these questions around in your mind. The memory of your visit to the castle will sink deeper and deeper until it's impossible to forget.

Some things are impossible to forget.

■ Give Meaning to Meaningless Words

How quickly can you name all the planets? Maybe you're not even sure how many there are!

Memorizing strings of words is something we are all confronted with at one time or another. If you can't recite the planets off the tip of your tongue, chances are you didn't memorize them the easy way when you were in school.

Memorizing a string of unrelated words requires a little elaboration, says Dr. Herrmann. You give the meaningless list some meaning.

Mnemonics put meaning where there isn't any.

Anyone who's studied music has used this technique. The phrase "Every good boy does fine" to any music student stands for E-G-B-D-F, the notes of the treble staff, says Dr. Herrmann. The first letter of each word corresponds to the letter of a musical note. It's called mnemonics. You can use the same approach to any list you need to learn—even your grocery list.

PUZZLE POWER

Just how good is your memory? Below is a quick test to find out. Don't be discouraged if you don't get the right answer; it's fairly tough. And remember, better memory may come with practice.

Total Recall

This is a test of your spatial memory—your ability to recall shapes and figures. Look at the eight shapes pictured here for a minute and try to add them to your memory. Then, turn to the solution to see how many you recognize.

To find the answer, see Solution #3 on page 455.

Oh, yes, the planets. Here's a mnemonic for that one in case you're ever asked to name them again: "Meek violet extraterrestrials make just such unusual new pets": Mercury, Venus, Earth, Mars, Jupiter, Saturn, Uranus, Neptune, and Pluto. ————■

5

Intelligence

Boost Your IQ at Any Age

Several years ago, a young psychologist was sent to a Connecticut school for the retarded to administer an IQ test to the students. When he walked into the school, he found it strangely deserted—the entire student body had just executed an escape.

It wasn't easy, but the kids were eventually rounded up and the psychologist was able to give them the test. Of course, after leading teachers, administrators, and the psychologist on a merry chase throughout the school and grounds, you'd think that the kids would do well on an IQ test called the "Porteus Maze." But they didn't. To the psychologist's astonishment, the same kids who had neatly evaded capture, although temporarily, could not even get through the first problem.

How could a group of children be clever enough to put one over on an entire faculty of educators, yet fail so miserably on a test that measures intelligence? It's ironies such as this that have given new thought to the way we define intelligence.

The New View of IQ

Twenty years ago, intelligence was measured purely by the score on an IQ test. Today, however, intelligence is viewed much more broadly. Educators, psychologists, and scientists now recognize that true intelligence is not just how well you perform on a test. It's how well you perform in life.

Most experts agree that an IQ test is only one aspect of intelligence. It merely measures, well, how well you do on tests—your ability to break things down into their component parts and analyze them, says Robert J. Sternberg, Ph.D., professor of psychology and education at Yale University and one of the leading experts in intelligence research.

But intelligence is also your ability to react intuitively and creatively to various experiences, says Dr. Sternberg. And it has a lot to do with what many of us call street smarts— your ability to *learn* from your experiences.

Intelligence has a lot to do with "street smarts."

"Intelligence boils down to your ability to know your strengths and weaknesses and to capitalize on the strengths while compensating for the weaknesses," says Dr. Sternberg, who has written numerous books on intelligence.

In other words, an IQ test may predict whether or not you're going to flunk school— not whether or not you're going to flunk life.

Smart, Smarter, Smartest

Although there is more to intelligence than your IQ score, how you fare on this test still, to some degree, plays a part in how fair a shake you'll get in life. "It's part of what gets you good grades, gets you into college, and keeps you there," says Dr. Sternberg. It can also help or hinder your chances in the job market.

Score 100, and your intelligence quotient—your IQ—is considered average. About 95 percent of us fall in the 70- to 130-point range. A score of 130 labels you as gifted. Only 2 percent of us fit into that category. Anything below 70 means you may have learning problems.

About 95 percent of the population is considered to have an average IQ.

So what makes some people smart and others not so smart? Part of it is genetics. Some scientists say that 50 percent of your intelligence comes from your ancestors. The other 50 percent is environmentally determined, meaning the way you are influenced by such things as childhood experiences, parental guidance, and schooling. How smart you are or how smart you become has a great deal to do with how you use this other half.

Fifty percent of intelligence is genetic; the other half is environmental.

And the good news is that your ability to boost your IQ doesn't end the day you graduate from high school or college. Scientists say we all have the ability throughout our lives to boost our intelligence.

You can boost your IQ at any age.

How? Through mental challenge. When it comes to getting into shape, the brain is no different from the body. The brain needs exercise to build mental muscle.

Mental Aerobics

Certain mental exercises can make you smarter.

How do you exercise an organ that's confined to your skull? You teach it to run in place. Dr. Sternberg says there are a variety of mental strategies you can exercise to give your neurons a good workout. They won't condition you to break world IQ records, but they can help you beat your own personal best. You can get smarter.

The following mental exercises and strategies offer unique or clever ways to approach and solve problems. If you can remember back to your days of IQ tests or SATs, some of them will sound familiar. The idea is to take these basic techniques and apply them as much as possible throughout your daily life. Only through constant challenge, reminds Dr. Sternberg, can you keep your mind in top form.

■ Search for the Not-So-Obvious in the Obvious

Dr. Sternberg tells this story of how some sharp thinking turned an ordinary problem into an extraordinary solution for one person.

The person in question was a top executive at a major firm who loved his job, his power, and his salary, but not his boss. His relationship with his boss eventually became so untenable that he went to see a headhunter about finding another job.

The headhunter was familiar with the executive's work record and assured him that any number of companies would welcome him on board. That night, as the executive told his wife

Man versus Machine: Who's Smarter?

So far, man is winning. But that's mostly because no one has yet figured out how to program a computer with common sense.

The problem is that a computer can add 2 plus 2 and come up with 4, but it cannot take various pieces of information (some of which may be only partially correct), analyze them, and arrive at a conclusion that is compatible with most—but not all—of the evidence.

Nor are most computers good at making analogies (a measure of intelligence on most IQ tests) or at figuring out what are called series completion problems. If someone says to you "Mary had a . . . ," you have a whole childhood on which to draw to complete the sentence. Because computers are an outgrowth of a lab, not a womb, they can't really know about Mary's little lamb.

Computers perform a lot like job candidates during an interview, explains Yale psychologist Robert J. Sternberg, Ph.D. "As long as they are asked questions for which they have been primed, they are able to answer in an intelligent way. But throw them a curveball and it becomes obvious that they are unable to think for themselves."

But don't declare man the victor over machines just yet. A new kind of computer system is being developed—one that "thinks" more like a human brain than any other system thus far: Instead of processing one piece of information at a time, it processes information simultaneously throughout its entire network—weighing, evaluating, and modifying the input just the way you do.

Recently one of these systems was loading information on people into its data banks. It paused for a moment and then typed out a single question: "Am *I* a person?"

So far, the answer is no. ∎

what he was up to, he lamented how he wished he didn't have to leave his firm. His wife, a psychologist who was teaching a class using Dr. Sternberg's program on how to be more intelligent, put some of her knowledge into practice.

It wasn't the firm he disliked, she reminded him. It was his boss. By taking his problem and redefining it, he then came up with a much better solution. The executive went back to the headhunter, withdrew his name, and asked the headhunter to find his boss a new job. The headhunter followed through and the boss was hired away for a top position by another firm. And to make a perfect ending, the executive was promoted into his boss's job.

His wife was one smart cookie.

By redefining a problem or situation and turning it around, you can often find a smarter solution, says Dr. Sternberg. When the obvious presents itself, keep your mind working on finding the not-so-obvious.

Think of how you can redefine problems in your own life. The problem, "How can I keep rabbits out of my garden?" might be recast as, "How can I preserve the local wildlife *and* my garden?" Or the problem, "How can I keep the raccoons from raiding my trash cans?" might be reslanted as, "How can my trash be handled so that it no longer attracts four-legged raiders?"

A wife solved her husband's job problem by figuring out a way to get his boss to quit.

Think of how you can define problems in your own life.

■ *Form Small Pieces to Shape the Big Picture*

Here's a classic example of a type of question that can pop up on IQ tests:

> A mother sends her son to the river to fetch 3 quarts of water. She gives him a 7-quart bucket and a 4-quart bucket. How can the boy retrieve exactly 3 quarts of water using only the two buckets?

It's a simple problem requiring a two-step solution. First he fills the 7-quart bucket, then uses it to fill the 4-quart bucket. He's left with 3 quarts of water in the 7-quart bucket.

This type of question trains your mind to break problems down and put them in sequential order to arrive at the right solution.

How does it apply to life? Let's say you want to write the Great American Novel. If you just sit down and start writing, you're not going to get anywhere—or at least anywhere with anything that's any good. Any novelist will tell you that writing a novel is a lot like putting together a puzzle. It has an outline. A cast of characters. Historical notes. Lots of index cards.

Large tasks that seem impossible can be made very manageable by breaking them down into a number of smaller tasks. Try it next time you're faced with cleaning out an attic filled with 20 years of memorabilia or planning a reunion for classmates spread all over the planet. Or even planning a gala party for 100 of your boss's closest friends. Carrying it off properly requires some smart thinking.

Large tasks that seem impossible can be tackled by breaking them down into smaller tasks.

■ *Use Analogies as Intellectual Barbells*

Think about this one: A candle is to tallow as a tire is to rubber.

Why? Because a candle is made of tallow and a tire is made of rubber.

As you learned in school, this is called an analogy—a comparison of two or more things that allows you to discover a relationship that exists among or between them. Analogies are found on IQ tests, and for good reason. People use them all the time. For example, comparison shopping is a way of making an analogy.

Let's say you need new front tires for your car and you only have $100 to spend. ABC tires cost $50 apiece and are guaranteed to last for 50,000 miles. DDD tires also cost $50 apiece but are guaranteed for only 45,000 miles.

By comparing the two—making an analogy—you determine ABC tires will get you the better mileage for your money.

How good are you at analogies? Dr. Sternberg gives a few examples that are typical of what might be found on an IQ test.

Smart people are good at analogies—and they use them all the time.

1. Spouse is to husband as sibling is to
(a) father, (b) uncle, (c) brother, (d) son.
   The answer is (c). A husband is a spouse. A sibling is a brother.

2. Owl is to foolish as lion is to (a) timid, (b) large, (c) wise, (d) temperamental.
   The answer is (a). An owl is supposed to be wise, which is the opposite of foolish. A lion is supposed to be bold, which is the opposite of timid.

3. Trap is to part as rat is to (a) goodbye, (b) whole, (c) bait, (d) tar.
   The answer is (d). "Part" is "trap" spelled backward. "Rat" is "tar" spelled backward.

4. Lion is to eagle as sphinx is to (a) pterodactyl, (b) dodo, (c) vulture, (d) phoenix.
The answer is (d). A lion and an eagle are both real animals. A sphinx and a phoenix are both mythical animals.

It's not as easy as you might have thought, is it? But the practice you get tusseling with analogies and their relationships will work your mind hard. And they're so effective you'll think you've found the equivalent of intellectual barbells. The practice will give you a real boost if you ever have to take another IQ test.

Practicing analogies will work your mind hard.

■ *Use Insight to Expand Your Vocabulary*

Probably the single most important way to increase your intelligence and boost your score on an IQ test is to sharpen the skills you use to build your vocabulary, says Dr. Sternberg.

Think about how you normally approach an unfamiliar word you stumble across in your reading. Ten to one, you don't look it up in a dictionary. If you're curious but don't have the inclination to get out of your chair and fish out the dictionary, you probably try to figure out the meaning of a word from the words and sentences that surround it—from the context in which it appears.

Learn words by figuring out their meaning through context.

For example, see if you can figure out the meaning of the word *oont* in this story developed by Dr. Sternberg.

There is no question but that the oont is king of the Asian and African deserts. Despite its strong, unpleasant odor, its loud braying, and

The True Mark of Genius

She had held human brain tissue before, many times. But this time was different. This time, there was genius lying in her palm. "It was the ultimate brain as far as our society is concerned," says neuroanatomist Marian Diamond, Ph.D., recalling that moment in the early 1980s.

In her hands, she held a slice of Albert Einstein's brain. Alone in her University of California at Berkeley lab, Dr. Diamond carefully placed the section under her microscope. She slowly turned a dial and suddenly one of the few geniuses of this century came into sharp focus. "I knew I was looking at something very precious," says Dr. Diamond.

She looked where even Einstein couldn't see. What she found confirmed what many others had thought all along. Einstein's brain was special. "More glial cells were found in a certain portion of his left hemisphere as compared to the same area of the brains of normal males."

Glial cells nourish and support neurons and are known to increase in number with learning and experience, something Einstein obviously had a lot of.

Other researchers know that the true nature of genius can't always be measured under a microscope's lens, even though *all* behavior is a product of nerve and glial cells.

Most people believe that to be a genius you must have a high IQ—140 or above. But researchers who study geniuses

its obnoxious habits of viciously biting, spitting when irritated, and quitting on the job, the foul-tempered oont is widely used as a beast of burden by desert travelers. Perfectly suited to desert conditions, it can store vast quantities of water in its body tissues.

You've probably guessed that an oont is a

say that to be a true genius, you have to be more than just smart. "We have to distinguish between a person who does well on conventional tests and someone who makes really unique contributions to knowledge," says Philip Powell, Ph.D., associate professor of educational psychology at the University of Texas at Austin.

"After 70 years of following a group of people with IQs over 180, we found that none of them turned out to be geniuses in their lifetime by anybody's definition," says David Feldman, Ph.D., professor of developmental psychology at Tufts University in Boston. "Genius is only very loosely related to IQ."

Geniuses are like oysters. They can turn a tiny grain of sand into a sparkling pearl. Geniuses are driven. They get an idea and they continue to build on it, layer by layer.

"The operative word when describing genius is novelty," says Dr. Powell. "A genius is a person who comes up with unusual or unique ideas or products that end up transforming a generation."

Who does he put in this elite group? Buckminster Fuller was one, he notes. So were Shakespeare and da Vinci.

And, of course, Albert Einstein.

camel. You figured it out by using an intellectual skill known as insight.

According to Dr. Sternberg, there are three kinds of insight. The first, called selective encoding, allows you to sort through all the words in the paragraph and sift out the relevant information: beast of burden, desert, store, water.

Learning words through context exercises your insight.

The second kind of insight, called selective combination, allows you to combine the information into a single entity: a beast that stores water and carries burdens through the desert.

Then the third kind of insight, selective comparison, allows you to relate this new knowledge to old knowledge. And you got your answer: a camel!

■ *Cram Your Mind with Knowledge*

Before you can use this third type of insight most effectively, however, you need to be well informed. If you had never seen a camel at the zoo (or in a picture) or read about it in books or at school, you would never have been able to figure out what an oont was.

A broad education is important to developing intellect.

That's why a broad education is so important to developing your intellect. But most of us are long out of school. How can we broaden our knowledge without going back?

Experts say we should make learning an important part of our life. Read frequently, keep your mind open to new influences, take courses at local colleges as the opportunity arises, and discuss ideas with others.

One woman broadens her knowledge by throwing dinner parties for people of divergent backgrounds.

Or fashion your own innovative strategy to broaden your knowledge. One woman, for example, makes it a point to invite people from widely divergent backgrounds to her house for dinner about once a month. In a few months' time, she's learned about narrative art from an old artist, Soviet education from a Russian exchange student, wool manufacturing from a textile designer, film production from a man who makes industrial training films, and sea life from a female scuba diver.

She makes learning enjoyable by combining it with three things in life that she truly loves: good friends, good food, and good conversation.

■ Practice Problems That Tease the Brain

Enjoyment is the key word here. If you like solving problems, puzzles, and quizzes, you can be a natural at boosting your IQ. But you need to work on the kind that make your mind work.

Solving problems, puzzles, and quizzes can naturally boost your IQ.

We've listed some fun brainteasers at the end of this chapter to help get you started. In the meantime, here's a single brainteaser to help measure what you've learned so far. According to Dr. Sternberg, solving it correctly requires such sharp skills that it's considered a sign of a high IQ.

Water lilies double in area every 24 hours. At the beginning of the summer there is one water lily on a lake. It takes 60 days for the lake to become covered with water lilies. On what day is the lake half-covered?

By employing your skills of insight, you should be able to figure out that the relevant information here is the first sentence: Water lillies *double* in area every 24 hours. Get it? The lake is *half-covered* on the 59th day.

■ Do the Same Kind of Mind-Teaser at Least Ten Times

Everything gets easier with practice. And that includes problem solving.

Everything gets easier with practice.

108

One way to improve your problem-solving skills, says Dr. Sternberg, is to do the same type of problem using the same mental strategy over and over.

If, for example, you want to work on developing the kind of insight that helps you find what's relevant (as in the water lilies riddle), you need to concentrate on a series of similar problems. Try this: According to the United States Constitution, if the vice-president of the United States should die, who would be the president?

Again, your strategy in solving this problem is to find what's relevant. See it? In this case it's "death of a vice-president." The death of a vice-president is relevant to the answer because it is irrelevant to the issue of who would be president. So your answer to who would be the president if the vice-president died is: the president.

Do a series of similar problems and by the time you get to the tenth problem, you'll be surprised at how quickly you're coming up with the correct answers, says Dr. Sternberg. Your mind will have figured out the "trick" to solving this kind of question and will now be able to spot the setup and work out the solution in seconds.

The trick to answering a trick question is knowing how to spot what's relevant.

■ *Race the Clock*

Another way to sharpen your mental skills is to work on how fast you can think. You can practice this by solving problems by the clock.

The next time you're doing a series of brainteasers, the Sunday crossword puzzle, or any game that taxes the mind, race the clock to get it done. Let's take a series of problems such as those at the end of the chapter as an example. Do the first problem and check your watch to see how long it takes you to figure it out. Then, just as you start the second problem, set a timer to ring just 2 seconds earlier. If you do that each time you start a problem, you'll have boosted your response time. Do this until the pace causes you to make mistakes, then ease up on yourself.

Learning to think fast takes practice. Use a clock to time yourself.

Cues on Taking an IQ Test

When Dr. Sternberg was little Bobby Sternberg, he checked out a library book containing IQ tests and took it to school to try it out on some of his seventh-grade classmates.

But this idea didn't get them better grades; it only got Bobby in trouble. As Dr. Sternberg tells it: "A guy I knew in Cub Scouts, who proved to be a fink, told his mother, who called the school psychologist, who then told me that he would burn the book if I ever brought it into the school again."

Dr. Sternberg will also tell you he didn't do extremely well on the test, either. But Dr. Sternberg has learned a lot about intelligence and IQ tests since his elementary years. Today Dr. Sternberg is a world-famous expert on intelligence who also happens to design intelligence tests that measure more than rote smarts.

So how does Dr. Sternberg suggest you ace a test the next time a potential school or em-

Forget everything you learned about acing a test.

ployer pushes one under your nose? By disregarding just about everything everybody has told you about taking the test.

Dr. Sternberg has found through his work that some of the conventional wisdom of the past really isn't so wise when it comes to test-taking strategy. Here's what he says should work for your benefit.

■ Put Your Work Pace on a Budget

> Don't feel pressured to work quickly through every problem on the test.

Don't feel pressured to work quickly through every problem, despite what the test booklet or anyone says. Your best strategy is to evaluate how much time to spend on each problem; then you can use that time to your best advantage. If you get familiar with the type of problems that will be on the test, you'll learn which kind you can work quickly and which will take more time. Use this as the criterion for budgeting your time.

Studies indicate that if you follow your instincts, you'll speed up where you can and slow down where you need to. If you work too quickly over problems that need careful analysis, you'll likely get them wrong.

■ Read Wisely, Not Thoroughly

It's not necessary to read everything carefully, but it is necessary to read wisely. Feel free to skim through easier questions until you get the gist of the main idea. Some people tend to read *everything* with equal care. But studies indicate that this is counterproductive, says Dr. Sternberg.

The Ideal Intellectual?

Several years ago, a quartet of scientists studying IQ did a survey among average folks on what they believed were the characteristics of an intelligent person.

They found that almost everyone has a preconceived ideal of how an intelligent person acts and interacts with others. They also found that most people had a relatively similar notion of what these behavioral characteristics should be.

Below is a partial list of some of the traits that came out of the survey. These are not necessarily true traits of the intelligent personality, note the scientists, but only what others think it should be. They say an intelligent person:

- Accepts others for who they are.
- Admits his own mistakes.
- Displays an interest in the world at large.
- Is on time for appointments.
- Has a social conscience.
- Thinks before speaking or acting.
- Displays curiosity.
- Does not make snap judgments.
- Is sensitive to other people's needs.
- Is frank and honest with both himself and others.

■ Put Those Vocabulary Books Away

Yes, most tests emphasize vocabulary. But cramming a bunch of words into your brain

Cramming is the surest way to forget.

111

just before the test is the surest way to forget them.

Instead, build your vocabulary by learning how to figure out the meaning of a word from the context in which it appears. The exercises for practicing insight detailed earlier show you how to do this.

■ Use Your Mental Strengths to Your Best Advantage

People are frequently taught to use specific strategies to solve specific problems when they're preparing for tests, says Dr. Sternberg. But there are usually multiple ways to solve problems. And his studies indicate that, for many problems, there is no *one* best way to answer them.

There is no one best way to solve a problem.

The strategies you use to solve a problem will depend on *your* mental skills. The skills you are most comfortable with are the ones you should use. If you are very verbal, for example, and you are solving a geometric problem, you might find the answer by analyzing the words used to describe the relationship of the shapes.

■ Make Living Your Training Wheels

Most test-training programs will tell you to train for your test by practicing the types of problems that will appear on the test. And it's true—this tactic can help you increase your test score. But keep in mind that intelligence is more than book learning. Actually learning how to interpret everyday events in context— the same strategy that you use for increasing your vocabulary—is likely to help you even more, says Dr. Sternberg.

Scoring well on an IQ test takes more than book learning.

■ Know How to Find What's Important and What's Not

Remember the question about the vice-president of the United States that we discussed above?

Often people are instructed that they should be sure to use *all* of the given information to figure out a problem. This isn't always true, says Dr. Sternberg. Many problems on an IQ test are specifically designed to see if you can focus on the important information. If you *don't* ignore the unimportant stuff, you're likely to get the answer wrong.

■ Consider All Your Options

Conventional test-taking wisdom holds that as soon as you see the answer to a problem in a list of possible solutions, you should check it off and move on. Not so, says Dr. Sternberg.

Frequently IQ tests are constructed so that at least one of the answer options is very close to the correct answer, he cautions. So if you don't consider all the possible answers, you're not as likely to detect the frequently subtle difference between what *looks* right and what *is* right.

The obvious answer isn't always the right answer.

Once upon a time, many people thought that the ability to solve problems was the sole measure of intelligence. Now we know that intelligence, like cars and ice cream, comes in many varieties. As long as you don't take puzzle solving too seriously, it can be lots of fun. Enjoy.

"Plane" Numbers

Can you replace the letters below with numbers, so that the addition will be numerically correct? (Hint: K = 9)

```
      M  O  M
      M  O  M
+        N  O
   _____
   B  O  O  K
```

Three Spring Chicks

Of three sisters named April, May, and June, none is yet 21. April is now as old as June was 14 years ago, and two-thirds of May's age. May, on the other hand, will be June's age when May is twice as old as she is now plus two years. Three years ago, May was as old as April is now. How old are April, May, and June?

To find the answers, see Solution #4 on page 455.

■ Do More Than Try to Psych Out the Test-Maker

Learning to second-guess the test-maker will help you get better scores, says Dr. Sternberg. But it can lead to falling into the trap of always trying to think like that. And trying to think the way you think somebody else thinks is, well, not thinking well. The true sign of intelligence is your ability to think in creative and novel ways. So it's fine to psych out the test-maker—as long as you place more importance on honing *your* way of thinking.

Think in creative, novel ways.

6

Clear Thinking

The Foundation of Smart Decisions

The sun was gleaming through clear Denver skies as United Airlines Flight 232 bound for Chicago took off on the afternoon of July 19, 1989. All aboard expected a routine trip. And so it was, until 3:16 P.M., when the tail engine suddenly exploded. Passengers rocked forward and attendants plummeted to the floor as the huge DC-10 pitched downward.

With the two remaining jets under the wings, the plane still had power enough to fly. But power wasn't the problem. The blast had demolished the aircraft's hydraulic system, causing a complete loss of control of the rudder, wing flaps, and ailerons. 296 people were caught 37,000 feet in the air—on a plane with *no* steering.

A call to United's emergency center in San Francisco was fruitless. Experts there had no idea how a faulty hydraulic system could be fixed in midair. Never before had such an occurrence been reported. Flight 232 was on its own. Captain Alfred C. Haynes had some fast thinking to do.

Clear Thinkers Sometimes Turn Out to Be Heroes

The situation called for an emergency landing, but the nearest landing strip was at Iowa's Sioux City Airport, 70 miles away. Although the steering was shot, Capt. Haynes found he could maintain some control by alternating speeds of the two wing jets.

For 41 minutes, Capt. Haynes and his three-man crew struggled to guide the disabled plane closer to the airport. On approach, Captain Haynes shouted through the intercom, "Brace! Brace! Brace!" Moments later the highly unstable aircraft somersaulted to the ground. Miraculously, 184 people survived, many without a scratch.

Clear thinking on the part of a jet pilot saved the lives of 184 people.

Officials agreed that the landing of the plane defied staggering odds. Capt. Haynes was commended for his exceptionally clear thinking and called a national hero—a label he still has a hard time accepting. "There is no hero," he told the *Washington Post* shortly after the incident. "There is just a group of four people, four people who did their job."

That's possibly so, but by some standards, Capt. Haynes is overly modest. "If you look at heroes in the movies, in a western or a crime drama or whatever, the hero is always the person who knows the right thing to do," says

Dorothy Tennov, Ph.D., Delaware psychologist and author of *Super-Self* and *Love and Limerance*. "Superman not only had great strength, he also knew how to use it," she says.

The Beginnings of Good Decision Making

Since the days of Aristotle, possibly even earlier, philosophers have been studying human reasoning—the ability to understand, draw conclusions, and make decisions. It's a complicated science, one in which there are many parameters and rules. But relax—you don't need a college course in logic to figure out which investments to make, which house to buy, or which set of parents you're going to visit on Thanksgiving.

In fact, taking a college course in logic may not help you make such decisions at all. Reasoning is something like swimming, says Amos Tversky, Ph.D., professor of psychology at Stanford University. "Knowing a lot of theory about swimming doesn't mean you can swim," he says. Similarly, you can be an excellent swimmer without knowing anything of the theory behind it.

The same can be said for knowledge. A college degree may prove you *have* the knowledge, but it's no guarantee you know how to *use* it—or use it wisely.

Reasoning is something we learn from living, says Dr. Tversky. As infants, we begin to reason much as we begin to walk. You have some built-in program, but every now and then

Logic is something you can't learn in college.

Book knowledge won't do you much good if you don't know how to use it.

you need a little help, so someone will give you a hand.

So here's a little help from some of the best-known hands in the business.

■ Ask Lots of Questions

Before you can make a good decision, you have to gather all the information—and you should do so with the zeal of a squirrel gathering nuts before winter. Although Capt. Haynes's time was extremely limited, he had to gather certain information before he could choose a course of action. How much damage had the explosion caused? Which controls were still available to him? What sites were open for an emergency landing?

Collecting the information you'll need to make a decision is perhaps the most crucial part of the process, says John C. Johnson, M.D., director of emergency medical services at Porter Memorial Hospital in Valparaiso, Indiana, and president of the American College of Emergency Physicians. "Usually mistakes aren't made because someone made a wrong decision—usually they happen because someone had insufficient or bad data," he says.

Lack of information in an emergency room could have tragic consequences, says Dr. Johnson. Imagine a badly wheezing child whisked in for care. If the attending doctor weren't thinking clearly, he might reason that the child was having an asthma attack and treat him accordingly. But a sharper doctor would *first* ascertain when the wheezing began and whether the child was playing with any small objects.

Getting all the necessary information is essential in making the right decision.

Lack of information can have tragic consequences.

He might discover that the child was choking— and save a life!

If you recall Sherlock Holmes, that master of reason and crime detection in Sir Arthur Conan Doyle's turn-of-the-century London, his credo was to gather information first and make judgments only afterward. When his sidekick, Watson, would jump to premature conclusions in the solving of a case, Holmes would set him straight. "It is a capital mistake to theorize before you have all the evidence. It biases the judgment," said Holmes.

You may never need to diagnose choking infants or solve murders, but if you want to make the best decisions, you're going to have to do some sleuthing. For instance, before you show up on election day to vote for candidate D or candidate R, find out as much as you can about each. Don't vote for D because he's handsome, kisses babies, and says he stands for a "strong America." Find out exactly where he stands on issues that are important to you. Or before you whisk home a cuddly little puppy that you fell in love with the moment it licked your hand, learn something about the breed and how much care it will take to raise. Find out how big it will get, how much it sheds, whether it's good with kids, and whether it's the kind of pooch that would go berserk living in your two-room apartment!

■ Look for All Possible Moves

In just about any given situation— whether it's deciding where to live or what kind of job to take—there are almost always a num-
(continued on page 124)

121

Great Goofs in History

History is full of great deeds, heroic men and women, and brilliant ideas. But the pages of time are also filled with enormous blunders, bad calls, and awful decisions. Below, a few candidates for history's greatest goofs, as nominated by Robinson V. Smith, professor of world history at Bentley College in Waltham, Massachusetts.

The Trojans Accept a Horse

Homer's *Iliad* may be largely fantasy; nevertheless, the ancient epic depicts perhaps man's earliest monumental muff. For ten years, Troy (in modern-day Turkey) stood strong against attacks from its Greek enemies. Finally, pretending to give up, the Greeks presented Troy with a giant wooden horse. The Trojans pulled their gift inside the walls of the city, and . . . you know the rest. Homer doesn't say whether the defeated Trojans had a word for "Ooops!"

Montezuma Greets a Man with a Beard

Montezuma II reigned over the powerful Aztec Empire. He was also a believer in Quetzalcoatl—according to legend, a white, bearded god. When Montezuma heard of a strange-looking army approaching his kingdom, led by a white, bearded individual, he did not send soldiers in defense but instead sent gifts in deference. Spanish conquistador Hernàn Cortès accepted the gifts, scratched his beard, and marched forward to victory.

Pope Leo Throws a Party

At the same time that Cortès was conquering Mexico, Pope Leo X, sort of a medieval Donald Trump, was whooping it up in the Vatican, running the papal treasury into bankruptcy. "God has given us the Papacy, let us enjoy it," shrugged his high-living Holiness.

The German monk Martin Luther didn't like what he heard and spoke up. The Pope was furious, and in 1521 excommunicated Luther. Pope Leo's actions split the Church in two, causing religious and political turmoil that continues in some places to this very day.

A Young Nation Feels Its Oats

The United States and Canada are such good pals today that it's hard to believe U.S. troops invaded Canada, *twice*. On both occasions, "the Americans were convinced that they could cut Canada off from Britain, and the Canadians would come willingly into their arms," says professor Smith. But that didn't happen. During the American Revolution, two invading Yankee armies were clobbered in Quebec. And during the War of 1812, American incursions into Canada resulted in the burning of Washington in retaliation.

Dred Scott Loses His Case

Back in 1857, the United States was not very united. Part of the problem was that the South favored slavery, the North did not. At one point, the Supreme Court was asked to decide whether a Southerner could legally keep his slaves even if he moved North. The Court ruled that a black man had "no rights which any white man was bound to respect." Therefore, slaves could be kept anywhere. It was this decision "that made the bloodiest war in American history inevitable," says Smith.

Adolf Wants to Visit Moscow

By 1941, Nazi Germany's blitzkriegs had rolled over nearly all of Europe. Only England stood, but the island-nation's power was draining fast. On June 22, Hitler decided to ease off on his offense against England and turn most of
(continued)

Great Goofs in History—
Continued

his guns east, attacking the Soviet Union. In so doing, Hitler allowed England to recoup power and created for himself a war with two fronts, a war he would eventually lose.

Surprisingly, Napoleon had made the very same blunder a century before, leading to his defeat at Waterloo. As philosopher George Santayana said, "Those who cannot remember the past are condemned to repeat it."

Japan Pulls a Fast One

The year 1941 turned out to be a banner year for goofs. While Germany was following Hitler's mad quest for the domination of Europe, militaristic Japan had grabbed vast regions of Asia and the Pacific. On the early morning of December 7, fearing potential U.S. intervention, Japan sent waves of planes in a surprise attack to knock out American naval forces at Pearl Harbor. President Franklin Roosevelt, calling it a "date which will live in infamy," asked Congress to declare war. Japan was soon to sorely regret its attack. ———■

ber of options available to you. But if you're like most, you don't seek out all the options. Rather, you end up forcing yourself into anxiety-ridden either/or situations. The cerebral world of chess offers a perfect example. According to Michael Valvo, one of America's top-rated chess players, the downfall of many in chess—as in life—is that they "concentrate on only two or three moves—while at least seven or eight are usually available."

One way you can limit your options is to spring upon the first solution to a problem that

Concentrating on only a few moves can lead to downfall.

124

enters your head. But "your first answer is likely not to be your best," says Jeff Salzman, vice-president and cofounder of CareerTrack, a Colorado-based company that consults with other companies on matters such as decision making. Considering how rushed today's world can be, you may be inclined to breathe a sigh of relief when the answer to a tough question is found. But you're more likely to find the *best* answer if you say, "Okay, I have one possible answer—let's see if I can find something better."

What do you do if all you can see is one solution? Regardless of whether it's chess, how to market a product, or how to pick a career, the answer is to "be creative," says Paul Slovic, Ph.D., professor of psychology at the University of Oregon and president of Decision Research, a nonprofit research institute in Eugene. If something has you stumped, "ask questions of friends, read, talk to experts—be a detective and investigate!" he says.

If only one solution is apparent, keep on investigating.

■ Use Confidence to Keep Your Cool

Imagine what was going through Capt. Haynes's mind when he found himself in the cockpit of a crippled plane with the lives of nearly 300 people hanging in the balance. Do you picture some horrible images running through his mind, hear him saying to himself, "What in the world am I going to do?", see him break out in a really big sweat? If you do, you're wrong. "I really didn't have any thoughts. There was nothing on my mind but what we were trying to accomplish, just the job at

Someone in control of a situation is in control of his mind.

hand—which was to bring the plane down safely," says Capt. Haynes.

You might think that Dr. Johnson, who oversees the care of roughly 90, sometimes critically injured, emergency room patients every day, might get a bit emotional at times. And you'd be right. "We can't be like RoboCop," he says. But he knows *when* to dwell on his feelings and when not to. When a bleeding patient is lying in front of him, "that is not the time to worry—that is the time to act," says Dr. Johnson. "After everything settles down, *then* you can think about it."

All right, it's one thing to say you have to be cool to make your best decisions—but how can you always be cool, especially in trying times? The key, our experts agree, is *self-confidence.*

And self-confidence, says Capt. Haynes, comes largely from training and experience. "There were 103 years of flying experience up there in that cockpit," he says. "We weren't sure if we'd get to an airport, but as far as getting the plane to the ground, I don't think it crossed any of our minds—we'd handle it."

Says Dr. Johnson, "To remain calm, you have to have confidence in your ability." But having self-confidence can be hard when you lack experience. This is why, says Dr. Johnson, "young doctors often get hung up wondering whether they're doing the right thing." His advice to them at such moments is to look to the good decisions they have made in the past to reinforce their confidence. You can do the same.

Self-confidence ultimately comes from accepting yourself and your decisions *regardless*

Wise decisions start with self-confidence.

Self-confidence comes from training and experience.

of what anybody else thinks or any mistakes you may have made, says Albert Ellis, Ph.D., president of the Institute for Rational Emotive Therapy in New York City.

A lack of self-acceptance, he says, is a "sickness" whose symptoms often include indecisiveness and muddled thinking. What's the cure? "You have to say to yourself—and believe—'I accept myself whether or not I perform well, just because I am a human being.' With that kind of self-acceptance, you're on the road to becoming a clearer thinker (and a happier person as well)," says Dr. Ellis.

> Accept yourself whether or not you perform well.

■ Turn Yourself into an "Amiable Skeptic"

The tough part about separating your emotions from your reasoning is that there are lots of people out there who'd *rather* you remain emotional! The multibillion-dollar world of advertising, for instance, is one in which emotions reign, says Diane Halpern, Ph.D., a professor of psychology at California State University in San Bernardino and author of *Thought and Knowledge: An Introduction to Critical Thinking*.

> Separate emotions from reasoning when making decisions.

Take cigarette ads (all $3.3 billion of them blasted at you last year). "They always show beautiful people having a wonderful time in healthful places. There's a crystal-clean lake, and everybody's in clean clothes, and the air is fresh and pure. The message is that smoking is clean and healthy," says Dr. Halpern. But is it? Of course not. Smoking causes cancer and heart disease. The side of you that is the critical

128

thinker undoubtedly *knows* that—but the emotional side of you (in cahoots with your addicted body) may be the one forking over the money to buy the next pack!

To prevent yourself from being lured into making bad decisions, "you must say to yourself 'I'm going to make the effort to be a more critical thinker,' " says Dr. Halpern. That means developing an attitude of "amiable skepticism," she says. If you see an ad promising that a certain product will, for example, "increase the size of your bust in 30 days!!"—ask yourself, Where's the evidence? If you read that a particular drug is "medically approved!!"—ask yourself what "medically approved" means. And if the same drug boasts positive results based on an "exciting new study!!"—ask yourself *what* exciting new study, and *who* funded it?

And don't think that advertisers are the only ones out there trying to grab your emotions. Politicians, says Dr. Halpern, can be worse!

Developing a Rational Lifestyle

Since we learned to reason the way we learned to walk, we've all tripped over a few decisions in our time. Nevertheless, the only way to become adept in the art of reasoning is to stand right back up and keep "walking." It's scary though; when big decisions come along, we often feel like crawling into a corner. These are the times we can use a few crutches. So grab hold of the following and you'll be back on your feet in no time.

Develop an attitude of "amiable skepticism."

When big decisions come along, we often feel like crawling in a corner.

■ *Create a Balance Sheet*

Say you're considering whether to sign a petition banning bicycles from your local park. Or whether to adopt a dog or a cat. Or whether to take a six-month sabbatical so you can travel through the Amazon. You naturally want to make the best decision. "To be rational about it, write down a list of all of the advantages and all of the disadvantages of each avenue," says Dr. Ellis, who is also the author of *A New Guide to Rational Living* and *How to Stubbornly Refuse to Make Yourself Miserable about Anything—Yes, Anything*. You can then rate the advantages and disadvantages, giving each item a score of, say, between one and ten.

> Rationality involves weighing the positives against the negatives.

Then do some quick arithmetic. "You'll normally find that one option comes out with a distinctly better score," says Dr. Ellis. If you *don't* make such a list, he warns, you risk allowing your emotions to zero in on only one aspect.

He gives as an example a young man he knows who purchased a flashy—but quite undependable—car simply because it massaged his ego to do so. Naturally, the young man soon found himself with a car he was *kicking* more than *driving.*

■ *Drop Your "Musts"*

While in the midst of trying to make a decision, *any* decision, listen to your inner self. Do you hear a cranky little voice inside saying, "I must have this . . . I must . . . I must . . . I *must!*" People are born with a tendency to take their important desires and turn them into "musts," says Dr. Ellis. "They become what I call 'musturbaters.' "

The problem with "musturbation" is that it limits your ability to think in an objective manner. The key to rational thinking and clear decision making is to remain *flexible,* says Dr. Ellis. So the next time you hear yourself saying "I *must!*"—step back and ask yourself, "*must* I?" Ask yourself if a sabbatical makes more sense *after* the kids get out of college, or if dependability overrides flashy when it comes to choosing the new car. (Chances are, it *does.*)

Satisfying a personal want is counter to rational thinking.

■ *Take a Knife to Big Decisions*

A big decision can be like an enormous chunk of steak. Try to swallow it without first cutting it up, and you risk choking, says Dr. Slovic, who recommends a technique he calls incrementalism. Say, for instance, that you're considering giving up your job as a salesman in Chicago to become a newspaper writer in Miami. The decision involves not only starting a new career, but selling your house, moving your family, and leaving all your friends. You've been agonizing over this one for some time.

Big decisions can be overwhelming. Cut them up like a piece of steak.

Decisions like this can be overwhelming, says Dr. Slovic. The thing to do if we feel overwhelmed is to cut up the dilemma like a piece of steak. Perhaps you can find a part-time newspaper job in Chicago, while keeping your present job, to see if newspapering will be as much to your liking as you think. Possibly you can take time off from work and spend it in Miami with the family to see how much everyone likes Florida living. You may be surprised. "We tend to think that we can predict new situations better than we actually can," says Dr. Slovic.

■ Seek a Second Opinion— but Not from a Twin

When time allows, it's generally a good idea to consult with other people before making important decisions, says Baruch Fischhoff, Ph.D., a psychologist at Carnegie Mellon University in Pittsburgh. "There are just too many things in this world that are too big for any one person to examine alone," he says.

There are many decisions that are too big for one person to examine alone.

But whose opinion do you ask? You *could* ask your best friend or someone else with whom you share common interests and values. But you can do *much* better by asking people who think differently than you do, says Janet Sniezek, Ph.D., assistant professor of psychology at the University of Illinois at Urbana-Champaign. "If you talk to people like yourself, they'll tend to agree with you. So you'll get more confidence, but not more accuracy," she says. Preferably, "find people of different backgrounds, different occupations, and different biases."

And if you want to get double your money with your second opinion, ask it *before* you reveal your own feelings, advises Dr. Sniezek. "Don't walk in and say 'I've decided that I'm going to get this operation—what do *you* think?'" Others' opinions are much more

Others' opinions are more valuable when you keep yours to yourself.

Make a decision and sleep on it. This may be the best advice.

valuable if they come without any influence from you.

■ *Let Recency Fade*

If someone gives you the old advice to "sleep on it," consider it good advice. *Your* opinions will be more valuable if you harvest them after allowing them time to ripen, says Donald A. Norman, Ph.D, professor of cognitive science and chairman of the Cognitive Sciences Department at the University of California in San Diego. Creative writers know the importance of allowing a story to sit for a day or two before picking up the pencil for a final edit. Only then can they see their work with a fresh eye. Similarly, your vision becomes clearer over time about decisions and judgments you need to make.

There's a good reason for this. "We're heavily influenced by recency," says Dr. Norman. For instance, if you had to travel to London two days after a major airline crash, you might decide to swim! "Leaving a little time to put recent things in the past can help a lot to clarify thinking," he says.

■ *Last Step: Try to Prove Yourself Wrong*

Most of us, when we make up our mind, set out immediately to validate what we think we "know," says Dr. Ellis. As time goes on, we find more and more "proof" that our assumptions are correct—because all we're looking for is proof! "But we tend to learn more by trying to falsify our assumptions," says Dr. Ellis.

Dr. Sniezek agrees. "People have mistaken beliefs about how much they know," she says. There's no better way to find holes in the fabric of faulty thinking than to ask yourself, "What are the reasons I may be wrong?" Try asking this question of yourself the next time you feel absolutely sure about something—you have nothing to lose but your possible error!

> People have mistaken beliefs about how much they know.

Why We Sometimes Make Mistakes

We live in a world of illusions, says Dr. Tversky. He's not talking about the visual illusions that we thrill to at magic shows where women get sawed in half. He's talking about cognitive illusions where reason and logic get sawed in half. As you will see, the conclusions we often make (believing them to be completely reasonable) are actually beyond reason.

■ Get a Fix on Probability

By grasping a basic understanding of the laws of probability, you can greatly reduce the probability that you will fall prey to cognitive illusions, says Dr. Tversky. That doesn't mean that you have to bone up on standard deviations, permutations, coefficients, and all the other torture tools of statisticians. It just means knowing a few simple rules.

> Cognitive illusions lead to mistakes.

For instance, suppose you've just met a woman named Linda. Linda is 31 years old, single, outspoken, and smart as a whip. In college, where she majored in philosophy, she was deeply concerned with issues of discrimination and social justice and also participated in anti-nuclear demonstrations. What do you think is more likely of Linda in the 1990s? That (1) she works as a bank teller? Or (2) she works as a bank teller and is active in the feminist movement?

If you chose (2), you are not paying attention to a simple rule of probability. The probability that statement (2) is true (that Linda is a bank teller *and* is active in the feminist movement) cannot possibly be greater than the probability that (1) is true (that Linda is a bank teller). But because the part about Linda being in the feminist movement looks so likely, you might have fallen prey to a cognitive illusion. Many people do, says Dr. Tversky.

■ *Figure Yourself as a Potential Statistic*

Do you always buckle your seat belt? Or are you the kind of person who says (or thinks) "Aw, these things don't happen to me, they always happen to somebody else." Honestly now!

A common illusion is the belief that you are somehow exempt from the rules of chance.

One of the most common illusions about probability is the belief that you are somehow exempt from the rules of chance. This cognitive illusion accounts for more than 11,000 unnecessary deaths a year because people don't wear their seat belts, says the National Highway Traffic Safety Administration.

No one realizes that anyone can become a statistic better than Capt. Haynes. When he addresses groups of young pilots, he warns them not to goof off during training. "Although

I've always taken my job very seriously, I thought it couldn't happen to me. I'd been flying for 34 years before the crash and hadn't even dented a wing tip," he says. "Be ready for accidents to happen—because they can happen to you!" he says.

■ Don't Get Trumped out of Your Money

Convincing yourself that bad things only happen to other people is no more of a cognitive illusion than is convincing yourself that fate has willed good things to come your way. This is the kind of thinking that often puts gamblers in hock.

One reason casinos and state lotteries make so much money is that players often don't understand the slim odds against their winning. And although games of chance are simply that—games of *chance*—some gamblers refuse to see them as such. Consider the roulette wheel. "People believe that after several reds a black number is due, or after several blacks a red is due. It doesn't work that way. The roulette wheel has no memory and no moral sense," says Dr. Tversky.

Games of chance are simply that—games of chance.

But failing to understand the odds against winning at roulette is not the only faulty thinking that goes on in Las Vegas and Atlantic City. "Most gamblers don't know the odds, but then they don't really care—because they think they're going to win anyway," says psychologist Durand F. Jacobs, Ph.D., professor of psychiatry at the Loma Linda University Medical School and cofounder of California's Council on Compulsive Gambling. Gamblers often have "reasons" that they're going to win, such as "the sun shined on my wallet this morning," he says.

For most people who occasionally stroll into a casino or play the lottery, gambling is a form of recreation. It's nice to fantasize about striking it rich, and "everybody should have a fantasy," says Dr. Jacobs. If you're a recreational gambler, just make sure you realize hitting it big *is* a fantasy—a cognitive illusion.

Hitting it big is a cognitive illusion.

■ Be Cautious of Words

The way you phrase a question can also create a cognitive illusion, says Dr. Tversky. Pollsters, for instance, know that the way a particular question is phrased can greatly affect people's answers. (Do you think those miserable, stinking flag-burners should be allowed to continue to desecrate our proud national symbol? Yes or no?)

People can be easily swayed into changing their minds.

Studies have shown how easily patients and doctors can be swayed into picking one therapy over another by a simple rewording of facts. Ask a group of doctors, for instance, how many would try therapy X, which gives the patient a 95 percent chance of survival. Then ask the same group how many would try therapy Y, which gives the patients a 5 percent chance of dying. Studies show that you'll get two very different answers—although the therapies have *exactly* the same success and failure rate!

The best way to make a decision when faced with such a question is to rephrase the question, says Dr. Tversky.

■ *Read Newspapers with a Rational Eye*

Another form of fallible thinking that tends to affect polls, airline ticket sales, and much more occurs in the area of perceived risk. For a while after the showing of the thriller *Jaws,* for instance, many people along the East Coast were afraid to swim in the ocean. Following major airline crashes, plane travel declines. Are these decisions *rational?*

Not really, says Dr. Slovic. People generally allow what was in yesterday's newspaper or what they last saw at the movies to have an undue influence on their thinking. What this often means is that dramatic and sensational events tend to dominate our mind. One study, for instance, found that newspapers carry three times as many articles about homicides as they do about disease-related deaths—even though diseases claim 100 times as many lives!

Both fact and fiction can have undue influence on thinking.

So we wind up fearing for our lives over things like shark attacks, tornadoes, and mass murders. And we tend to downplay the dangers we don't read about as much, things like riding in a car without using a seat belt, smoking, and eating a lot of the wrong things.

What can you do? Get the facts, says Dr. Slovic. And be rational about the horror stories you see on the news.

■ *Get the Big Picture on Big Numbers*

Brace yourself—we're going to talk about numbers. Remember those problems in school that went something like this: One train leaves

Chicago 3 hours before another train leaves Pittsburgh; it is traveling at 57 miles per hour, whereas a train leaving Buffalo 2 hours later . . . yak, yak, yak. In the real world, such problems are (thank goodness!) rare, but number problems are *all* around us—we just don't recognize them as such!

According to Steven Sherman, Ph.D., professor of psychology at Indiana University, one of the more common errors in thinking is in failing to account for something called a "base rate." To illustrate how this works, consider Professor Yang. Professor Yang teaches in a large American University. He is Asian, very literate, likes to take nature walks, and writes poetry in his spare time. Would you think that Professor Yang is more likely to teach math or Korean literature?

If you think that Professor Yang is more likely to teach Korean literature, you're not considering the base rate. That is, if the number of Korean literature professors and the number of math professors were roughly equal, you might be wise to assume that Professor Yang teaches Korean lit (given his Asian background and interests). But all things are *not* equal. In any large American university, there may be 100 professors of math for every professor of Korean literature (a rather obscure field of study in the United States).

Now that you know this, if you had to put $20 on what Professor Yang teaches, would you say math or Korean literature? If you chose math, you'd probably win your money—and you can say you understand base rate. Easier than train problems, isn't it?

> A common error in thinking is in failing to account for "base rate."

When Fumbles Are Not Our Fault

To err is certainly human, but not *all* erring is human, says the University of California's Dr. Norman, author of *The Design of Everyday Things.* All too often we wind up kicking ourselves for our botches and blunders, even when they are not our fault. In fact, says Dr. Norman, many of the world's problems are attributable to that sometimes infernal creation of the Modern Age: The Machine.

> Too often we kick ourselves for botching up something that was not our fault.

"A lot of mistakes are due to the way things around us are built—they often don't take into consideration the way people function," says Dr. Norman. Take, for instance, the average stovetop. You typically find four burners laid out in a rectangle. Somewhere near the burners, you find the controls—four buttons laid out in a *straight line.* What happens is that "we often wind up doing the right thing to the wrong element," says Dr. Norman.

So you reach for the control that you *think* will heat up a certain burner, but it winds up heating *another* burner. What do you say? "Gee, how stupid I am!" That's wrong, says Dr. Norman, "It's not your mistake. It's the designer's!"

■ Dot Your Home

What can you do in the face of these mechanical nightmares? Start by visiting your local stationery or office supply store and purchasing some stick-on dots of various colors,

140

Color coding your life can help you outsmart modern machinery.

says Dr. Norman. Then, dots in hand, take a tour of your house.

Zero in on all those mechanical bugaboos. Your stove controls are in a straight line but your burners are in a rectangle? Try sticking a different-colored dot beside each of the burners and then put corresponding dots on the controls, suggests Dr. Norman. "It'll be surprisingly easy to remember which are which because you yourself made the decision," he says.

Your telephone answering machine has a dozen little buttons so that you're always pushing the wrong one? Try a little red dot over the rewind button, and perhaps a blue over the play (do the same for the VCR). Your ceiling fan and overhead light have identical chains? Stick a blue dot on the end of the fan chain (blue for its cooling action). Before you know it, you'll develop a reputation among friends as someone who is "good with machines!"

■ Find Guinea Pigs for Your Inventions

Getting too close can make you lose your objectivity.

If you're wondering why product designers seem to always put the buttons in the wrong places, it's because they become so intimately involved with their projects that they lose objectivity, says Dr. Norman. That's why, he says, "designers should never evaluate their own products." That's something to remember should *you* ever go into design work—find someone to experiment on!

Living (Well) with Your Decisions

Most decisions you'll make in life are not final. Luckily, that's true for the bad ones as well as the good. Money lost can be regained. Friendships tarnished can be mended. And tasteless gifts can be returned. Nevertheless, you've probably agonized wondering whether a particular decision was the right one.

Capt. Haynes, of course, had to make decisions of the nonreversible kind. And he agonized. Following the crash landing of flight 232, "All of us at first asked 'What if?' 'Should I have?' or 'Maybe I could have?' I'd replay the scenario in my mind every day," he says. Eventually, however, the agonizing ended. "Every day I convince myself more and more that there was nothing else we could have done," he says.

> "What ifs" can only add to the agony of making a wrong decision.

How often this is the case—that things don't turn out quite perfectly even after you've made all the best decisions!

■ Develop a More Eastern Attitude

According to Dr. Slovic, many of us, particularly in the Western world, go by the notion that for every problem there is a right answer. If you think long and hard enough, so the notion goes, you'll find that right answer. But what if, by chance, things *don't* work out? You wind up feeling that you made a bad decision. And you agonize.

In many Eastern cultures, however, a more easy-going approach prevails, says Dr. Slovic. Someone adhering to this Eastern philosophy would not think in terms of good or bad decisions. Rather, for any given problem, he would simply strive to make the best decision he could at the time—for that's all anyone can do. "It might help people in the West live a little easier with their decisions if they could develop this kind of outlook," says Dr. Slovic.

> Eastern thinking says there is no good or bad decision.

Confucius summed up this attitude when he said, "Things that are done, it is needless to speak about . . . things that are past, it is needless to blame." But thoroughly Western Harry S Truman also grasped this philosophy. He wrote: "Once a decision was made, I did not worry about it afterward."

■ Find Confidence in Your Mistakes

Not worrying about mistakes is one thing, but that doesn't mean you shouldn't give past mistakes some thought. You'll likely be missing out on a good learning opportunity if you simply erase mistakes from your mind. Often, says Dr. Johnson, "mistakes are a better learning experience than success."

As he explains to young emergency physicians, "If you make a mistake, sit back and analyze it. Ask yourself what data you could have gathered to make a better decision." Above all, he says, "Don't lose confidence because you made a mistake. In fact, have *more* confidence because you've learned in the process!"

Often, mistakes are a better learning experience than success.

■ Find Your Decision Pattern

If you're really serious about learning from your mistakes *and* your successes, consider keeping a "decision diary," suggests Dr. Fischhoff. One thing that may happen is that you'll start to see patterns. You may find that you make your best decisions early in the morning, or while taking walks in the woods, or in the

143

shower. One man who did this discovered that he generally makes lousy decisions while on the telephone. So he decided (while off the telephone) to no longer make any decisions on the telephone!

■ Don't Get Sunk by Self-Delusion

Another thing that a thought diary can help you with is something Dr. Fischhoff calls hindsight bias. As an example of how this bias works, he points to the number of political pundits who said *after* the Berlin Wall fell, "Oh yeah, I *knew* what was going to happen." In fact, no one knew. Hindsight bias makes us rewrite the past, convincing ourselves that we knew much more than we did. The danger with this self-delusion is that it makes us think we can predict the future. "Now all these pundits are saying that they know what's going to happen next in Eastern Europe," says Dr. Fischhoff.

Believing we can read the future can lead us up blind alleys where life may take us by surprise. This commonly happens to unwary investors who convince themselves that they "knew" the stock market was going to soar when it did. So they plunk down lots of money just as the stock market takes off again—in the opposite direction. "If you have a surpriseless past, you're likely to have a surpriseful future," says Dr. Fischhoff. By keeping a record of your thoughts and decisions, you'll have a clearer idea just how much you can trust your predictive powers.

> Hindsight bias is a self-delusion that makes you think you can predict the future.

> Record your thoughts and decisions and you'll have a clearer indication of predictive powers.

144

The older you get, the better you'll be at making good decisions.

In the end, clear thinking is something that comes with practice—and age. Capt. Haynes was 58 when he had to decide how to land his crashing airplane. But making decisions is something he's used to. He's been doing it since childhood. "My folks gave us a reasonably free hand to make up our own mind. I didn't have someone over me to make all my decisions for me," he says.

Today, says Capt. Haynes, he actually *likes* making decisions. He likes it so much that when back home in Washington he often exchanges his captain's uniform for another kind of uniform—that of a Little League umpire.

Which, you may wonder, is more difficult—making calls in the cockpit of a speeding jet or calling balls and strikes from behind home plate? "More difficult? . . . Calling balls and strikes," says Umpire Haynes.

Logic Makes a Great Team Player

Goof-ups are a part of the human condition.

Life can never be botch-free. Goof-ups just seem to be part of the human condition. No matter how much we try to be perfect, logical thinking machines, we cannot. Is that reason to be glum? Before answering, let us briefly introduce you to a perfect logical thinking machine—Deep Thought, the world champion computer chess player.

Deep Thought is a tremendously powerful computer. It can evaluate a mind-boggling 700,000 positions per second, far beyond what

PUZZLE POWER

If you can get the right answers to the puzzles below, you're thinking clearly. If you can't, get a good night's sleep and try again tomorrow!

The Right Direction

If Boston is east of New York, cross out all the A's. If not, cross out the R's. If Paris is south of New York, cross out all the O's. If not, cross out the I's. If Sri Lanka is in Asia, cross out the B's and U's. If not, cross out the C's. The remaining letters will tell you whether you've found the right answer.

C A A O I I A B U R R I A U E I B B C I A U T

Race Pace

In a marathon, which you watched from the sidewalk, Sam was faster than Jack. Denise beat Jim, but lost to Jack. Who came in last?

"Buy" the Letter

At one particular fruit stand where clear thinking doesn't always reign, an orange costs 18 cents, a pineapple costs 27 cents, and a grape costs 15 cents. Using the same logic, can you tell how much a mango would be?

To find the answers, see Solution #5 on page 455.

a human can. It can look as far as five or six moves deep on either side of the board, far beyond what a human can. But guess what? . . . Deep Thought has yet to beat the world champion *human* chess player. In fact, during their last match, Soviet Gary Kasparov gave Deep Thought a beating that its little microchips will not soon forget.

How is that possible? It's not because the human champ can think any faster or more logically than the machine, says Michael Valvo, international computer tournament director for the International Chess Association. That wouldn't be possible. But the human has something the machine has not—"an ability to see patterns and not just individual moves, and an ability to intuit a solution," says Valvo.

The point is, logic doesn't seem to work well in a vacuum. Thinking logically and rationally is darned important to making decisions and good judgments, but intuition and creativity are important, too. Get them all working together as a team, and your brainpower—like Kasparov's and like Capt. Haynes's—will really be revving!

Intuition and creativity play big roles in good decision making.

Learning

Teach Yourself New Tricks

The judge pushed her reading glasses down her nose with a long, red-lacquered nail and looked directly at the defendant. The mother of four grown children, the Honorable Linda K. M. Ludgate, judge of the Berks County Court of Common Pleas in Pennsylvania, was clearly accustomed to weighing guilt and innocence from more than just the obvious.

"Was it your family that was having problems around the time of your arrest?" she probed.

The defendant nodded. "Yes, your honor."

Ludgate took a deep breath and exhaled slowly. Another tough case. The defendant's father had allegedly killed the young man's mother, then dropped dead himself. Now the son was in court, accused of stealing four steaks and a tenderloin from a local supermarket.

"You have my condolences, young man," said the judge. She

147

looked at his lawyer. "Nevertheless, I'll see you both back in court at 1:30 so you can enter a plea."

A Lifelong Learner

Linda Ludgate is a judge, a lawyer, a mother, a wife, a prison reformer, a YWCA volunteer, and—above all—a lifelong learner. She started college at 30, began law school at 35, and was elected to the bench at 47.

How did she achieve so much so fast after such a late start? Through her indomitable desire to learn, learn, *learn!* No matter where she's lived, how much money she has had, whether or not there has been a college nearby, or how many people tried to discourage her, Ludgate sought and found knowledge.

Ludgate's path to the bench was not easy. The youngest of 14 children, she got married right out of high school, had children, and realized somewhere between the 2,000th and 3,000th diaper change that if she didn't want her brain to go soft from all the grunge work that being a homemaker—however rewarding—entailed, she'd better start doing something about it.

So she did. She hit the local library, familiarized herself with how it worked, then set up her own learning program. Her goal was to read six nonfiction books every week. If she reached her goal, she could treat herself to a novel.

Her independent study combined with her activities as a local prison volunteer whetted her appetite for more knowledge about govern-

The desire to learn can help you accomplish anything you want at any age.

One woman didn't start college until age 30. She became a judge 17 years later.

ment and the history of the American judicial system. So at the age of 30 she signed up for an American history course at a local college in upstate New York. When her husband was transferred to Reading, Pennsylvania, the county seat of Berks County, she enrolled at a local college as a full-time student in the criminal justice program. She graduated—with highest honors—three years later and was accepted at Temple University law school in Philadelphia, to which she commuted an hour each way every day.

After graduation, she worked in the public defender's office and then on her own as a practicing attorney. Within ten years she was sitting on the bench.

The Adult Advantage

Ludgate's success may be unusual, but her self-directed approach to learning isn't. Learning does not end the day you get out of school. For a lot of people, it's where the desire to learn *begins*. It seems the freedom to pursue what you want, when you want, and how you want can stimulate the desire to learn.

Researchers at Iowa State University discovered this several years ago when they asked 214 people over the age of 55 to describe their learning activities. They found that every single person was engaged in at least one learning project, while most said they got involved in three or four learning projects a year. And the older they were, the more interested in learning they seemed to be.

The older people get, the more interested they become in learning.

What this suggests, says D. Barry Lumsden, Ph.D., a professor of higher and adult education at the University of North Texas, is that most older adults are eager to learn. It also suggests that many aging adults find the structured learning of formal education stifling.

■ Do What You Want to Do

Eighty to ninety percent of all adult learning in this country is self-selected, concurs Alan B. Knox, Ed.D., a professor of education at the University of Wisconsin at Madison. That's because there's no one to tell them what to do. Being able to choose what you want to learn and how you're going to learn it is what adult education is all about. It's what makes learning easy—and fun.

If, for example, you're interested in investing your money, you can read books or take a course to learn about the stock market. If you want to learn how to sail, you can grab a couple of books on knots, weather, and sails, sign up for a lesson or two, and go to it. The pressures you may have experienced during your formal education no longer exist. You're free to please only yourself.

■ Use Learning to Fill a Personal Need

Experts say adults usually start a learning project in response to a need for self-improvement, self-esteem, or personal recognition. And our desire for knowledge changes as we move from one stage of life to another. Childbirth, job loss, divorce, a friend's death, or a move

Learning is more appealing when you can choose your subjects.

across town are all likely to set in motion an urge to learn something new.

Most women who give birth for the first time, for example, devour books and magazines and quiz friends and relatives endlessly to learn how to rear happy, healthy children.

■ Build on Your Past Experiences

If you're shying away from learning as an adult because you weren't too thrilled with learning as a kid in school, listen to this: "You can learn many things quicker and better as an adult than you did at age 15," says Dr. Knox. That's because your experiences over the years contribute to basic knowledge about given topics. When learning something new, it gives you a running head start that somebody without that background doesn't have."

Having studied chemistry in high school, for example, can make it easier for you to learn how to bake bread as an adult, because you've already learned a lot about how one substance interacts with another. The foundation is there; all you have to do is build on it.

Think about it. If you studied chemistry, you know that if you add yeast to flour, it creates carbon dioxide bubbles that cause the dough to rise. If the bread doesn't rise on your first try, or something else goes wrong, you'll be able to review what you did and analyze what went wrong. You'll figure that either your yeast was too old or the temperature at which the chemical reaction occurred wasn't right. So you should be able to make an adjustment or two and get the bread right on the second try. If you don't know anything about chemistry,

You can learn many things more quickly as an adult than you did at age 15.

Life experiences go a long way in making learning easier.

(continued on page 155)

What's Your Learning Style?

Each of us has our own natural learning style that reflects the quality of our mind, says Anthony Gregorc, Ph.D., educator and author of *An Adult's Guide to Style*. It reflects the way we absorb new information, process it, and use it to form new ideas.

"I started out with learning styles—or mind styles as I call them now—about 20 years ago," says Dr. Gregorc. "I was principal of a lab school for gifted kids and I was watching youngsters in grades 7 through 12 who were not being very successful. We had tried all kinds of curriculum revisions, so what I started to do was observe them in relation to their teachers—to really watch their behavior, to see how they learned."

His approach was somewhat unusual, says Dr. Gregorc, because educators rarely study learners to see how they learn. "We normally take the position that a learner is a learner and if he only tries he can adapt to just about anything," explains Dr. Gregorc."The implication that's at the root of this is that all of us have the capacity to learn in specific ways. It's just that we haven't been taught to.

"As I observed these youngsters, however, I found that they all had different kinds of styles. And when we tried to get some of them to learn in a style that was different than their own, there was a resistance to it.

"I didn't find the resistance was due to 'laziness' or 'contrariness,' " he hastens to add, "or things of that type. I simply found that there were indeed ways of processing information that are different."

The learning styles that Dr. Gregorc discovered among his students—which have since become standard among

United States educators—fall into four basic groups: concrete/sequential, abstract/sequential, abstract/random, and concrete/random.

The idea, explains Dr. Gregorc, is that most of us obtain new information best in one of two ways: either *abstractly*, through the use of our emotions, intellect, and intuition, or *concretely*, through the use of our physical senses. Then when we get the information, we assimilate it in one of two other ways: either *sequentially*, in a step-by-step, methodical way, or *randomly*, in a scattered, nonlinear way. We can all learn in any fashion, but we each have a natural proclivity toward one. How do you know which learning style is naturally yours? The following examples should give you an idea.

All of us remember the kid in high school science class who would logically and precisely examine a lab specimen, write up his report, and get an A. He's an example of a concrete/sequential learner—he learned best by seeing and doing. And we can remember the girl in English class who could always interpret the meaning of a *Moby Dick*, and explain its plot, point by point. She was an abstract/sequential—she naturally understood literature.

And remember the kid who was always into half a dozen things at once? His desk was always a mess, his attention could be caught for only a moment, and he was always thinking up new things to do. He learns what he wants when he wants—an abstract/random. And the kid who was voted "most likely to succeed in business"? She's the one who was always dreaming up new schemes to make money, then talking other kids into chipping in their allowances or lunch money—a concrete/random learner, an independent thinker and self-starter.

(continued)

153

What's Your Learning Style?—*Continued*

Once you have an idea of your natural learning style, capitalize on your strengths and don't fight your weaknesses, advises Dr. Gregorc.

The concrete/sequential learner, for example, learns best when he can examine things with his own two eyes. He prefers a quiet, ordered, predictable, and stable environment in which he can work methodically to his heart's content.

The abstract/sequential learner learns best from words and pictures of things, rather than the things themselves. He prefers an intellectual environment in which he can share his thoughts and ideas with others, although he needs solitude in order to concentrate on a particular task. An environment full of distracting sounds will make him a nervous wreck.

The abstract/random learner learns best when he can use his feelings to absorb ideas, information, and impressions as they flow around and through him. He prefers a harmonious environment that allows him both mental and physical freedom. Restrictions, rules, and negative feelings from those around him can make him anxious and/or frustrated.

The concrete/random learner prefers to learn independently. He needs his own "space" and the freedom to exercise his curiosity. He thrives on competition, but he cannot stand rules, regulations and orders, or being limited or confined in any way.

"The reason that we learn the way that we do is that we're actually 'wired' to learn and process information in a particular way," explains Dr. Gregorc.

All of us naturally lean toward one of these categories, says Dr. Gregorc. Once you identify your style, learning automatically can become a whole lot easier.

you'll probably just give up in frustration and claim you're a lousy baker.

Or suppose you want to learn how to ride a motorcycle. If, like most people, you learned how to ride a bike as a child and how to drive a car as an adult, you already possess the fundamentals of handling a motorcycle. It'll make learning the rest, like working the gears and balancing the weight, easier.

■ *Do It Your Way*

Do you want to learn how to grow prize-winning roses? Are you interested in finding out how to sail? Or how about learning a new skill—word processing, perhaps—related to your job?

Whatevever it is, as an adult you have the opportunity to suit yourself.

As an adult, learning is dictated by personal desire.

Do you prefer to learn by reading a book, listening to others, watching how something is done, or conducting an experiment with your own two hands? Do you like to learn on your own or in a group?

Do you generally start with the big picture and add pieces? Or start with pieces and discover the big picture?

Once you've figured out how your mind learns naturally, use that approach on anything you want to learn. You'll be surprised at how easy it can be.

Endless Opportunities

"The potential for learning continues right up to the minute you breathe your last breath,"

156

The potential to learn continues right up to the moment you draw your last breath.

says Jerold Apps, Ph.D., professor of adult education at the University of Wisconsin at Madison. "There aren't any limits." You don't get dumber as you get older, you only get smarter.

So why then do many adults seem to have the idea that they're too old to learn? Attitude, says Dr. Apps. Most adults still need to overcome a couple of attitudinal problems before they can really get on with the business of learning effectively.

■ Get Past the Barrier That You Can't Learn on Your Own

Many adults seem to think that you need a teacher standing in the front of a classroom in order to learn. Yet, as Dr. Apps points out, "You've had to learn thousands and thousands of things on your own just to have survived in this society."

You don't need a classroom setting to learn. You can be your own teacher.

Ronald Gross, a learning expert who co-chairs the University Seminar on Innovation in Education at Columbia University, agrees. "One of the biggest myths in education is that it's the teacher who accounts for learning, not you," says Gross, who models workshops and tapes after his book *Peak Learning*.

■ Get Past the Barrier That You Have to Learn Systematically

"Another myth is that learning has to be systematic and planned in advance," says Gross. "We think that way because our teachers always had a syllabus and had it all planned out, right? But that's not the way it works in the real world."

Think about how you learned to do your taxes. Most of us didn't develop a week-long plan in which one day we learned about deductions, another day we learned about exemptions, and another day we learned about capital gains. Most of us probably just sat down with our income tax return and referred to the accompanying booklet whenever we had a question. If the booklet didn't answer the question, we called the IRS. And if the IRS didn't answer the question—or didn't answer the question in a way we could understand—then we called a friend. Or an accountant. It didn't take a teacher with a lesson plan to show us.

Boosting Your Knowledge Naturally

Reading, writing, and arithmetic. They're the basis of learning—and for good reason. Without them you can't even get through life. (You can't assemble a bicycle, correspond with a friend, or figure out how much change you should get when making a purchase.) Get good at them and everyday life gets a lot easier. Get *great* at them and your potential to learn knows no bounds.

Reading, writing, and arithmetic—without them you can't get through life.

■ Read Everything You Can Get Your Hands On

Start your morning with a story and end your day with nonfiction. Stick plays into your lunch hour and recite poetry after dinner. Take notes, reread important paragraphs, and question the author's statements. Argue with him in the margins. What's he trying to say? How does it relate to your own experiences? Does what he has to say make sense?

■ Learn Faster by Reading Smarter

"People ask me, 'Should I take a speed-reading course?' " notes Gross. "I usually say, 'well, before you put a lot of money and effort into learning how to read fast, how about just learning how to read smarter?' "

For example, you want to bone up on a subject—say, birds of the southeastern United States—so you go to the library and you find the book. All 500 pages. The best way to tackle a 500-page book is not to be able to read it four times as fast as you can read right now, says Gross, but to be able to figure out if the book even contains what you need to know *and*, if it does, to know how to figure out which pages you really need to read.

A table of contents can be your shortcut to what you want to know.

Use the table of contents to "X-ray" the book and diagnose what you want to read, says Gross. Then just skim through the index and look for things you already know a little something about, and flip to the parts of the book where they're discussed.

Is there anything really interesting that you want to explore? If there is, read those sections and move into other areas that stimulate your interest, suggests Gross. But feel perfectly comfortable skipping the parts that don't really look interesting. Remember, your interest is dictated by what you need to know. So if a particular section doesn't intrigue you, it's probably not something you need to learn.

■ *Fascinate Yourself with Your Vocabulary*

Think of yourself as a word sleuth, suggests Dr. Apps, and everywhere you go, anytime you hear a new word, write it down on a small card you can easily fit in your pocket or handbag. When you have several, track down their meanings. Look them up in an abridged dictionary such as the one most of us have at home, the monster unabridged dictionary in the local public library, or—for a really fascinating commentary on their historical roots—in the library's copy of the *Oxford English Dictionary* (*OED*).

Keep a list of words you're unfamiliar with.

The *OED* comes in 20 volumes plus supplements. That may sound a bit intimidating, but it's one of the few places in the world that will tell you the origin of the word "diesel" (Rudoph Diesel, who invented the engine of the same name) and also how the diesel is engineered. In fact, it not only gives exhaustive explanations of words, it also traces their literary meaning back to their first written record.

The point of all this is that it makes updating your vocabulary interesting.

■ *Get to the Root of Your Latin and Greek*

Approximately 60 percent of the English language is made up of prefixes and roots taken from Latin and Greek words, Dr. Apps points

160

Sixty percent of the English language is derived from Latin and Greek.

out. So if you take some time to pick up a Latin or Greek primer at the library and learn the most common prefixes and roots, you'll be yards ahead of anybody else when it comes to figuring out the meaning of a word.

Take the word "asexual," for example. Ten to one you know what "sex" and "sexual" mean, right? But what happens to the meaning when you add the "a-" up front? Well, if you know that "a-" in Latin and Greek means "not," then you can pretty well figure out that asexual means "no sex." And you'd be right on the money. The actual definition is "lacking sex."

Or how about the word "misanthrope"? You may know that "mis-" in front of a word usually means "wrong." And if you've studied a list of Latin and Greek roots, you know that "anthrop" means "human being." Put them together and what do you get? A "wrong human." Again, that's pretty close to the actual meaning. A misanthrope thinks that being human is wrong. He's someone who dislikes people.

■ Write about the Texture of Your Life

Sharpening your writing skills requires a bit more work. And a blank piece of paper can be an intimidating object when you know you have to fill it with words. Where do the words come from? How do you get started?

A blank sheet of paper can be intimidating when you must fill it with words.

Try keeping a pocket-sized notebook with a page reserved exclusively for jotting down ideas and possible topics as they occur to you, suggests Natalie Goldberg, a writing instructor

Are You Plugged In to the M-Field?

Is windsurfing easier to learn today than when it hit the scene 20 years ago? Yes, says biologist Rupert Sheldrake, but it has nothing to do with improvements in the sport. It's simply because the sport isn't new anymore.

According to Sheldrake, author of *The Presence of the Past,* how easily any particular individual learns any particular task is based upon how many times someone—anyone—has done it before.

And why not? "If we tune in to our own memories, then why can't we tune in to other people's as well?" Sheldrake asks. "I think we do, and the whole basis of the approach I am suggesting is that there is a collective memory to which we are all tuned. It forms a background against which our own experience develops.

"This concept," he adds, "is very similar to the notion of the collective unconscious. . . . The main difference is that [the collective unconscious] idea was applied primarily to human experience and human collective memory. What I am suggesting is that a very similar principle operates throughout the entire universe, not just in human beings."

But how? Sheldrake's ideas have provoked a storm of controversy among scientists on both sides of the Atlantic. He hypothesizes the existence of *morphic fields* (M-fields) around every person, tree, rock, and grain of sand on the planet. The M-field sets up a soundless resonance that—along with genetics— influences and shapes every fiber of every being. This is only a theory, of course, but if it's true, the guiding resonance in the M-field of our muscles could make windsurfing easier and easier to learn. ∎

Improve your writing
skills by jotting ideas
as they occur to you.

at the University of New Mexico and author of
*Writing Down the Bones: Freeing the Writer
Within.*

"Making a list is good," writes Goldberg in
her book. "It makes you start noticing material
for writing in your daily life, and your writing
comes out of a relationship with your life and
its texture." Until you develop your own list,
however, she suggests, among other things,
that you might try writing about one of the
following:

• Tell about the quality of light coming in
through your window.

• Begin with the words "I remember" and
write down memory after memory.

• Take something you feel strongly about,
whether it is positive or negative, and write
about it as though you love it.

• Write about "leaving." Approach it any way
you want. Write about your divorce, leaving the
house this morning, or a friend dying.

■ *Write for a Specific Period of Time*

Commit yourself to
writing on a routine
schedule.

Commit yourself to writing for a specific
period of time—10 minutes, 20 minutes, half
an hour—the amount doesn't matter as much
as the commitment. But to keep your mind
moving through these first thoughts, here are
Goldberg's suggestions.

• Keep your hand moving. (Don't pause to
reread the line you have just written. That's

stalling and trying to get control of what you're saying.)

• Don't cross out. (That is editing as you write. Even if you write something you didn't mean to write, leave it.)

Keep the ideas flowing. Don't pause to reread what you have written.

• Don't worry about spelling, punctuation, grammar. (Don't even care about staying within the margins and lines on the page.)

• Lose control.

• Don't think. Don't get logical.

• Go for the jugular. (If something comes up in your writing that is scary or naked, dive right into it. It probably has lots of energy.)

■ Write from Within

You also have to remember that writing from within follows no formula, cautions Gold- berg. "You can sit down and have something you want to say. But then you must let its expression be born in you and on the paper. Don't hold too tight; allow it to come out the way it needs to rather than trying to control it. Yes, those experiences, memories, feelings are in us, but you can't carry them out on paper whole the way a cook brings out a pizza from the oven."

Writing follows no formula.

She suggests you start simple and don't worry about being awkward. "You are stripping yourself," she writes. "You are exposing your life, not how your ego would like to see you represented, but how you are as a human being." Then, most important, she adds, "Learn to trust the force of your own voice."

■ *Picture a Way to Relate to Numbers*

Sharpening the 'rithmetic part of your skills may take a little more effort than writing. Although we were taught the basics—2 plus 2 equals 4—in school, many of us never learned how to translate numbers and everyday statistics into ideas and concepts that we can think about and use.

Without some acquaintance with probabilities and an ability to estimate risks, says Temple University mathematician John Allen Paulos, Ph.D., we can't even figure out where the world is dangerous and where it's safe.

Understanding probabilities and estimated risks is essential.

"I think an ability to estimate numbers, probability, and risk is very important in our culture," says Dr. Paulos. "I know people who can compute anything you give them, but ask them how high the Empire State Building is and they'll say, 'Ten miles high.' Ask them how many people there are in the United States and they'll say, 'A couple of billion or maybe 20 million' and not have a clear idea of the difference.

"Or ask them how likely something is—one out of ten or one out of a million; it makes the same impression on them. Most people's quantitative vocabulary is limited to 'more' or 'less.' "

Without some feeling for probabilities, automobile accidents, for example, might seem a relatively minor risk of domestic transportation while being killed by terrorists might seem to be a major risk when going overseas. Yet

45,000 Americans out of a population of nearly 250 million are killed annually in automobile accidents, while from 1978 to 1988 (before the plane disaster over Lockerbie, Scotland), only 17 Americans had been killed by terrorists. And 28 million Americans travel every year.

165

When figuring probability, your risk of being killed in an automobile accident is 1 in 5,555. As for being murdered by a terrorist, the risk is 1 in 1 million.

The point is that our "innumeracy"—as Dr. Paulos calls it—blinds us to reality.

Innumeracy blinds us from reality.

To overcome your innumeracy, says Dr. Paulos, you need to develop a way to relate to numbers so they become more meaningful. One way is to paint a picture in your mind.

"For 1,000," says Dr. Paulos, "I think of a section of Veterans Stadium in Philadelphia that has a thousand seats. In my mind's eye, I can see what a thousand is. For 10,000, I think of the number of bricks in the side of a large garage near my house."

The larger numbers, such as a million, a billion, and a trillion—numbers frequently thrown around by politicians trying to explain the national deficit—can be made more vivid by equating them to various times. "A million seconds is 11½ days," says Dr. Paulos. "A billion seconds is 32 years. And a trillion is 32,000 years."

■ *Learn the Numbers*
That Define the World

Another way to get a feel for numbers is to familiarize yourself with some basic statis-

Familiarize yourself with some basic statistics.

166

Many people have no idea what the population of the United States is.

tics, says Dr. Paulos, especially about the world around you.

You don't need to know a lot of figures, says Dr. Paulos, just a few standard benchmarks—the number of people in the United States (248 million), the number of people in the world (5.2 billion), the number of miles from coast to coast (3,050). So when you're reading a newspaper story about the 113 million people in Eastern Europe you'll know that population represents almost half of the United States.

Take a trip to your local library and browse through a few books like the *World Almanac*, *Information USA*, or Dr. Paulos' book, *Innumeracy*. Then commit a few of the numbers that define the world to memory. Any subsequent material you learn that uses numbers—whether from a newspaper or a textbook—will bring with it a depth of meaning that you would otherwise have missed.

Learning: As Easy as Child's Play

A child's natural curiosity is what allows him to learn so much so fast.

Next time you're in the presence of toddlers, take time to sit back and observe them. You'll most likely notice they can't sit still—that they want to constantly move, feel, touch. What you're observing is their natural inquisitive nature, an overwhelming desire to explore the world around them—to *learn*.

Try to think of yourself as a toddler. How you learned to walk. How you learned to speak the thousands of words and inflections of your native tongue. Walking and talking are probably the most monumental learning achievements you'll ever accomplish, says Columbia University's Ronald Gross.

For young children, learning comes naturally. Even before they can read, for example, they can pick up a second language effortlessly. But for an adult, it takes lots of effort—even with a book and a tutor!

Why does learning seem to get harder as we get older?

"Number one, when you're a child, mistakes don't count," observes Gross. "Children have no inhibition about mistakes, they have no problem about doing and failing, about saying the wrong word or falling down.

"Number two, they are doing it usually in the company of someone who cares about them. There is a very strong emotional component. The brain isn't being asked to work in isolation from feelings.

"Number three, childhood learning is usually associated with a multisensory condition— touching and feeling and hearing and seeing.

"And, most important, although it is taken for granted, kids *want* to learn—they feel a strong impulse."

Whether it's instinctual, developmental, or social, the impulse comes from within the child, explains Gross. He proceeds at his own pace and tends to choose his own times so he is actually unconsciously—but very effectively—shaping the learning to his own style. "This is what I call the flow state of learning.

"Now look at all those conditions and then contrast them with what we try to do when we take complete control over learning in schools," says Gross. "In schools we find that everything

The rigidity of traditional education can inhibit learning, some experts believe.

Beating the Fear of Foreign Language

You're going to Italy next week and your only knowledge of Italian is pizza, pasta, and Gucci. You'd like to at least be able to say "please" and "thank you" and "Where is the bathroom?" but your experience with high school French is a reminder that a foreign language is not for you.

So how can you learn enough Italian so you at least don't get stuck eating the same food at every meal? Start by getting rid of the notion that you can't learn a language, or at least enough of a language to communicate effectively, says Claire Kramsch, Ph.D., a professor of German and foreign language acquisition at the University of California at Berkeley. Then get some introductory language tapes—you can probably borrow some from your local library—and immerse yourself in the language, conversation-style.

Avoid language tapes with drills, advises Dr. Kramsch. (It's probably why you hated languages in school in the first place.) Since the meanings of so many words and phrases are dependent upon the social context in which they are used, you need to hear language "live," not parroted in isolation.

is prescribed. The teacher's in charge and there's a curriculum and there's a place and a time and an evaluation and isolation from other people and other senses and 'Sit still!' and 'Don't you know?' "

Gross gives an exasperated sigh. "People who have thought the most deeply about this and examined all the existing evidence pretty well agree that these conditions actually begin to inhibit, sabotage, undermine, and otherwise disturb the natural learning process.

Instead, get tapes that include social situations and conversations between people—between waiters and diners, parents and children, retailers and customers, friends and lovers.

If possible, listen to radio shows that are broadcast in the language you're trying to learn, suggests Dr. Kramsch. And visit ethnic restaurants, shops, and neighborhoods. Tune your ears in to the foreign conversations around you.

After you've developed a small working vocabulary, says Dr. Kramsch, see if you can find some books or newspapers written in the language you want to learn. Obviously you won't be able to understand an entire article or even an entire paragraph. Avoid trying to translate every word, says Dr. Kramsch. Try to get the gist of the material by following what you do know.

You improve your ability to speak a language, says Dr. Kramsch, by always being into it at a level just over your head. It's the struggle to make sense out of what sounds like nonsense that eventually teaches you the language.

But all is not lost forever. Gross says that, as adult learners, we can recapture that flow state of learning we experienced as a child.

■ *Visit a Nursery School*

What better way to get a feel for the ease of learning than to observe it firsthand?

Psychologists tell us that nursery school children learn faster than at any other time in

170

Nursery school children learn faster than at any other time in their lives.

their lives. But what's happening? What are they doing that's making them learn so fast? What can you get out of watching them?

"I'll give you an example," says Peter Kline, author of *The Everyday Genius* and director of the National Academy of Integrative Learning in Rochester, New York. "I was watching an 11-month-old child who was getting to know a vacuum cleaner. He would pick it up, and he would kick different parts of it, put it in his mouth, sit on it. He would do everything to that vacuum cleaner that you could possibly imagine."

If you watch children learn to walk, he says, you'll notice that they all go through several steps in the process—balance, forward motion, developing a system, and so forth.

The idea is to let go of learning inhibitions. Use your imagination; it can be your biggest learning tool.

■ Start a Learning Log

A learning log should be a diary of your thoughts and feelings.

"To me, the most comprehensive learning strategy is the learning log, because it can take so many different forms," says Gross. "It can be kept in a notebook, on audio or video tapes, or on a computer." Some people paint their logs on canvas or express it through dance.

Your log should be a diary of your thoughts and feelings about the things you've learned and experienced throughout each day—along with the questions that those things and experiences have raised in your mind. It allows you to learn about things with the freedom of a child.

"The learning log is based on the fact that you need to process information and understand it to get anything out of it," says Gross. "It provides activity that stimulates and guides you in doing that.

"If you don't have such an activity," he adds, "you're literally going to go through your life asleep. You're going to have new experiences, but you're not actually going to be distilling them.

"We all know people who have worked 30 years in the same job and haven't learned anything since their first year. And we know other people who are constantly learning. Just walking down the street they'll be asking questions: 'How does this work?' 'How does that work?' 'How did it come to be?' 'What would it be like if . . . ?' "

Some people can spend 30 years in a job and never learn anything new; others learn constantly.

The learning log kind of forces you to resurrect that inquisitive nature you had as a toddler, explains Gross. It forces you to question and examine everything.

■ *Don't Hesitate to Ask "Why?"*

"A famous astronomer taught one of our seminars at Columbia," recalls Gross, "and I asked him what he wanted his students to get out of the workshop. Did he want them to be smart enough to read *Scientific American* or what? He told me he didn't care if they got to know more science. He wanted them to learn the importance of constantly asking why about *all* kinds of things. From why is it hotter in the summer and cooler in the winter to why do I feel this way on Tuesday mornings." Asking

Always ask, "Why?"

why is one of the most important ways to improve your mind. And putting it in your log is one of the best ways to ensure you'll keep it there.

■ Make a Map in Your Mind

Did you ever sit through a class or a meeting scribbling words you were hearing on a notepad and surrounding those words with boxes and circles? You may not have known it, but you were making a knowledge map.

Knowledge mapping is the brainchild of psychologist Donald F. Dansereau, Ph.D., a professor at Texas Christian University. "Knowledge mapping is sort of like graphic language," says Dr. Dansereau. And it's much more effective than note taking when it comes to comprehending and analyzing a subject.

Let's say you're studying the German occupation in Europe during World War II. You scribble down the United States and its allies on one part of a page and draw boxes around them. You scribble down Germany on another part and box it. As you read about key people and places you do the same. Pretty soon you have a whole page full of boxes—graphic representation of what you need to know. Then later when you study, you look them over, see how they relate to one another, and connect them with lines or links that indicate that relationship.

Knowledge mapping is simply an alternative to the strings of words we usually use to write down information, says Dr. Dansereau. It

Knowledge mapping is more effective than note taking when it comes to comprehension.

can be used for anything—to indicate questions in the learning log of an independent learner or to replace massive note taking during a lecture.

"I was watching a show on PBS the other night on weather patterns, for example," says Dr. Dansereau. "It was a very interesting show, lots of graphics, nice flow and narrative." But, he said, most of what he saw was forgotten as soon as the broadcast was over.

"What I would have done if I had really wanted to retain the information was to take that information immediately after I saw the program and map out what had occurred." He would have jotted down each piece of information that interested him on a 3-by-5 card. Then after the show, he could have laid them out on the coffee table and moved them around to see how one piece of information related to another.

Knowledge mapping is a smashing success, says Dr. Dansereau. "We're finding in our research that maps are better than words in a lot of situations. Most folks who use maps tend to learn better, although the people who tend to benefit the most are people who have low verbal ability. The technique organizes the material so that people who aren't 'good' with words can use their spatial skills and not get lost in word clutter.

Those who use knowledge maps tend to learn better.

"Knowledge mapping reduces word clutter," Dr. Danserseau points out, because "it uses links rather than whole strings of words to show relationships. A lot of the words in language are kind of just words to carry you along the page—as opposed to words that have any

Those who benefit most are those with a low verbal ability.

substance. And a lot of people just get hung up in that clutter and don't really get to the meat of the matter."

"I'll frankly admit that in some ways it's better than writing," says Gross. "If you make a knowledge map in your learning log, for example, and then add to it over a period of a week or two, you'll focus on different aspects each time you pick up a pen.

"You'll have a wonderfully rich display of what you're learning from all different points of view," he concludes. "It can be marvelously illuminating."

■ *Start a Learning Co-Op*

Another trick that can help you recapture the natural way of learning is a technique called "scripted cooperation." It plays on the observation that people learn better when they work together rather than in isolation.

"One thing we've discovered is that it's fine to tell people to study together and work together, but you really need to have a good script for them to follow," says Dr. Dansereau. "A script in this case is very much like a play script—it prescribes the role that they're supposed to take, the flow of dialogue, and the actions that are to take place.

"If you and I were cooperative learners, for example, one simple script might be that we'd both read a body of material. Then we'd put it away and I would attempt to recall the information to you, and you would sit there and listen and try to notice any gaps. You'd point

People learn better when they work together rather than in isolation.

those out to me and we'd brainstrom about how to fill them.

"After that we would both talk about it. How can we remember this material? How can we elaborate on it? Does it fit into anything else we know? Then we'd go back and read the next section of material and we'd reverse roles. You'd be the recaller and I'd be the listener. And we'd follow the script once again."

If you wanted to learn about canning and freezing vegetables, for example, you and a friend could both read one of the county extension service's bulletins on preserving foods. Then put the bulletin away and have one of you recite the major points. The other would act as critic. When you've finished recalling as much information as you can, start to ask yourself questions that the material provoked but didn't answer. Do vegetables that are stored in the basement keep longer than vegetables stored in the refrigerator? Do lima beans retain taste better than string beans when frozen?

Then decide where you can get your questions answered. The county extension service? The home ecconomics unit of a local college or high school?

Read another bulletin on food preservation and reverse roles. By the time the two of you are finished, both of you should be ready to can like a couple of experts!

Two things happen when you use scripted cooperation, explains Dr. Dansereau. One, as you're learning material together, you're learning it better than someone who is learning on his own. And, two, when you're in a situation in which you must learn on your own, the co-

Act out a lesson with someone else, then reverse roles.

Learning with others helps you learn better when you're on your own.

operative learning experience will help you learn *better*. The experience intensifies your ability to learn, he says.

■ *Recruit Three Learning Aids*

Here's a form of scripted cooperation with a spin. It comes from Peter Kline.

Let's say you've decided to take a course at your local community college. The first thing you should do after you've signed up for the course, says Kline, is to go out and find three kinds of people.

The first is someone who is taking the course with you. Build up a relationship with this person so you can talk about your studies and share ideas.

The second person is someone who knows nothing about what you're learning but would be interested in hearing you talk about it. You'll tell this person everything you learn as you take the course. Because this person isn't a professor or fellow student, you know that if you make a mistake he's not going to know—or probably care.

The third person you're going to find is somebody outside of the course who is an expert. Let's say you're taking an accounting course and you hire a CPA to do your taxes. You make an appointment, you go in, and you say to this person, "I want you to tell me the three most important things about accounting in your opinion. And do it in 2 minutes, because I'm paying for your time."

Kline chuckles. "That person is going to boil down an enormous amount of information.

Build up a relationship with those who can help you with your studies.

And all three of these people will be extremely helpful to you in terms of thinking about what you're learning."

■ Take Advantage of Free Advice

"Let's say you go to a cocktail party and you meet an accountant there," suggests Kline. "You say, 'What do you like about accounting? What attracted you to the profession? What are some of the things you've learned by being an accountant? What do you think most people don't understand about accounting?'

If you're studying accounting, rub elbows with accountants.

"Just get them into a conversation. It's not like you're asking them to reveal professional secrets. You're just asking them about what they do. And they'll love it. Most people just love to talk about their work. They'll give you a whole education."

At the same party or in another situation you may meet another accountant or several accountants. Make sure you strike up a conversation. You're bound to get some conflicting points of view, and that may help you wrestle with some heavy issues that come up in your class, says Kline. And actively struggling with those issues will help you learn even more.

■ Get Some New Friends

Of course, running into accountants at parties is only possible if you move in the right circles. As you branch out into new learning endeavors, you may also have to acquire a whole new bunch of friends.

The problem is that your social group perceives you in a certain way, says Kline. "Let's say you're a housewife and you want to become a lawyer. You can go to law school, but you may find that your friends are subtly making you feel uncomfortable about that. And they are because they realize that law school is changing you, and that makes them uncomfortable."

The solution? "You need to think about building a social life around what your aspirations are and what you're doing," says Kline. "It's not 'get rid of the old and get new,' but you need to form relationships with people who are really going to be excited about what you're doing and not just say, 'What do you want to do that for?'

"The people who are supporting you are going to continually give you new ideas about how to do what you're doing better," he adds. And those are the kinds of friends you need if you're serious about learning.

Your social group perceives you in a certain way.

■ Send Yourself Positive Messages

"A lot of people won't try something new because they think they can't do it," says Kline. "They say, 'I can't draw,' or 'My grammar's not good.' It's a bias you picked up as a grown-up. As a child, you'd give anything a try!"

An "I can't" attitude is a mindset that will guarantee you can't do something, says Kline.

What's amazing, he adds, is that if you flip that around and experiment with saying things like "I'm a really excellent artist," or "I'm developing a million-dollar marketing plan," you'll find that you actually begin to do that.

An "I can't" attitude is a mindset that guarantees that you can't.

"It's almost uncanny how it happens," says Kline. "And the more you play this little game with yourself, the more you'll find that you actually can do something. It's like a hypnotic suggestion. If you're sure that you can't learn something, it doesn't make any difference what you do—you're still not going to be able to learn. If you're sure you can learn, however, these hypnotic or subliminal messages are going to help you start thinking of ways to help you learn."

The easiest way to do this is to make an audio tape that repeats the positive message over and over. "You can make it a subliminal tape by turning it down and playing it on a little cassette player while you listen to music on the stereo." It'll sound like people whispering in the background.

Kline says subliminal tapes can work. "They've cut shoplifting in stores by 40 percent because the stores are now playing subliminal suggestions that say, 'I will not shoplift.'

"I use subliminal tapes myself," he adds. "And practically everything I can do today is something that I was sure I could never do."

Make a subliminal tape to send yourself positive messages.

■ *Find a Positive Environment*

All the learning tools in the world aren't going to do you much good if you aren't in a learning environment, says Anthony Gregorc, Ph.D., an educational consultant in Columbia, Connecticut. It doesn't matter whether you're learning in a college classroom, your living room, or on the job, the point is that the part of you that learns is like a seed, while the en-

180

A friendly environment feeds and challenges us.

vironment around you is like the ground and air.

"A friendly learning environment feeds us and provides what we need," says Dr. Gregorc. "It also challenges us positively and appreciates and accepts our gifts or the fruits of our labor.

"A hostile environment doesn't feed us. It's bland. It puts roadblocks in our way that prevent us from growing. It's a sterile environment, a 'We-don't-do-that-here' environment. It's also an environment that doesn't want your gifts."

But you must be honest in evaluating, he says. You might want to believe the environment is hostile but in reality the environment is friendly and you're a wimp.

Environment is the root to satisfaction or dissatisfaction, says Dr. Gregorc. It's why we change jobs. And in a learning situation it's why we give up.

Opportunity Keeps on Knocking

Social conversation is a great learning tool.

"Learning is hanging out and talking to people, being resourceful and imaginative and going to where the information is or the people are," explains Gross. "It's kind of flopping around and soaking it up and not feeling that you have to get it in a systematic fashion or in a logical order. And not feeling that you have to learn all of it or it's not going to be worth anything."

■ Take Advantage of Community Resources

One of the best sources of knowledge is your own community, says Gross. Libraries, friends, community organizations, professional organizations, religious groups, Y's, every community has a million of them. To find them, use the Yellow Pages—a tool that Gross describes as a better catalog of learning opportunities than even the best college catalog.

■ Go to Extremes

While at the library, stroll through the juvenile section and look at a few books on the subject you want to study.

"I love to start people off with something for young children," says Gross. "It's a much better place to start than any college textbook. It's going to be readable, it's going to be expert, it's going to be fun—and you're going to get an immediate sense of accomplishment" because you'll learn something.

"But I also like to pick up some advanced journals that I can't even understand yet," adds Gross. "I just flip through them to get a feel for what the subject I'm studying is like at the most advanced level—to see where I end up if I get to be an expert."

Read up on a new subject at a level you can understand.

■ Hang Out in Specialty Stores

Visit bookstores and shops that specialize in the subject that you're studying. "They're one of the richest resources you can find," says Gross. Specialty shops will have a better collection of books and tapes and other material than even the library. A Civil War store, for example, is likely to have a better, more up-to-date collection of Civil War books than the local library. And it's going to have people working there who are avid about the subject.

"Specialty bookstores are also the nexus of contact on their particular subject," reminds Gross. "They have bulletin boards with meetings and all kinds of stuff that you can get into. So you can get with people who are enthusiastic about the subject and go to events and seminars and workshops."

Hang around places where you can join a network of enthusiasts.

■ *Fall in Love with Learning*

"The philosopher Alfred North Whitehead said that there are three stages of learning," recalls Gross. "The first stage is the stage of romance where you fall in love with a subject. You're really enthusiastic, you're all keyed up, you're running around, everything's wonderful.

There are three stages of learning. The first is romance.

"The next stage is the stage of precision. You have to learn the periodic table, you have to learn formulas, you have to learn whatever it is you set out to learn.

"And then there's the third stage where you've mastered the skill and you can do creative things with it." You can play the piano without having to look at the keys, or type a letter without making a mistake, or write a computer program without using the manual.

Part of your learning experience as a kid was dealing with word problems and number problems. Remember these?: "If one train left Chicago at noon, and another left San Francisco at midnight, and. . ." Below are some problems of a different sort. See how you do.

Fail, Pass

It's hard to go back to school after vacation, but you have to get to work sometime. Go from FAIL to PASS in only four steps, changing one letter at a time to make a new English word at each step.

$$F \quad A \quad I \quad L$$
$$\text{\_\ \_\ \_\ \_}$$
$$\text{\_\ \_\ \_\ \_}$$
$$P \quad A \quad S \quad S$$

Brainteaser

You can substitute one letter for the first letter of each word in the following pairs and make two new words. (For example, RACE and CLAY could become PACE and PLAY.) Insert the new letter on the line between the words. The new letters will spell a new word reading down.

TALL	____	LABEL
SOUND	____	COUGH
SLIT	____	HIM
ALL	____	ARE
ROSE	____	TETHER

To find the answers, see Solution #6 on page 456.

184

Learning is a lifelong affair.

The idea is, don't expect too much much too fast.

"Don't make the mistake of getting too serious and heading for stage three from the very beginning," says Gross. Go through the state of romance—take it lightly, allow yourself to be infatuated." And don't be in a hurry to rush to the next stage.

After all, learning is a lifelong affair.

Creativity

Recognize and Maximize Your Talents

The thousand years after the collapse of the Roman Empire were truly a dark age, one in which rats, war, and hunger prevailed, while art, music, and science languished. But in the year 1400 the people of Florence were talking excitedly about *la Rinascita*, the rebirth. A new age was coming, and out of this small Italian community an explosion of creativity would rock the entire world.

Within a mere 25 years, the artists and architects of Florence would produce some of the world's most spectacular artworks. Donatello would sculpt the statues of St. Mark and St. George. Gentile da Fabriano would paint the frescoes of the Adoration of the Magi. Masaccio would paint the Brancacci Chapel. Ghiberti would carve the north doors of the Baptistery. A generation after

Scientists may never fully understand the nature of creativity.

It's impossible *not* to be creative.

all this, a young Leonardo da Vinci would arrive in Florence to forge his artistic career.

How is it possible that one small city, with a population of roughly half that of modern-day Jackson, Mississippi, could produce such a stunning array of masterpieces and so many world-class artists? This is but one of many questions that scientists grapple with when trying to figure out the nature of creativity. But the answer may be as elusive as Mona Lisa's smile.

Scientists who use the example of Florence typically say that creativity comes from one's surroundings. They point not only to Renaissance-era Florence but to ancient Athens and modern Manhattan as fertile gardens of creative thought. But, of course, not all creative superstars grew up in these surroundings, leading other scientists to argue that creativity is more a personal affair.

On one point, however, all scientists seem to agree. Although only a few of us have the stuff to be another Leonardo, Aristotle, or Andy Warhol, every one of us has creative abilities and potentials. "It's impossible not to be creative. Everyone's creative. Life doesn't allow you to be noncreative," says James L. Adams, Ph.D., a professor at Stanford University who teaches creativity. And there are tried-and-true ways in which we can nurture the creativity within us.

"Don't think of creativity as something you either have or don't have—it can be influenced even by small things in your life. It can be facilitated," says Alice M. Isen, Ph.D., a professor of psychology and behavioral science in the Johnson Graduate School of Management at Cornell University.

Come Out, Come Out, Wherever You Are

Why bother to unleash your creativity? All right, maybe that's a dumb question. After all, with more creativity, you might make big bucks on Madison Avenue, discover a cure for cancer, pen the Great American Novel, paint wonderful murals, or write poems that bring tears to people's eyes. But all that is *just* the beginning.

Creativity is not merely a means to an end. It is much more than producing a work of art or even winning a Nobel prize. Or even winning a *hundred* Nobel prizes. Creativity, says David Feldman, Ph.D., a developmental psychologist at Tufts University in Boston, is nothing short of "a vital life force." It is, he asserts, "the human process par excellence."

Is Dr. Feldman being a bit, well, overly creative with his definitions? Not at all, according to Ellen Langer, Ph.D., a Harvard professor of psychology. Dr. Langer doesn't even like the word "creativity" because she finds it too limiting. "It makes people think of a final product," she says. Rather, she sees creativity as a process, and she prefers to call it "mindfulness" (which, with a capital *M*, is also the title of her book).

Several of Dr. Langer's studies show how thinking creatively, er . . . mindfully, can literally transform people. In fact, people who tap their creativity may even *live longer*, says Dr. Langer.

In one study, elderly nursing-home residents were divided into two groups. Members of one group were given a creative task and encouraged to make decisions on their own.

> **Creativity is not merely a means to an end.**

> **Learning to think creatively can literally transform you.**

The other group's members were not. After an 18-month period, 13 of the 44 residents given no task had died (30 percent), while only 7 of the 47 given a creative task had died (15 percent). The results were surprising, says Dr. Langer.

What kind of task were the elderly residents given to do? No, they were not asked to replicate the ceiling of the Sistine chapel, nor were they asked to whip up musical scores for symphony orchestras. They were merely asked to take care of their own potted plants. That may not sound like a tremendously creative task to you, but in a nursing home, where residents often have nothing but boredom to keep themselves occupied, nurturing a plant can mean a whole lot, says Dr. Langer.

"People tend to think mindlessly of Picasso—but creativity can be more mundane than that," Dr. Langer says. Creativity *can* be as simple a thing as caring for a houseplant.

Different Strokes for Different Folks

With all you stand to gain by letting your creative juices flow, isn't it time you tried to become more creative? Ah, but the question is ... How? And Where? And won't the world laugh at me if I play the tuba? Good questions. A look at what others are doing might give you some creative answers.

■ Creative Expression Is Vital to Your Mental Health

To Karen Earl-Braymer, a secretary for a Pennsylvania publishing company, creativity

Nursing home residents who were allowed to express their creativity lived longer.

Creativity can be as simple as caring for a houseplant.

means spending much of every evening, needle and thread in hand, embroidering landscapes and other intricate designs onto canvas. "Everybody likes to be special in some way. This is my chance to be unique. And it makes me feel good to create something of beauty," she says.

To Steven Guy, a dentist from Silver Spring, Maryland, creativity is singing in a barbershop quartet. "Sometimes I can hardly wait to get the root canals done and get out of the office and sing. I love to sing and entertain!" And while Dr. Guy is performing with his foursome, the "Maintenance Free Music Company," his business-manager wife sings her heart out with dozens of others in "The Heart of Maryland" chorus.

These pastimes are more than mere amusements, says David F. Duncan, Dr.P.H., an epidemiologist with the Illinois Primary Health Care Association. "A creative approach to life is essential to mental wellness," he says. That creative approach can manifest itself in "anything that is an expression. It may be painting, music, repairing clocks, or fixing walls in your house . . . anything that puts you totally there and gets your full attention," he says.

> Everybody can have his own unique way of expressing his creativity.

■ *Find Your "Creativity Intersection"*

Your creativity will probably flourish in an area where you exhibit some talent *and* where you enjoy yourself. This area is your "creativity intersection," says Teresa Amabile, Ph.D., an associate professor of psychology at Brandeis University in Waltham, Massachusetts. As good fate would have it, this intersection is a
(continued on page 192)

Can an Organization Be Creative?

The *creative organization*. Is that anything like a *jumbo shrimp*? Yes, it is indeed an oxymoron, a contradiction in terms. At least that's the opinion of Jeff Salzman, vice-president and cofounder of CareerTrack, a Colorado-based company that offers business seminars around the world.

Organization tends to kill creativity, says Salzman, and it's for exactly this reason "that the most creative organizations are the ones that aren't overly organized."

Organizations that aren't rigidly structured are often the most successful of all organizations, he says. That's especially true in today's fast-paced competitive business environment.

That's not to say that Salzman tells companies to let employees come and go as they please or do whatever they want. He tells them that if they give employees a certain amount of freedom, they'll get back a certain amount of creativity in return.

Does your company stifle your creativity or does it give you enough freedom to flourish? The answers to the following questions should give you a clue.

Are you allowed time to think up new ideas? One way to strike a balance between freedom and organization is to give people a certain percentage of their time, maybe 15 to 20 percent, in which to do nothing but explore new projects of their own choosing, says Salzman. That's what the 3M Corporation has done for years—with enormous success.

Does your company reward you for good ideas? People enjoy being creative, but incentives never hurt. But money isn't the only reward. Some companies offer more vacation time, the opportunity to work at home, a new title. Even a simple pat on the back helps, says Salzman.

Does your company encourage positive brainstorming sessions? Many companies use brainstorming sessions as tools for getting creative ideas flowing. "But most companies don't run them properly," says Salzman. The only way to run a successful brainstorming session is to "suspend *all* criticism," he says. The leader of the session must be "ruthless" in stopping criticism. During the brainstorming session *all* ideas are good ideas.

Does your company encourage quiet hours? Of course, many people come up with creative ideas on their own. For this reason, "you need pockets of serenity where people can relax and think," says Salzman. It takes time to get into a creative state of mind. But in many organizations, interruptions are constant. Many companies foster quiet hours where, for at least an hour or several hours each day, no one knocks on doors or screams down hallways.

Does your boss get you out of the office to get ideas? No matter how quiet the office, it's not a good idea to keep employees working too long at their job. Gordon Bowen, senior vice-president and creative director of Ogilvy & Mather Worldwide, one of the world's largest advertising agencies, says, "Probably the most important thing I can do to generate ideas among my people is to get them out of here, out of the cloistered world of Madison Avenue.

"Let's face it, you don't create from nothing; you create from what you know," says Bowen. He fosters creativity among his staff by encouraging them to "go to see films, shows, football games, soccer matches . . . have dinner at grandmother's"—anything, he says, to broaden their world.

Is your workplace a fun place? "You don't have to be a psychologist to see that people will want to go to a place where they're having fun," says David J. Abramis, Ph.D., an assistant professor in the School of Business Administration at California State University in Long Beach.

(continued)

Can an Organization Be Creative?—*Continued*

Fun work? Are we back to oxymorons again? Not at all! Work should be fun, and making it fun may help people to be more creative, says Dr. Abramis.

Be a little zany, be playful—special events, contests, parties, "weird dress-up" days. "Make a conscious effort to have fun," says Dr. Abramis. Not only does it foster creativity, but people who try to make work fun find they themselves have more fun on the job! ⟶ ▪

large one—we tend to like what we do well, and do well that which we like.

"I'm 65 now. I started drawing in grammar school. I enjoy it. I've always wanted to draw," says Jack Davis. But is Jack Davis any *good* at drawing? Well, one *might* say that after doing 36 covers for *Time* and 22 for *T.V. Guide*, drawing countless goofy cartoons for *Mad* magazine, and illustrating issues of *Playboy*, *Esquire*, and *Life*, that Davis has found his creativity intersection!

In Davis's case, his creativity intersection became his career. But that's not to say that for you it couldn't be simply a rewarding hobby!

> Talent alone will not make your creativity flourish.

Friends of Creativity

Jack Davis, by the way, is one of those creative people who lives far from Florence or

New York. But some of the same stuff that sparked an artistic revolution in fifteenth-century Italy may also be available to freelance artist Davis in his little seaside town in Georgia.

■ *Treat Time as a Friend*

One thing Davis enjoys in his quiet little town is time. There's an old Chinese saying: "You cannot win if you treat time as the enemy." How true that is when it comes to creativity. Just about any creative endeavor you can think of requires practice, revision, and nurturing. That is, time.

Some creativity experts reason that time is what gave Renaissance Florence's artists an edge. They say that because Florence was one of the wealthier cities of the age, rich patrons were available to support artists. These same artists, if they had lived near, say, Madrid or Moscow, might have had to toil in the fields for long hours each day to feed themselves. (Imagine trying to paint the ceiling of a cathedral after 9 hours of pulling up potatoes!)

Jack Davis appreciates the fact that *he* doesn't have to pull potatoes, for he knows the importance of allowing time to nurture his creativity. "I spend a lot of time thinking about ideas. Then maybe I'll scribble-scrabble till I find something. I'll play with it awhile, then tighten it up," he says.

Other creative stars also emphasize the importance of allowing time for ideas to blossom. "I work for two months just jotting down ideas before I ever start work on a book," says

> Just about any creative endeavor requires practice, revision, and nurturing.

> Creative ideas need time to blossom.

Phyllis A. Whitney, best-selling author of *Rainbow in the Mist*, *The Singing Stones*, and 70 other novels.

And Dave Barry, the nationally syndicated humor columnist and author of zany books such as *Claw Your Way to the Top: How to Become the Head of a Major Corporation in Roughly a Week*, similarly emphasizes the importance of allowing ideas to ripen. "A blinding flash of light doesn't hit me and I just sit down and write great stuff. I think what makes my writing funny is that I distill it," he says. Between flashes and distillation, Barry says, "I'll interrupt myself a hundred times a day to eat, clip my toenails, and pick my teeth."

When picking his teeth doesn't bring creative results, Barry will sometimes pick the guitar. "I'm bad, but I'm loud," he says. And when *that* doesn't work, he may just put off his writing for another day. "It's amazing how much easier things are the next morning," he says.

■ *Find Others to Inspire You*

Find a role model who can give you creative inspiration.

It certainly takes more than time to be creative (or mountains would write novels). Another creativity booster is having "creativity heroes . . . models of creativity in areas of interest to you," says Dr. Amabile. "If possible, hang out with them, see how they operate," she says. If that's not possible, "read about them, and study their works." Dr. Amabile's creativity hero? "For me, it's Woody Allen."

For Leonardo da Vinci, it was the versatile artist Verrocchio, with whom Leonardo worked and studied as an apprentice. And for Jack

Davis, his creativity hero has long been Walt Disney. "You have to study other people's work, enjoy it, and be inspired by it," he says. Davis lists Popeye, Little Henry, and Mickey Mouse as a few examples of other people's work that serve to inspire him.

■ Learn with the Best

Finding a good instructor is one of the most important steps you can take toward nurturing your creativity, says Ronald Hays, director of the Master of Creative Arts in Therapy program at Philadelphia's Hahnemann University. Perhaps above all, he recommends that you find an instructor, in whatever field you choose, who is "nonjudgmental and supportive."

An instructor should be nonjudgmental and supportive.

■ Take It Easy on Yourself

It's also important to be supportive and nonjudgmental of *yourself,* says Hays. So you want to play the tuba? "If that's what you've always wanted, find yourself an adult education class or someone who'll teach you. But don't aim right away to play the thing in an orchestra—just play," he says.

Be supportive and nonjudgmental of yourself.

■ Don't Worry about What Others Think

Dave Barry says that too much concern about what others think of your creative efforts is a good way to stifle your creative self. "I

196

To be brilliant you have to be willing to be stupid.

think people limit themselves by saying 'Ah, no one will like that. That's not good.' "

Gordon Bowen, senior vice-president and creative director for Ogilvy & Mather Worldwide advertising agency, says "to be brilliant, you have to be willing to be stupid—you have to be able to take risks, sometimes flop, and say, 'hey, that's okay.' "

Dr. Guy, who has practiced dentistry for 20 years, says he doesn't worry too much about being seen as a "goofball" for singing in a barbershop quartet while wearing "incredibly corny" costumes. "This one guy asked me 'How do you switch from being such a goofball on stage to being a dentist?' I told him 'I don't. I'm a goofball all the time!' "

The Tricks of the Trade

Five . . . four . . . three . . . two . . . one . . . blast off! You've set aside the time, you found yourself a creative hero, and you have the right frame of mind to launch yourself into the creative outer limits. Now what? Now you're ready to learn the tricks of the trade. Yup, baseball pitchers learn to put a twist on their fastballs, reporters learn their own shorthand, and creative artists have *their* little tricks as well.

■ Develop an Area of Expertise

Ideas are drawn from a vast knowledge base.

Well, this first point isn't so much a little trick as a big one: You have to know your stuff. "People don't invent new concepts out of nowhere. It's vital to have a big knowledge base from which to pull ideas," says John Feldhusen, Ph.D., professor of education, educational studies, and psychological science at Purdue University. "Know and master as much as possible in an area of your talent," he says. That's a first step to coming up with great ideas. Pablo Picasso, for example, didn't father a new school of art without a solid familiarity with the old.

■ Tap into Your Unconscious Mind

Let's look at a few smaller tricks, the first from Phyllis Whitney. "I have a system I use when I come to a snag—I lie down, close my eyes, and ask the questions that I need answered. And I get the answers—in color!" says the prolific novelist. "I watch it happen," she says of the complicated plots of her mystery novels that appear to her when she closes her eyes. "I know my characters, and I watch them perform before my nose."

The process of which Whitney speaks is called visualization. Among brain experts it's a respected technique for tapping into the powers of the unconscious mind. For the creative artist, it can be a powerful tool. "Who knows where the images are coming from? I don't care. All I know is that they come," says Whitney.

Brain experts believe visualization can be a powerful tool for finding ideas.

■ Know When the Critic within You Must Sleep

When you abandon your visualization to get down to work, leave your critical side behind. It's important, as mentioned earlier, not to be too judgmental of your creative efforts, especially when starting off. But even for the pros, there's a time to be critical and a time not to be.

When Phyllis Whitney is tapping out one of her stories, she says she "puts the critic to sleep." It's when you're working at trying to be creative that "you don't want a critic over your shoulder," she says. Tough scrutiny of what you've done can always come afterward.

Learn to put the critic in yourself to sleep.

■ To Explore Your Mind, Explore the World

What you do in your spare time will also affect your creativity. "People who are open to new experiences are more likely to be creative," says Robert R. McCrae, Ph.D., a research psychologist with the Laboratory of Personality and Cognition at the Gerontology Research Center of the National Institutes of Health. "Creativity requires lots of material to play around with. If all you do is see the same people, eat the same food, and read the same book over and over, you won't have much material to work with," he says.

Too much sameness in your life will hamper your creativity.

"Everything is grist" for your creativity, says Whitney. "I recommend constantly putting something new into the hopper. I can still be fresh and excited at my age (87 years) because I've just seen something new." And by "something new," Whitney emphasizes that you needn't travel to the mountains of Nepal or the valleys of Peru.

"To the person who sits there in a small

town and says nothing ever happens—I say that person can walk to the other side of town and really look at things," says Whitney."There's always something new to see—wherever you are."

At New York City's J. Walter Thompson advertising agency, one of America's largest, group creative director Linda Kaplan says, "Ideas come from life." It's from life, she says, that she came up with the ideas for such jingles as "I don't wanna grow up, I'm a Toys 'R' Us kid," and slogans like "I'm going to get you with a Kodak disc." More specifically, "I get my ideas from just about anywhere ... from a movie I might have seen or something I saw on my way to work. I had an idea the other day in exercise class listening to rap music," she says.

■ *Sharpen Your Natural Curiosity*

Creative people tend to be extremely responsive to the world around them, says Dr. Feldhusen.

People who note details that most of us miss enhance their creativity over time, he says. You can train yourself to do this, to look more closely at the world. For instance, look out your window. You may see a squirrel up in a tree and say "Oh, how nice, a squirrel." *Or* "you can notice how the squirrel will look for a nut, how he postures his body, uses his forepaws, and how he cleans himself off," says Dr. Feldhusen. If you do *that,* you'll be on your way to becoming more creative.

Seeing the world with such intense curi-

People who notice details most of us miss are more creative.

(continued on page 202)

Creativity on the Rocks

"No poems can please for long or live that are written by water drinkers."

So said the Roman poet Horace some 2,000 years ago, and since then plenty of writers have taken this saying to heart.

Ernest Hemingway, F. Scott Fitzgerald, Eugene O'Neill, William Faulkner, Sinclair Lewis, John Steinbeck, Tennessee Williams, and Edgar Allan Poe all were great writers. And they all were great drinkers.

The famous poet T. S. Eliot was known to have said that he couldn't write a poem unless he had a few drinks. Is there something to the idea that creativity flows along with the booze? Or is the notion just a creative excuse to drink? According to experts in the field, this is clearly a story with two sides.

Yes, for some people, it is true that there are several ways in which alcohol may bring forth creativity, at least writing creatively, says Donald W. Goodwin, M.D., professor and chairman of the Department of Psychiatry at the University of Kansas and author of *Alcohol and the Writer*.

The first and most evident way that alcohol may enhance creativity in some people is to "blank out the censor, or the part of you that says 'that's no good,' " says Dr. Goodwin. "Writers often have a highly developed critic in their head, and sometimes the critic becomes so powerful that it inhibits their writing. Alcohol has the nice effect of eliminating this critic," he says.

Second, "alcohol allows the writer to deal with those memories that may be painful or uncomfortable. It anesthetizes whatever part of the brain is responsible for guilt and anxiety," says Dr. Goodwin. Because much of creative writing comes from a writer's memories of his own life, increasing access to those memories is bound to boost creativity, he says.

Third, alcohol may make other people and events seem more intriguing to the drinker, says Dr. Goodwin. "Two martinis may make things that don't seem too interesting all of a sudden seem very interesting," he says. This newfound "sense of wonder at the world" can turn on the writer's creativity.

Last, drinking, like writing itself, can put you in a "trancelike state," says Dr. Goodwin. So having a few drinks offers the writer, deeply entrenched in his work, a way to stop writing without coming out of the trancelike state that he has become accustomed to. As Hemingway said, "Drinking is a way of ending the day."

But with all this said, alcohol is still no magic elixir. On the contrary—it's more a Pandora's box. "Alcohol in some instances can stimulate creativity, but overall it will kill it," says Arnold M. Ludwig, M.D., professor of psychiatry at the University of Kentucky Medical Center.

Dr. Ludwig closely studied the careers of a number of past writers, performers, and artists and came to the conclusion that heavy alcohol use eventually resulted in a deterioration in performance in 75 percent of the cases. "The profound effect of alcohol is clear," says Dr. Ludwig. As far as creativity is concerned, "it has a detrimental effect in the vast majority of people," he says.

Dr. Goodwin isn't sure that he agrees with Dr. Ludwig on the long-term detrimental effects of alcohol on creativity. (He points out that the alcoholic playwright Eugene O'Neill saw his writing dry up when he did.) Dr. Goodwin does agree, however, that heavy drinking, even if you think it can boost your creativity, should be avoided. For, while it's questionable whether alcohol abuse will boost or kill your creativity, one thing is dead sure: It can kill *you*.

As the great writer Sinclair Lewis once asked (in a bit of a hyperbole), "Can you name five American writers since Poe who did *not* die of alcoholism?"

202

Many of us lose the natural curiosity we had as children.

osity is something that children do naturally, but somewhere down the line many of us lose that ability, says Dr. Feldhusen.

■ Look Deep within Yourself

Looking wide-eyed at the world is important to cultivating creativity, but so is looking deep within yourself, says Peter Cooley, Ph.D., poetry editor of *The North American Review*, author of five books of poetry, and English professor at Tulane University. To really tap your innermost creativity, Dr. Cooley says you need to "go down into yourself and think about things other people don't think about." The creative outpouring, he says, will follow.

If writing poetry is where you want to put your creative energies, looking within yourself is as integral as pages to a book, says Dr. Cooley. "Writing poetry is entering into a state of being. When it's going well, it's writing *you*—you're not writing it. The outside world doesn't exist. All that exists is what you're spinning on paper. It's a wonderful, almost religious, experience."

Good writing writes itself.

■ Creativity Thrives in Happy People

Obviously, Dr. Cooley is describing a pleasant experience. And the creative experience *is* a pleasant one. So what better way to prepare yourself for it than to put yourself in a happy state of mind *before* you try to tap into your creativity? For years now, Dr. Isen has been battling the popular (but terribly mistaken) belief that creativity comes best to those who are sullen, lonely, and depressed.

The stereotype just isn't right, says Dr. Isen. She, along with her colleagues, has conducted several studies to prove her contention that "If you induce positive feelings in people, it can enhance their creativity."

Stereotypes about creativity have been proven wrong.

One such study presented two groups of students with a problem: Each student was given a candle, a box of tacks, and a book of matches and was instructed to attach the candle to a corkboard so wax wouldn't drip onto the floor if it were lit. The solution calls for a bit of creative trickery: emptying the box and tacking it to the wall to serve as a platform for the candle. The answer came easily to students who had just come from yucking it up over television "bloopers" (75 percent figured it out). But among those who had just sat through a film on mathematics, few (20 percent) figured it out.

Other studies looking at other creative tasks, such as making unusual word associations, show that merely handing someone a piece of candy or having him read and think about a few pleasant words can increase creativity. Dr. Isen's advice, based on these studies, is to "let yourself feel good."

When you're trying to bring out your creativity, think pleasant thoughts, such as the last time someone paid you a compliment. Be careful, however, not to conjure up nostalgic thoughts, warns Dr. Isen. Thinking of good times you had with a deceased friend can very quickly turn from a pleasant thought to an unpleasant one.

When you're trying to be creative, think pleasant thoughts.

By the way, Dr. Isen does not deny that

204

many creative people (such as Edgar Allan Poe and Vincent van Gogh) were very sad people. "Sadness may also enhance creativity under certain circumstances or for certain people," she acknowledges. However, "if you have your choice—why not take the fun way?" she asks.

■ Use Pencil and Paper to Clear Out Your Mind

Whether or not you think of writing as fun, giving it a crack may enhance your creativity. "Writing things in stream-of-consciousness fashion is a way to clean out your mind," says Dr. Cooley. And poets and writers are not the only ones who stand to benefit by letting their feelings out on paper.

Alan Rogers is president of New York City's Mind Computer Institute. He writes computer programs designed to help people— primarily business people—think more creatively. The programs are based on what Rogers calls *journaling,* which is close to what Dr. Cooley calls stream-of-consciousness writing.

"Our best thinking—the really creative work—comes out of the nonconscious part of the brain," says Rogers. Unfortunately, it's hard to tap into this part of the brain. Writing your thoughts can help enormously. "Keep writing until the flow is exhausted, put it aside, take a break, then come back and write some more," suggests Rogers. No matter what the problem, you'll come up with more creative solutions if you write it out, he says.

If it helps, you may want to pretend that you're writing a letter to a good friend or to

Externalizing your thoughts on paper will help creativity flow.

someone whose advice you respect, says Rogers. The important thing is to *externalize* your thoughts. Externalizing them on paper helps your mind to reorganize those thoughts and helps the creativity flow. "I've seen many people try this—it really works," says Rogers.

Healthy Body, Creative Mind

Whether writing down your thoughts, playing the tuba, or spreading paint on canvas, your creative side is more likely to flourish in a body that is well exercised and well rested.

■ Exercise Gives You the Creative Edge

"A sedentary body makes for a sedentary mind," says Bruce W. Tuckman, Ph.D., professor of educational research at Florida State University.

That is the conclusion he draws from several studies measuring creativity in the fit versus the not-so-fit. In one study, Dr. Tuckman took over 100 youngsters and got them started on a jogging program. After 15 weeks, the children did significantly better on a number of creativity tests than did children who hadn't been doing aerobic exercise. Four other studies he was involved with gave similar results, says Dr. Tuckman.

Theorizing that exercise may directly stimulate those parts of the brain related to creativity, Dr. Tuckman says the results of his studies are clear: "Get yourself in shape and you're

Children who jogged did significantly better on creativity tests.

The Pangs of Unemployed Creativity

Having gobs of creativity "is not all a bed of roses," says Patti Hulvershorn, director of Ability Potentials of northern Virginia, a consulting service for people looking to better uncover their aptitudes.

The number of jobs in our society that require heaps of creativity is limited, says Hulvershorn. That makes for frustration and boredom among people who are endowed with more creativity than they can use. "Creativity needs expression—if you don't give it expression, it'll get to you," she says.

Some people feel so frustrated, they may even break the law and face arrest. In the city of Los Angeles, for instance, graffiti artists, often under the cover of night, spray-painted a total area of over 1½ million square feet in one year, reported city officials.

"We need to develop alternatives to get to the root cause of graffiti," says Delphia Jones, director of Operation Clean Sweep, Los Angeles's graffiti control program. At least part of this root cause, she says, is a need for creative expression. "One thing I'd like to see is more arts programs in the schools," she says. ————■

likely to be more creative." He says that moderate exercise is all you should need to stimulate your creativity. One great way to get moderate exercise is to enjoy a brisk 45-minute walk five or six days a week.

■ **The Well-Rested Reap Bigger Rewards**

After all that exercising, you'll likely be ready for some relaxation. Getting the proper amount of sleep is essential to the creative mind, say some scientists. If you don't believe them, ask one of 12 Englishmen who pulled an all-nighter as part of a study on sleep and creativity at Great Britain's Loughborough University. When compared to fellow countrymen who had a full night's sleep, the 12 who lacked sleep scored quite poorly on a number of standard creativity tests.

Those who got a good night's sleep were more creative the next day than those who pulled an all-nighter.

Meeting Your Creative Goal

As an accomplished writer, Dave Barry is often asked by aspiring writers how they too can become syndicated in 150 newspapers, write best-selling books, and win a Pulitzer prize. They typically aren't thrilled with the answer he gives them: "Writing can be laborious, boring drudgery. A real drag. But if you want to be a writer, you have to write!"

■ You Have to Have Discipline!

"It won't do you much good to be this imaginative, creative person without being disciplined. You can't be a writer without making deadlines. If you don't show up at rehearsals, you can't be an actor," says Barry. It's lack of discipline that prevents many from fulfilling their creative dreams, he says. "A lot of people just want the end product without doing the work."

Stanford's Dr. Adams, author of *The Care and Feeding of Ideas,* agrees with Barry. "Most

Lack of discipline can prevent you from fulfilling your creative dreams.

problems don't have to do with a shortage of ideas," but with how to turn those ideas into reality, he says.

■ *You Have to Be Committed!*

Great ideas won't turn into anything but old memories unless you're committed to the necessary time and energy it requires to turn them into reality, says Dr. Adams, a former engineer who helped design the first Venus and Mars spacecraft for NASA. "Many people say they're going to write a novel and then they put aside 3 hours a week for it—that's not enough," he says. "You can't create anything unless you set aside the time to do it."

You can't write a novel in 3 hours a week.

■ *Originality Is Only Half of the Equation*

Over several decades, Jerome Markowitz has poured time, energy, and brainpower into developing more than 30 U.S. patents, mainly in the area of electronic music. The accomplished inventor today is the CEO of the world's largest company producing classical organs, the Allen Organ Company in Macungie, Pennsylvania. How did the inventor of such innovations as the gyrophonic projector (a rotating speaker system) come up with so many patentable ideas?

"The first thing is to identify something that will fulfill a need. God knows the world is full of things that are needed," says Markowitz, who developed an interest in both music and

For a creation to make a difference, it has to fill a need.

electronics in his youth. Developing an electronic organ that sounds every bit as good as a pipe organ wasn't easy, but the inventor took it one step at a time. "First, I'd listen. Then I'd figure out what was needed. Sixty percent of a problem is identifying what is needed," he says.

■ Think Like a Dolphin

Once you know what you need, go get it as a dolphin would. No, to think like a dolphin doesn't mean to concentrate on where your next fish meal is coming from. Rather it means to think more flexibly—and to become more creative in the process. The metaphor is a bit of creative thinking on the part of Dudley Lynch, business consultant, president of Brain Technologies Corporation of Fort Collins, Colorado, and lead author of *Strategy of the Dolphin: Scoring a Win in a Chaotic World.*

Think more flexibly and you'll become more creative.

Lynch hit upon the dolphin idea while reading about observations of the marine mammals "at work" at Hawaii's Oceanic Institute. He noted that when a dolphin performs his tricks and the trainer withholds his fishy treats, the dolphin doesn't sulk, sigh, or quit. When dolphins don't get what they want, "they break out of the water with a whole new set of dazzling tricks," says Lynch. "If dolphins can do it, why can't humans?"

The strategy that Lynch advises for enhancing creativity starts with "picking with care the issues or challenges where you seek to be genuinely creative." Our lives today are complicated. Realize that you don't have time

Pick your challenges carefully. You can't be creative on every issue.

to be creative on every issue— nor do you have to, says Lynch. But once you've decided that a particular issue deserves your creative energies, "then lock on tenaciously—the world doesn't surrender its secrets easily." And when those secrets don't come at first—don't sulk or quit!

The Great Creativity Killers

Question: What do you call a tree that grows from an acorn?
Answer: An oak.

Question: What do you call a funny story?
Answer: A joke.

Question: What do we call the sound made by a frog?
Answer: A croak.

Question: What do we call the white of an egg?
Answer: ?

Did you say "A yolk?" If so, you're guilty of mindlessness. (Look again at the last question.) Mindlessness is no crime, but it is the greatest obstacle to creative thinking, says Harvard's Dr. Langer, who provides the yolk example above (and others) in her book *Mindfulness.*

■ Don't Succumb to Mindlessness

*Mindless*ness is rigid, reflexive behavior. It is not being in tune with the world around you.

A Touch of Madness

Creative geniuses over the centuries have tended to be a bit, well, *strange.*

In *The Worldly Philosophers,* historian Robert L. Heilbroner describes Adam Smith, the brilliant eighteenth-century philosopher and economist: "The inhabitants of Edinburgh were regularly treated to the amusing spectacle of their most illustrious citizen . . . walking down the cobbled streets with his eyes fixed on infinity and his lips moving in silent discourse. Every pace or two he would hesitate as if to change direction or even reverse it. . . . Accounts of his absence of mind were common. On one occasion he descended into his garden clad only in a dressing gown and, falling into a reverie, walked fifteen miles before coming to." This is the man often referred to as "the father of modern-day economics"!

Such eccentricity is not uncommon among creative geniuses. Accounts of emotionally disturbed writers, poets, composers, scientists, and philosophers are easy to find in history books. We could start with Vincent van Gogh, Franz Kafka, Eugene O'Neill, Ernest Hemingway, Charles Darwin, and Ezra Pound, but the list goes on and on. "While not a prerequisite, a touch of madness could enhance creativity," theorizes Arnold M. Ludwig, M.D., professor of psychiatry at the University of Kentucky Medical Center.

The seeming link between madness and creative genius is hard to figure, says Dr. Ludwig. Madness may sometimes provide the motivation or the imagination for new discoveries. Or it may allow the artist to escape the cultural constraints that favor conformity.

But certainly you don't *need* to act crazy to be enormously creative. Many creative individuals from the history books are believed to have led "sane" lives. These include Albert Einstein, Walt Whitman, Carl Jung, Aldous Huxley, and Duke Ellington, says Dr. Ludwig. ————■

Constantly pay attention and question the world.

*Mindful*ness, on the other hand, is the essence of creativity, says Dr. Langer. It is nothing less than the key to a more enjoyable, fulfilling, and successful life.

The way to be more mindful is to "constantly pay attention," and to "question the world," says Dr. Langer. The kind of attentiveness you might have while walking through the streets of some far-off exotic city is the same kind of attentiveness you should *always* have, she says.

Beyond that, "intentionally deal with novelty," says Dr. Langer. "Ask yourself what a new way of doing something might be. Ask yourself how your closest friend or a parent might deal with a situation, or how someone from another culture might handle something . . . try to look at problems from multiple perspectives," she advises.

■ *Expect Criticism (For It Will Come)*

You must also be aware of how culture looks at *you*. Creativity and change are practically one and the same—"they both imply new directions," says Stanford's Dr. Adams. The *problem* with new directions is that they fly in the face of the old. And the prevailing culture, with a vested interest in maintaining the status quo, is likely to view these new directions with a disapproving eye.

Negative feedback is a hazard of creative thinking.

"Creative people must come to a realization of the way the world responds to creativity," says Dr. Adams. The more creative a person is, the more likely he is to encounter negative feedback, or even hostility, from those around him. This is particularly true in large organizations such as corporations and universities, says Dr. Adams. "A lot of people give up when the world doesn't love them," he says. But if you want to put your creativity into action, you can't give up.

■ Fight Your Fears

Even in the absence of criticism from others, just plain fear of making a mistake has killed many a creative endeavor. Fear is probably the most common block to creative energies, says Dr. Adams, who also wrote *Conceptual Blockbusters: A Guide to Better Ideas*. Most of us grow up in an environment where we are rewarded for "right" answers and punished for "wrong," he says. As adults, our fears of doing wrong sometimes get blown up in our mind to the point where our creativity can become frozen.

Most of us grow up being rewarded for "right" answers and punished for "wrong" answers.

How do you thaw it out? "One of the better ways of overcoming such a block is to realistically assess the possible negative consequences of an idea," says Dr. Adams. Ask yourself "What are your catastrophic expectations?" Write it out, listing all the things that would happen if *everything* went wrong as a result of your creative idea. You may discover, says Adams, that the risks aren't as terrible as you thought.

■ Break Through Your Mental Blocks

Criticism and fear, says Dr. Adams, are not the only things that can suffocate your creativ-

Daydreaming: It's Not for the Lazy

What do people daydream about? "Their unmet wants and unassuaged fears," says Eric Klinger, Ph.D., a psychologist at the University of Minnesota at Morris and author of *Daydreaming: Using Fantasy and Imagery for Self-Knowledge and Creativity.* Daydreams are inherently spontaneous bursts of imagination in which you work out problems, dream up solutions, and plan for the future. You roll in and out of them so often that, more than likely, you spend half of your waking hours in a dream.

Don't believe it? What do you do when you brush your teeth in the morning? When you drive your car? When you pour a cup of coffee?

"Daydreaming seems to be a natural way to use brainpower efficiently," explains Dr. Klinger. "I think that the brain machinery is set up in such a way that when we're not using full capacity, we automatically cut out and start working over other things. Our minds wander into a review of the past or rehearse what's coming up."

You might replay an argument you had with a friend, then visualize how the two of you will go to lunch and work it out. Or, if you're planning a dinner, you might recall the

ity. All of us develop mental sets, or mental habits, that inhibit us from free thinking. But there are exercises you can do to help you notice your confining mind sets, and once you've noticed them, you may be able to break through them, says Dr. Adams.

One exercise Dr. Adams suggests in his *Conceptual Blockbusters* book is to make a list: Spend 3 minutes writing a list as long as you

foods your guests like to eat, take a mental inventory of what's in your pantry, and then plan what you'll need to pick up at the market.

What we daydream about, although it's usually related to pursuing a personal goal, reflects our social differences, says Dr. Klinger. A businessperson is far more likely to think about a new product line, for example, while a day care worker is more likely to daydream about conflict resolution on the playground.

"But daydreamed thoughts are not random," Dr. Klinger points out. They occur when you run into emotionally arousing cues that trigger a new thought related to an ongoing concern.

For example, you might encounter the smell of fresh bread as you pass a bakery, remember how your mom used to bake a half-dozen fluffy loaves once a week, then daydream about a bread-baking bash before the holidays and wonder if you can squeeze it in.

In each instance, think of daydreaming as personal brainstorming, says Dr. Klinger. Then use what it reveals.

can of the potential uses for an ordinary yellow wooden pencil. You'll be surprised to find how imaginative you can be when trying to squeeze out a few last uses! "List making works by forcing the mind to dwell upon alternates to a greater extent than it normally would," says Dr. Adams.

List making works by forcing the mind to dwell on alternatives.

Another exercise that may shift your mind into a more imaginative state would be to spend

5 minutes writing a short and serious love poem, suggests Dr. Adams. Or spend 5 minutes designing on paper a better desk lamp, one that is both functional and attractive. If you have a friend who can do these exercises with you and with whom you can compare, so much the better.

■ *Creativity Has No Room for Insecurity*

Lack of confidence is deadly to creativity.

Like lack of patience, lack of confidence can be deadly to creativity. If you believe that solutions are possible, then your creativity will find one, says Jeff Salzman, vice-president and cofounder of CareerTrack, a Colorado-based company that consults with other companies on matters such as developing creativity. "You must anticipate achievement, for confidence is absolutely essential," he says.

A Word about Flying Elephants

If anything remains to be said about creativity, the man to say it is Joe Grant. You may not know the name, but you certainly are familiar with his work. Grant designed many of the characters and coauthored the scripts for such animated classics as *Fantasia, Snow White,* and *Pinocchio.* He started with Walt Disney studios back in the 1930s, and, at age 83, he's still creating.

Below are two problems that you won't be able to solve simply by using your three R's. In order to find the right answers you'll need to tap into your creativity. Get ready...get set...create!

The Straight and Arrow

This looks easy, but you may find otherwise once you try it. The challenge: Draw four straight lines through these nine dots without retracing or lifting your pencil from the paper.

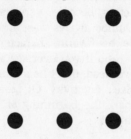

Find the Key Clue

Imagine you are the person in this illustration. You must tie the two ends of the suspended strings together without removing them from the ceiling. The strings are located so that you cannot reach one while holding the other. The room is completely bare, but you have the resources available that you would normally carry in your pocket or purse. What's your plan?

To find the answers, see Solution #7 on page 456.

■ *Involve Yourself Totally*

To be truly creative, you have to be drunk with your idea.

To be truly creative, says Grant, "you have to be drunk with an idea. . . . There has to be something stirring inside of you that you must do." When he works on a script, such as when he was writing and illustrating *Dumbo,* he says he becomes so totally involved that "the characters become very real, almost human." Dumbo always was, and probably always will be, his favorite character, says Grant.

So if you ever see a baby elephant flying overhead, don't be alarmed. It's only someone else's creativity. Or possibly your own! Let it mark the beginning of your personal renaissance! ───────■

Emotions

Use Mood to Your Mind's Advantage

The knee bone's connected to the thigh bone. The thigh bone's connected to the hip bone. And the hip bone's connected. . . . But hey, the popular little ditty already told you that.

What the songs don't mention, but what you ought to know about, is that all-important connection between heart and mind— between your emotions and the way you think.

That's right. Your moods can have a giant impact on your mental performance. Some emotions, as you might guess, can affect your thinking ability for the good. But others can have the impact of a Mack truck coming at you head-on. In fact, science is just beginning to understand the awesome power emotions hold

219

over the way we think, the decisions we make, our rationale, and even our creativity.

Feelings—Nothing More Than Feelings

"All the emotions have some influence on the way you think," explains Mara Julius, Sc.D., a research scientist at the University of Michigan School of Public Health and a leading researcher on the physical and mental effects of anger. "Some—particularly negative emotions like anxiety, anger, or fear—can actually *slow* your abilities to rationalize, solve problems, and make decisions. That's because it's hard to concentrate when you're feeling these emotions. When you're feeling rage or hostility, it overwhelms you. In some people, feeling rage will slow down some aspects of the thinking process. In others, it will completely stop it. You cannot separate your anger from your thinking."

Not all emotions, however, are destined to rain on your parade. "There are a number of studies that suggest that when you're feeling positive, you think more broadly, more creatively," says Margaret S. Clark, Ph.D., a psychologist and researcher at Carnegie Mellon University in Pittsburgh. "You can see more 'connections' than you might normally see and make decisions more quickly."

Why? Nobody has all the answers. "It could be because you're feeling more confident in yourself and therefore in your abilities," says Dr. Clark. "Or it could be that you don't want

Negative emotions can actually slow your ability to rationalize.

Studies suggest that when you're feeling positive you think more creatively.

to spend as much time making decisions because you don't want to ruin the good mood
you're in."

■ *Tap into Your Own Emotions*

Much of this research on happiness and
thinking is being done by Alice M. Isen, Ph.D.,
a leading cognitive psychologist who also
teaches at both the arts school and the Samuel
Curtis Johnson School of Management at Cornell University.

"The studies I've done indicate that when
people are infused with positive feelings, they
become more innovative and creative," she
says. "They are better able to solve problems
that require creative solutions. In a negotiation
situation, they are better able to stand back and
come up with an innovative response that's
most beneficial to everyone."

Not that it takes much to induce these
positive feelings. In her tests, people reportedly
felt happy after they were given a small bag of
candy or a free sample of an item or were
shown a short comedy film. "As a result, they
gave more creative answers to word-association
tests or other tasks," she says.

Everyone, in some way, has experienced
both the positive and negative impact of mood
over mind. Think for a moment (no emotion,
please) about a time when some no-good
blankety-blank cut in front of you in line, stole
your parking space, or did some other dirty
deed that got under your skin—and into your
mind. You were mad. So mad, in fact, that you
couldn't even discuss what to make for dinner,

Studies show that
positive people are
more innovative and
creative.

Anger inhibits your ability to think about anything else.

By learning to control your emotions, you can manipulate your thinking ability.

let alone do your income tax return—which, of course, you didn't. (And it's a good thing, too, because you'd probably be in the auditor's office right now.)

What you *were* thinking about—probably the *only* thing you were thinking about—is how angry you were at that blankety-blank. Maybe what he did ruined your entire day. But even if your anger lasted only for a few moments, your emotions overwhelmed your thinking ability. And for a lot longer than you probably realize.

Now think about a time when things were going great. You were feeling on top of the world—strong, vital, and *especially* smart. And you acted that way. You felt smart, so you *thought* smart. Ideas seemed to flow more readily. Decisions were made faster, problems solved more easily. Life's little, or even big, hassles rolled off you like water over a dam.

Aah-h-h! If you could only bottle that feeling.

In a way, you can. Not that wearing rose-colored glasses is suddenly going to make you another Einstein. But by learning how to control your negative emotions and capitalize on your positive feelings, you *can* enhance certain aspects of your thinking ability.

What's Love Got to Do with It?

Plenty. That's because Cupid's trusty arrow is more like a double-edged sword, which only seems fitting since love is perhaps our most complex emotion. Only love can send your heart aflutter one day—and smash it with the force of a gorilla in golf shoes the next. Make you feel like the luckiest soul alive—or the unluckiest, cursed to feel as if rainy days were forecast with you in mind.

We're talking some serious emotional extremes on the heart here. So what's this got to do with your mind?

■ Realize It's Not All Polka Dots and Moonbeams

"Love is perhaps the only emotion that can either really benefit or really hurt your thinking ability, but a lot of that depends on how you *view* love," says Dr. Julius. "The problem with a lot of people is that in the initial stages of a relationship, they tend to overlook certain things that they normally wouldn't. You do that because you're in an emotional state, and it affects your normal way of thinking. Then the relationship develops and the initial infatuation cools and those little things that you initially overlooked suddenly become *very* apparent— maybe even more so than they normally would be in other people." That's another change in your usual way of thinking.

Your view of love determines the effect it will have on your thinking.

The answer: Keep love in perspective. Sure, it's wonderful that you just met Mr. or Ms. Right—and you should relish the emotional bounty you've just received. Feel positive about yourself. And think positively because you're happy. But understand, from those very first heartfelt thumps, that even Mr. or Ms. Right isn't *totally* perfect.

Employees Who Laugh, Last

Executives aren't exactly trading their horn-rimmed glasses and wingtips for Groucho noses and clown shoes, but they're not fooling with findings—from both the business and medical communities—that the employee who laughs, lasts.

Research shows that workers who enjoy on-the-job yuks are least likely to feel yucky about their jobs and are more productive, motivated, happier, and healthier than those who grimly keep their nose to the grindstone. Even in the executive suite—or actually *especially* there—possessing the right sense of humor is becoming increasingly important for job advancement.

"Americans, particularly those in business, have always placed a very high value on a sense of humor," says Robert Orben, a humor consultant who, nearly 30 years ago, sparked a new breed of consultants when he began teaching executives how to use humor effectively at the workplace (he's also served as director of President Ford's speech-writing department). "Maybe it's because business executives are under more constant low-grade stress than ever before—with no down time to look out at sunsets or listen to the birds. But humor has become a boom industry in the workplace because having a sense of humor, particularly in difficult situations, implies control. If someone is able to joke in a tough situation—and he's not a total buffoon—then the perception is that he has control of the situation. He has the answer. He can beat the problem."

One recent survey of 341 employees in a wide variety of occupations found that those who felt they had fun at work proved to be better performers than employees who were satisfied with their job but had less fun.

One source of fun at work is joking and using humor, says David J. Abramis, Ph.D., a psychologist at the School of Business Administration at California State University, Long

Beach, who did the survey. "Essentially what I found is employees who had the most fun at work were more highly motivated workers," he says. "They were satisifed not only with their job but with their life in general." Several studies suggest that laughter can promote creativity. This may occur because humor allows people to be looser and perhaps less tense.

A hearty laugh is also great medicine for your body. When you laugh, the brain may be stimulated enough to pour out enkephalins and endorphins, brain chemicals that help reduce stress. Laughter stimulates the heart and lungs—temporarily increasing the heartbeat, contracting arteries, more thoroughly oxygenating blood, and even boosting production of immune cells. Some say that laughing can even provide a good massage to facial muscles, the diaphragm, the thorax, and the abdomen. When laughing stops, arteries and muscles relax, reducing blood pressure. Besides the obvious cardiac and circulatory benefits, scientists believe this few-second process also aids in digestion. Better yet, laughter and other positive emotions may even strengthen the body's natural defense system, making it more resistant to disease.

To a corporation, this can translate to happier, healthier, and *smarter* employees requiring fewer medical expenses and absences from work. "Not only are people who use humor more secure in their jobs, they may be more valuable," says John A. Jones, Ph.D., a University of Illinois researcher who has been studying the use of humor in the workplace since the 1970s. "There is considerable evidence to show that a sense of humor is an attribute of personality that people tend to remember and respond to very positively. And employers want that in their people. Everyone wants it." ———■

■ *Take Off Your Blinders*

"You must take an objective look at both the person you've fallen in love with and yourself," advises Dr. Julius. "You *can* be in love and realize that person has shortcomings—everybody does. If you realize this from the very beginning, then love won't have such damaging effects on your thinking, or your relationship, later on."

In fact, the *earlier* you see these "imperfections" in your "perfect" mate, the better the chances are for a "truer" love later on. "When people tend to overlook negative aspects early on in a relationship, it's not necessarily that they don't see them, it just doesn't seem to affect their idea of love or satisfaction in that relationship," says Dr. Clark. "But it does seem to predict the success of that relationship three years later."

In fact, realizing that love sometimes can be as thorny as the rose that represents it may be an indicator of how long it lasts. Judy Pearson, Ph.D., a professor of interpersonal communications at Ohio University and author of *Lasting Love: Married 40-Forever Years,* found that most couples married four decades plus—and reported to *still* be happy—realized from the onset that they would face difficulties.

Overlooking another's shortcomings makes for a destructive relationship.

Only the Lonely

The "L-word" can slice your self-esteem quicker than a sushi chef. When you're feeling lonely, your creativity, problem-solving ability, and other aspects of clear thinking can get clouded or otherwise hampered because you're too busy thinking you're a loser. And when you think you're a loser, you think *like* a loser.

"Loneliness is associated with a wide variety of things," says Warren Jones, Ph.D., a psychologist at the University of Tennessee who is a leading researcher on the emotional and mental effects of loneliness. "There are studies that suggest it plays a role in suicide and drug addiction. What I know from our studies is that in one sense or another, lonely people feel miserable and, as a result, have more stress and psychological problems." And that's a devastating one-two punch on thinking ability.

■ You've Gotta Have High Hopes—But Not Too High

"One of the reasons why so many people feel lonely or even desperate in regard to relationships is because they have this unrealistic idea that relationships should be this kind of glowing, storybook love," says Dr. Jones. This is particularly true of women and those around the age of 30 and over who are still in search of Prince or Princess Charming. "When they're not finding what they're looking for, they become depressed or miserable and that clouds their mind."

Usually, adds Dr. Jones, this type of loneliness affects people in one of two ways: They either blame the environment—"there aren't any good men or women around"—or they blame themselves.

227

Loneliness casts a cloud over creativity and clear thinking.

Prince Charming exists only in the fairy tale.

"Regardless of the truth, the better alternative is to blame the environment," he says. "When you do that, at least you still can have hope that you can someday meet someone. You can keep trying. When you blame yourself, you lose hope. And that is even more devastating to the way you think."

So Why So Shy?

One reason that Dr. Jones knows so much about loneliness is because he's one of the nation's foremost authorities on shyness. Shy people, he says, often tend to be lonely people. And they also tend to have problems remembering.

Shyness is exaggerated self-consciousness.

"Shyness is a feeling of exaggerated self-consciousness," he says. "You become so keenly aware of yourself as an object of other people's social perceptions that it interferes with your ordinary ability to remember and your ability to perform whatever it is you need to do. You're so worried about the impression you're making that you focus on your image rather than the task at hand—the names of people you are introduced to, for instance. And when you can't focus, it hurts other aspects of your thinking ability. You can't even remember a name you just heard."

Not that some shyness isn't to be expected. Almost everybody feels shy—call it nervousness or whatever—at the thought of having to give a speech. You might even feel shy about attending a cocktail party with people who may intimidate you. That's perfectly normal. In fact, those types of situations can even *enhance* your mental ability by making you care *more* than usual about the impression you're giving, so you pay closer attention than you normally would.

"But if you feel shyness in getting together with some friends, with people you should feel comfortable with, then it can be a real problem with devastating effects," says Dr. Jones. "Severe shyness can interfere with your problem-solving and decision-making abilities. Shy people are also less likely to go after a challenge, be it at work or even in relationships."

But it doesn't have to be this way. You can learn to use your shyness to your advantage.

Severe shyness can interfere with problem solving and decision making.

■ *Know You Are Not Alone*

First understand that if you're seriously shy, you're not going to eliminate it. "But you can learn to deal with it," says Dr. Jones. And it starts with the realization that you are not the only shy person in the world, or in the room, or at the party—whatever the circumstances may be.

The excessively shy often worry about themselves so much because they feel they're the only ones feeling the way they do. "But this is just not true," says Dr. Jones. "In fact, shyness is common among a lot of people—more than you might imagine. And there is some sense of relief in just knowing this."

Shy people spend too much time thinking about themselves.

It may sound unlikely that a thought like this will put you more at ease, but it does work, says Dr. Jones. Try it the next time you feel shyness pulling the shade on you.

230

■ *Make Like Barbara Walters*

When you realize you're not alone, you're ready for the next step: Find that shy someone else and strike up a conversation.

"What shy people seem to be most afraid of is not knowing what role they're supposed to take," says Dr. Jones. "They don't know *how* to act."

The classic example is a cocktail party where you know only the host or hostess. Look around the room and try to identify another person who looks as uncomfortable as you, someone who looks just as shy. "Approach that person because he or she is the most approachable," advises Dr. Jones. "They'll probably be most grateful that you struck up a conversation."

> Talk to someone who looks as uncomfortable as you feel.

You'll also be in control, because it was you who adopted the role of the interviewer. If *you* ask the questions about *their* lives, you take the pressure off yourself.

If you practice this in a "safe" environment before trying it out at the party, says Dr. Jones, you'll probably be more effective.

Anger Control

Most negative emotions hurt your thinking ability, but the most devastating is anger, says Dr. Julius. "Anger is probably the worst because it can be all-consuming," she says. "Jealousy, bitterness, resentment, and frustration all cloud your thinking. But when you're angry, you are paralyzed with that feeling. It is totally destructive."

> Anger is the one totally mentally destructive emotion.

But let's face facts. It's an anger-filled world we live in, and no matter how hard you try not to, you *will* get angry. So how do you handle it?

■ *Count to 100—Then Let 'Em Have It*

"The worst thing you can do is deny or suppress your anger. But you *can* delay it," says Dr. Julius. "Acknowledge your anger, but say to yourself, 'Okay, I'm angry, but right now I cannot deal with it.' What you want to do is give yourself some time to cool down, to put things in perspective.

"By giving yourself time, you will be able to better formulate a solution—without emotion. And your thinking will be clearer," she says. "You also might learn something about motives, which may help you to handle your anger better."

Not that you should roll over and play dead, mind you. That alone will make you angrier—only this time at yourself (which can be worse on your brain than being angry at someone else). The old advice of counting to 10 (or 100 if you're *really* upset) does hold true.

"Usually, the best thing to do is keep quiet at first but certainly make your feelings known later, either in person or in a note," says Dr. Julius. Fighting fire with fire—and that's what usually results from *immediate* responses that mostly serve to fan the flames—often makes the situation worse because you say or do things you may regret later.

Let's take, for instance, that blankety-blank who stole your parking space. Your initial reaction—a result of your emotions dominating

Time makes room for thinking of an unemotional solution.

Fighting fire with fire makes a bad situation worse.

your thoughts—may be to give him a black eye. A fair exchange for his blackening your mood, eh? Suppose, though, you later find out that he raced into your parking space because he needed to make an emergency phone call for an ambulance because some guy up the road had a heart attack. He'd be a hero with a black eye, and you'd feel like a red-faced fool. Now imagine what that would do to your thinking ability!

■ Ask Yourself: "Is It Really Worth It?"

Of course, most times when some blankety-blank steals your parking space, it isn't for such a noble cause. Still, your anger isn't going to change the situation—but it's certainly going to take its toll on *you*. Instead of playing Mike Tyson (or wishing you could), realize he's a jerk and you're not going to change that. So why should *you* suffer?

Don't waste anger on things you can't control.

"Make a *real* effort not to get angry over situations you have no control over, and you'll probably feel better about yourself," says Dr. Julius. "At the least, it won't affect your thinking as much."

Oh, Jealous Heart

Jealously is a lot like anger—only it feels a lot worse. Yet jealousy isn't totally bad—at least thinking-wise.

"Jealousy comes about when we feel threatened that something important to us might be taken away," says Peter Salovey, Ph.D., a psychology professor and researcher at Yale University. "When you're jealous, you're thinking about impending loss and, at same time, the blow it will be to your self-image." Your thoughts are totally self-absorbed: "Just what is it about this other person that's so attractive to the one you love?" you ask yourself. "What does this person have that I don't?"

So what, you're probably wondering, is so good about thoughts like that?

■ *Take Advantage of a Bad Situation*

Jealousy and envy, explains Dr. Salovey, trigger a type of thinking about yourself that you normally wouldn't practice. "What jealousy does is invoke thoughts of what is important to you; it makes you ask questions of yourself, and as a result, you learn a lot about what makes you tick emotionally."

Jealousy forces you to ask questions about yourself.

And that can be good because it makes you think differently. "People can learn a great deal about themselves and the world from feeling jealous," says Dr. Salovey. "Feelings of jealousy are usually giving you a message that things aren't going right—and if you don't take some action, you can lose that relationship or whatever it is that is making you feel jealous."

■ *Get Your Mind Working on What's Right*

Of course, jealousy does carry with it a lot of heavy artillery. And feelings of anxiety and

Wallowing in jealousy causes a total loss of concentration.

self-doubt top the list. By allowing yourself to wallow in feelings of jealousy, your mind can think of nothing else but your problem. You experience a total loss of concentration.

"When you're feeling jealous about a relationship or envious because someone else at work got that promotion you wanted, you should think of yourself in a more complex way and focus on *other* aspects about yourself and your life that you are succeeding at," suggests Dr. Salovey. "Don't think of yourself only as an employee who didn't get promoted. Think about what's good in your life—maybe about what a good spouse and parent you are or how good you are at the job you're doing right now."

Focus your attention on anything that is alien to what's making you jealous.

The Good in Grief

Anger may provide the strongest reaction to your thinking process, while love may be the most confusing. But the most draining of emotions is grief, which robs you of both energy and brainpower day after day after dreaded day.

Grief has the potential to cause long-term, thought-damaging depression.

Unlike anger, jealousy, and other short-term emotions, grief can last a year or more, says James R. Averill, Ph.D., a psychology professor at the University of Massachusetts in Amherst and an expert on stress and emotions. "In some people, it lasts a lifetime." And in extreme cases, that translates to a lifetime of impaired concentration, thought-damaging depression, or even a consuming effort "to find what was lost."

Why some people quietly suffer, maintaining some semblance of a "normal" life while others literally crumble from their grief is not fully understood. "We do know there are different stages of grief—shock, denial and protest, depression (which lasts the longest), and recovery—though they don't always come in that order," says Dr. Averill.

Throughout these stages, Dr. Averill says it's not unusual for the bereaved to have trouble concentrating or performing other thought processes. After all, attention is focused on the deceased or on whatever was lost. "The quicker they can get to the recovery stage, the better off they will be," he says.

■ Surround Yourself with Friends

"The typical reaction to bereavement, especially in the elderly, is to withdraw, to become isolated from a social network," says Dr. Averill. "But during isolation, an organism shuts down to a great extent—you can't function normally. Social animals like chimpanzees have been known to withdraw and die."

No matter how much you just want to be left alone and grieve, try to maintain social interaction, he says. "The best thing to do—for everyone, but *particularly* the elderly—is to prepare for the inevitable. You know death is going to happen and that grief will follow, so *before* the other person dies, it's very important to establish interests and contacts outside the relationship that can be maintained afterward," says Dr. Averill.

"This is especially important for people who are caregivers. When they suffer a loss,

Prepare yourself for the inevitable and the grief that will follow.

(continued on page 240)

Drugs That Alter Your Feelings

You're in charge of your emotional life, right? Unfortunately, if you're taking one of the following drugs, the answer may be no. In some cases, entire classes of drugs carry the potential side effects.

Drug or Drug Class	Used For/As
Drugs Reported to Cause Nervousness (Anxiety and Irritability)	
Amantadine	Parkinson's disease, viral infections
Amphetaminelike drugs	Appetite suppressants
Antihistamines	Allergies
Caffeine	Stimulant
Chlorphenesin	Fungal and bacterial infections
Cortisonelike drugs	Inflammation
Ephedrine	Asthma/decongestant
Epinephrine	Glaucoma, asthma/ decongestant
Isoproterenol	Bronchodilator
Levodopa	Parkinson's disease
Liothyronine (in excessive dosage)	Hypothyroidism
Methylphenidate	Stimulant
Methysergide	Pain reliever
Monoamine oxidase (MAO) inhibitor drugs	High blood pressure/ antidepressant
Nylidrin	Dilates blood vessels
Oral contraceptives	Birth control
Theophylline	Asthma/bronchodilator
Thyroid (in excessive dosage)	Hypothyroidism
Thyroxine (in excessive dosage)	Hypothyroidism
Drugs Reported to Cause Emotional Depression	
Amantadine	Parkinson's disease, viral infections
Amphetamines (on withdrawal)	Stimulant
Benzodiazepines	Minor tranquilizers

Drug or Drug Class	Used For/As
Carbamazepine	Convulsions, nerve pain
Chloramphenicol	Antibiotics
Cortisonelike drugs	Inflammation
Cycloserine	Tuberculosis
Digitalis	Cardiovascular disorders
Digitoxin	Cardiovascular disorders
Digoxin	Cardiovascular disorders
Diphenoxylate	Diarrhea
Estrogens	Hormone replacement therapy
Ethionamide	Bacterial infections
Fenfluramine (on withdrawal)	Appetite suppressant
Fluphenazine	Tranquilizer
Guanethidine	High blood pressure
Haloperidol	Tranquilizer
Indomethacin	Inflammation/pain reliever
Isoniazid	Tuberculosis
Levodopa	Parkinson's disease
Methsuximide	Convulsions
Methyldopa	High blood pressure
Methysergide	Pain reliever
Metoprolol	High blood pressure
Oral contraceptives	Birth control
Phenylbutazone	Inflammation
Procainamide	Irregular heartbeat
Progesterones	Hormone replacement therapy
Propranolol	Cardiovascular disorders
Reserpine	High blood pressure
Sulfonamides	Antibiotics
Vitamin D (in excessive dosage)	Supplement
Drugs Reported to Cause Euphoria	
Amantadine	Parkinson's disease, viral infections
Aminophylline	Bronchodilator
Amphetaminelike drugs (some)	Stimulants
Antihistamines (some)	Allergies

(continued)

Drugs That Alter—*Continued*

Drug or Drug Class	Used For/As
Drugs Reported to Cause Euphoria—*Continued*	
Antispasmodics, synthetic	Muscle spasms
Aspirin	Inflammation, fever/ mild pain reliever
Barbiturates	Sedatives
Benzphetamine	Appetite suppressant
Chloral hydrate	Sedative, hypnotic
Clorazepate	Minor tranquilizer
Codeine	Pain reliever
Cortisonelike drugs	Inflammation
Diethylpropion	Appetite suppressant
Diphenoxylate	Diarrhea
Ethosuximide	Convulsions
Flurazepam	Hypnotic, bedtime sedative
Haloperidol	Tranquilizer
Levodopa	Parkinson's disease
Meprobamate	Convulsions/tranquilizer, muscle relaxant
Methysergide	Pain reliever
Monoamine oxidase (MAO) inhibitor drugs	High blood pressure/ antidepressant
Morphine	Pain reliever
Pargyline	High blood pressure
Pentazocine	Pain reliever
Phenmetrazine	Stimulant
Propoxyphene	Pain reliever
Scopolamine	Muscle spasms
Tybamate	Tranquilizer
Drugs Reported to Cause Excitement	
Acetazolamide	Convulsions, glaucoma
Amantadine	Parkinson's disease, viral infections

Drug or Drug Class	Used For/As
Amphetaminelike drugs	Stimulants
Antidepressants	Prevent or relieve depression
Antihistamines	Allergies
Atropinelike drugs	Muscle spasms
Barbiturates (paradoxical response)	Sedatives
Benzodiazepines (paradoxical response)	Minor tranquilizers
Cortisonelike drugs	Inflammation
Cycloserine	Tuberculosis
Diethylpropion	Appetite suppressant
Digitalis	Cardiovascular disorders
Ephedrine	Asthma/decongestant
Epinephrine	Asthma, glaucoma/ decongestant
Ethinamate (paradoxical response)	Hypnotic
Ethionamide	Bacterial infections
Glutethimide (paradoxical response)	Sedative, hypnotic
Isoniazid	Tuberculosis
Isoproterenol	Bronchodilator
Levodopa	Parkinson's disease
Meperidine and monoamine oxidase (MAO) inhibitor drugs	High blood pressure, antidepressant, pain reliever
Methyldopa and monoamine oxidase (MAO) inhibitor drugs	High blood pressure/ antidepressant
Methyprylon (paradoxical response)	Hypnotic
Nalidixic acid	Antibiotic for urinary tract infections
Orphenadrine	Allergies, muscle spasms
Scopolamine	Muscle spasms

they feel it as a double whammy. They suffer a personal loss in that someone they loved has died. But they also feel a loss in that they are, in a sense, losing their profession, their reason for being. They need to find another mission. And that is easier when they are involved with other people or activities."

■ *Prepare to Grieve over Any Big Loss*

Grief isn't limited to physical death. Any emotional loss, such as divorce, can result in the very same feelings—and effects on thinking ability.

"The important thing to remember in those situations is that feeling grief is perfectly normal," says Dr. Averill. "You'd be surprised at how many people think they are literally going crazy for feeling grief in those circumstances. But they *should* be feeling that way, because they are suffering a loss, even if the relationship wasn't that good."

In fact, this is true *especially* if the relationship wasn't as good as it could have been. "Stronger grief reactions frequently occur when the relationship was ambivalent," says Dr. Averill. "If the relationship was good, there are no guilt feelings or feelings that you 'could have' or 'should have' done things differently."

Grief can be worse in an ambivalent relationship because of guilt.

Don't Worry, Be Happy

Think of your brain as a computer. And computers (even the *really* good ones) have a limited capacity for what they can do. So if you're busy fretting, fuming, or worrying, all that mental turmoil takes up valuable space that otherwise could be used more constructively—like by thinking more effectively.

Think of it this way. *Whatever* you're thinking about occupies "work space" in your brain, and your conscious brain has a somewhat limited work space. "If part of that work space is taken up with worries or whether you're making a good impression, then there's less room for other things in your brain," says Charles Carver, Ph.D., professor of psychology at the University of Miami in Florida. "If you're angry, your mind is preoccupied with that anger. If you're worried, your mind is preoccupied with worry, and if you're sad, it's preoccupied with that sadness. The more you are preoccupied with personal problems, then the less work space there is to deal with other things that come along, like making decisions or other forms of thinking."

Whatever you're thinking takes up valuable "work space" in your brain.

Then it stands to reason that positive emotions would also take up this valuable work space, making you preoccupied with your feelings of joy. Right? Not exactly.

When you're feeling positive emotions, some psychologists believe, your behavior is "greased"—it's smoother. When you have bad feelings, your problems require attention and thought—and that's a lot of space. Good feelings tend to soak up less mental space. So there's more room for other functions.

Bad feelings interfere with your thinking ability more than good feelings.

What all this means is that bad feelings affect your thinking ability *more* than good feelings. Reason enough to get a better outlook on life.

242

■ *See the Glass as Half Full*

Bernie S. Siegel, M.D., world-famous surgeon-turned-author, has seen first-hand (and documented it in his books, *Love, Medicine, and Miracles* and *Peace, Love, and Healing*) how the power of positive thinking has kept cancer patients doomed to premature death from meeting—at least temporarily—the Grim Reaper. He tries to get people to see that if they change their view of the world, they change. The day you take responsibility for your life and you *do* something about it is the day you set yourself free. You are participating in your future.

That's not to say that your thoughts will suddenly make your cancer—or any real problem, for that matter—just up and disappear. "But I've seen people diagnosed with cancer change their views and deal with illness positively. And I've seen those people enjoy productive, fruitful lives instead of just waiting around to die. And I've seen their condition improve as a by-product. You have to realize you *do* have options."

And not only if you have cancer.

To explain how emotions, thinking, and health go hand in hand, Dr. Siegel tells the story of a woman who was driving down a highway when a wiring problem caused her to lose control of her car. "She was listening to one of my tapes while she was driving, when suddenly the car started to accelerate," relates Dr. Siegel. "She was going 55, 75, then 90 miles per hour; her car was out of control. She was in a panic, thinking she was going to die.

You have to take responsibility for your life.

Your thinking should control your emotions, not the other way around.

"She was in a situation where her emotions were controlling her thinking. Then she changed and made her thinking control her emotions. She realized that she *did* have options. She said she switched the tape on in her head and went through her options: downshifting, turning the car off, putting on the emergency brake, thinking of the negatives of each (ruining the transmission, locking the steering column). Eventually, she stopped the car before it crashed by downshifting.

"In a sense, it was her changing her way of thinking that changed her life. Instead of letting her emotions control her, she controlled her emotions and was able to think more clearly."

■ Realize Life Is Full of Options

Say you're feeling desperate because you're stuck in a dead-end job. You can sit around moping because your boss hates you, or you can realize that you're really not stuck.

"Sure, you have to earn a living, but there are a lot of different ways to do that," says Dr. Siegel. "You don't have to do it in *that* particular job. If you behave like the victim of your situation, then you are promoting your problem. When you decide to leave, or heal yourself, then you become empowered and your situation changes."

Behaving like the victim of a bad situation promotes the problem.

■ Liberate the Child in You

If you are the cause of your problem, then you are also the solution.

244

"Liberate the child in you," suggests Dr. Siegel. "Stop thinking intellectually, and start thinking intuitively. Think from your heart, not from your head.

"When you think intellectually, others are controlling your life because you want to gain their acceptance and fit in," he says. "But when you liberate that child, you say how you appear to others is *their* problem. You're back to thinking in a different way, a more productive and healthier way."

If you find this a bit difficult or awkward, says Dr. Siegel,"think that you have a limited time on this planet. It'll make you worry less about what you're doing. And you're being selfish. You're allowing yourself to love the world wholeheartedly on that day or for that moment."

As an example, Dr. Siegel tells the story of a college student who proposed an idea as a class project and was told by the professor that it was a dumb idea. "The professor gave him a C on the project and told him it would never work," relates Dr. Siegel. "But he didn't worry about it. He believed in himself and after college pursued his 'dumb idea'—Federal Express.

"It's the same with people with cancer," says Dr. Siegel. "Some go home and die while others make the most of the time they have left. They liberate the child in them and do all the things they've always wanted to do. Some get into canoeing or get involved in politics or whatever. They make their lives more productive by thinking more positively, even with negative circumstances. And as a result, they enjoy their life more."

Feeling in a funk? Sometimes the ticket out may be a simple distraction. Here's a word game that should keep you occupied for a while.

The Missing Link

This spider web contains eight five-letter words. Each section contains four letters that have been jumbled. They all contain one missing letter, which should be placed in the space with the question mark. Figure out the missing letter and reassemble the eight words.

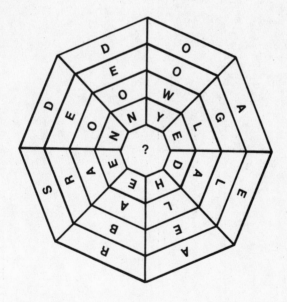

To find the answer, see Solution #8 on page 456.

What it all comes to, it seems, is feeling happy—about yourself, your life, your environment. As one other popular ditty told us a long long time ago: You've got to accentuate the positive. ————■

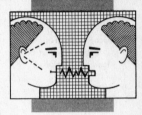

Communication

Wise Ways for Using Words

Ugh. Uh. Ugh uh. Ugh uh uh. Uh uh ugh. Ugh ugh ugh ugh. Uh uh uh uh. Ugh.

Back before the wheel was invented, when saber-toothed tigers roamed the land and volcanoes spewed molten lava, communicating with fellow humans was tough. Indeed, what you see above might have passed for a deep and meaningful sharing of thought.

Nowadays, of course, we have an enormous array of words with which to form speech. Not only that, but we can write those words, read them, send them by phone or facsimile machine, transmit them by radio or television, or even beam them, via satellite, across the globe in seconds.

So why is it still so tough to communicate? Why is it that, like, sometimes, you know, it's, like, so hard to say what, you know, we want to, like, *say*? Why is it that with lovers, friends, and foes alike, sometimes the only thing we can think of to say is . . . "Ugh"?

247

248

An Essential Mind-Building Skill

Good communication is simply a matter of learning the skills.

For most of us, the answer is simple. The reason—perhaps the only reason—that we have a hard time communicating is that we've never had the opportunity, or perhaps the inclination, to learn the skills available to us.

"Very few people would try to repair an automobile or build a house without first reading a manual or taking a course, yet people have relationships without knowing anything about the principles or techniques of effective relationship building," says Allen Fay, M.D., a New York City psychiatrist and author of *P.Q.R.: Prescription for a Quality Relationship.*

Better communication skills can help you succeed financially.

Building relationships is only one thing that can come from having sharp communication skills. Such skills can also help you to succeed financially, advance your career, influence other people, even change the world to a better place. We share a planet with billions of fellow human beings, and surely relating well to them is essential to just about any endeavor.

"Tragically, these skills are not taught in school," says Dr. Fay. "We learn our math, our grammar, and our history—and these are very important. But in my opinion, they don't compare to the importance of communication skills, which have more to do with personal success and happiness than anything else," he says.

But imagine that things were different. Imagine that you *had* gone through years of schooling in communication skills. What might you have learned?

Jane, Meet Dick

Meeting someone for the first time and getting to know that person can be a pleasure, or it can be abjectly terrifying. Generally, the more experience you have at meeting and greeting, the easier it becomes. But regardless of seasoning, how well you've mastered certain basic skills will largely determine your level of ease or pain—and your success at making new friends.

Interaction with people improves with experience.

- **Learn to Ask the Right Questions**

The surest way to build a bridge between you and someone you've just met is to find a common interest. "You're looking for something to hang the conversation on, something you can both relate to," says Matthew McKay, Ph.D., co-director of San Francisco's Haight Ashbury Psychological Services, and Families in Transition.

How do you find a common interest? By *asking questions*.

"A lot of people get stuck in conversation because they don't ask questions," says Dr. McKay. When a conversation is flowing, enjoy the flow, but when the words start to trickle, it's time to take remedial action. Ask questions about the other person. It shows that you are interested, and it helps you to zero in on your common interests, says Dr. McKay.

Finding a common interest is the foundation to building relationships.

When you get the answers to your questions, listen for "free information," says Dr. McKay. For instance, you ask, "Where is your office?" To which you get the response, "It's at 14th and McDoogle—you know, in that hideous gray building with no windows." You just got free information—this person seems to like fresh air and scenery. That gives you common ground. Consider following up with something like, "Yeah, I know what you mean. I wish I could spend all my time outdoors. Do you like camping?"

■ *Know What It Takes to Be a Good Listener*

Listening is crucial to conversation.

The reason you talk is because you want someone else to listen, and the reason that someone else talks back to you is—you guessed it—to be listened to. "Listening is core to communication. It is the first part of a process," says T. Thorne Wiggers, Ed.D., coordinator of outreach and consultation, and a counseling psychologist for the George Washington University Counseling Center. Unfortunately, the process of communication often breaks down because one party isn't listening properly.

Suspend your own judgments until another has his say.

What is listening properly? "Part of the trick of good listening is being able to suspend your own judgments until the other person has had his say," says Dr. Wiggers. All too often we are ready to jump into a conversation responding to what we *think* the other person is saying, not what he really is saying.

■ *See Eye to Eye*

Listening works best when you *show* that you're listening. The single most powerful (yet simplest) way of letting someone know you're being attentive is to look attentive! That means making good eye contact. A pair of roving eyes can stop conversation dead, says Dr. McKay.

Other ways to let someone know you're listening include leaning forward slightly, nodding or paraphrasing, and asking clarifying questions, says Dr. McKay.

251

Roving eyes can stop a conversation dead.

■ *Practice the Art of Disclosure*

When you respond to someone else's statement about his or her beliefs with a statement about your own, you are revealing something about yourself. The process of revealing yourself is called disclosure. It's easy to disclose if you are talking about something like your enjoyment of camping, but going further can be hard.

The process of revealing yourself is called disclosure.

"Disclosure is one of the most difficult parts of communication. It is revealing who you are, your feelings, thoughts, and ideas. In our society, we're generally not taught how to do this," says Robert Jaffe, Ph.D., a psychotherapist in private practice in Sherman Oaks, California.

Perhaps the first hurdle in disclosing is to realize that nothing bad will happen to you if you do, says Dr. Jaffe. Many of us were brought up in environments where we were told to repress our thoughts and feelings: "Stop crying like a baby! That's just a little scrape—go back out and play!" Know that you might have been treated this way, and that it's now all right to express your feelings—provided you feel safe in assuming you won't mind being yelled at for doing so.

Most of us learn at an
early age how to sup-
press our thoughts.

Disclosing doesn't mean that you share
your deepest and most intimate thoughts with
someone on your first or second outing. You
have to slowly open yourself up to another person, gauging how the other person responds,
and moving with that person at roughly the
same rate, advise the experts.

As Aristotle said many centuries ago,
"Wishing to be friends is quick work, but
friendship is a slow-ripening fruit."

■ Hold Off on the Self-Criticisms

It is wise, when first getting to know someone, to focus on the more positive aspects of
your personality. Say to someone who has
known you for years, "Gee, I can't seem to hold
a job," and it probably won't paint you as a loser
in his eyes, because he knows so much more
about you. But say the same thing to someone
who hardly knows you, and that person may
think of you forever as "The Unemployable
One." First impressions tend to last.

First impressions tend
to last.

Keeping Friendship in Repair

Maintaining a friendship involves time,
energy, and a will to make things work. As
writer Samuel Johnson advised, "A man, sir,
should keep his friendship in constant repair."
Of course, he could have been talking about
either sex. But what does it take to keep a
friendship in "constant repair"? Sometimes
it's knowing how to say the right thing at the
right time.

■ *Empathy Works Better than Sympathy*

An important part of a successful relationship is empathy, says Dr. Wiggers. Empathy is "the ability to put yourself in someone else's shoes, so that you can understand his situation and his feelings," he says. Too often, empathy is confused with sympathy, which is feeling sorry for someone.

Say your friend, Paul, comes to you with a problem. His dog died, he got reprimanded at work, and he had a fender bender—all in the same day. You might be inclined to say, "Oh, that's so awful what happened to you; I'm so sorry. I feel so-o-o bad for you." That's sympathy. You may think it's helpful, but it's probably not. "Sympathy takes away from the other person's experience," says Dr. Wiggers.

Sympathy takes away from another's experience.

That is, by getting upset yourself over Paul's problems, you are "jumping into your own stuff," says Dr. Wiggers. You'll be a much more helpful friend if you say something like, "It sounds like you've had a real tough day, Paul. Would you like to talk to me about it?" That's empathy. "By empathizing you don't take the feelings away from the other person," says Dr. Wiggers.

Empathy encourages shared feelings.

■ *Don't Steal the Show*

Perhaps a greater obstacle to forming lasting relationships is the tendency some people have to steal the show by constantly turning the focus of the conversation on themselves. In the example above, a show-stealer might have said to Paul, "Gosh, Paul, too bad. You know, I lost my dog when I was ten years old. Well, we did get another dog, Snooky. Talk about cute! Did I ever tell you about the time [laugh] that Snooky. . . ."

People need attention. It's perfectly all right to tell a friend what you're thinking or feeling in response to something said, but do it in a way that tells him you care about him and that you're listening to him. Be aware of any tendency to pull the ball into your own court," says Jane W. Bunker, Ph.D., a psychologist in private practice in Palo Alto, California, and consultant to the student health center at Stanford University. "And remember that you deserve time to be listened to as well."

Monopolizing a conversation is the biggest obstacle to forming lasting relationships.

■ Communication Is a Two-Way Conversation

The same kind of person who might have swiped the ball from Paul might also take other opportunities—or any and all opportunities—to grab the spotlight and start yapping "me me me. . . ." Chances are, this person will probably have a hard time with relationships. "Be aware if you're someone who talks all the time and everybody listens to you," advises Dr. Bunker.

Long, drawn-out monologues don't foster relationships.

"Pay attention to whether you're taking up all the air time. Ask yourself if there's balance in the relationship," says Dr. Bunker. "It's not a healthy relationship if you're the one doing either all of the talking or all of the listening."

■ *You Have to Be Assertive*

If Paul and his friend are going to have a successful relationship, it should not be the friend (let's call her Helen) who takes all the responsibility. Friendship is a shared project. Sure, Helen should attempt to listen more and speak less, but it's important that Paul let Helen know that's what he wants. What we're talking about here is called assertiveness.

> Both parties in a friendship must take responsibility.

"Assertiveness is helpful to communication. If someone takes a passive stance all the time, not communicating what he wants, then others can assume whatever they want and nothing will ever change," says Dr. Wiggers. In the case of Helen and Paul, it's perfectly all right for Paul to say, "Hey, I need to talk about this—we can talk about your life later."

> It's okay to be assertive when someone else is stealing the show.

■ *Don't Step on Others' Toes*

Be careful, however, to distinguish between assertiveness and its unruly cousin, aggressiveness. Assertiveness is "the ability or capacity to act in your own interest, to ask for what you want or you need, all done in a way that does not compromise the rights of others," says Dr. Fay. Aggressiveness, on the other hand, is expressing your needs while stepping all over others' toes.

For example, let's imagine that Helen and Paul get married and remain married for 20 years. Paul has never once taken out the garbage or done the dishes. Helen is fed up. Angry.

Reconcilable Differences

Take a peek inside the home of Mr. and Mrs. Average American Couple. . . .

WIFE: Honey, let's sit and talk for a while.

HUSBAND: What about?

WIFE: Oh, nothing in particular. We just haven't talked all day, so I thought it would be nice if we could chat.

HUSBAND: Uh . . . okay.

WIFE: So, tell me, Sweetheart, how was your day?

HUSBAND: Fine.

What's going on here?

Well, you've undoubtedly heard about the gender gap—that mile-wide canyon teeming with irreconcilable differences between men and women. But the problem here may not be so wide, or so irreconcilable. Mr. and Mrs. Average American Couple may not have a gap to fill, but rather a cultural boundary to cross! So says Deborah Tannen, Ph.D., a professor of linguistics at Georgetown University and author of *You Just Don't Understand: Women and Men in Conversation.*

Although Mr. and Mrs. Average were both raised in the same country, "they were essentially brought up in different cultures," says Dr. Tannen. Little boys typically grow up surrounded by large groups of other little boys, usually playing games. Little girls, on the other hand, spend most of their

She has three options, says Dr. Fay. First she can be *un*assertive, which means she'll say nothing, boil in silence, and probably develop indigestion. That's clearly no good.

time in small groups or in pairs. Rather than fooling with bats and balls, little girls spend much of their time sitting around and chatting.

So what happens when two people from two different cultures share a relationship later in life? "Women expect men to be new and improved versions of their childhood best friends, which means sitting around and talking. But for men, it's doing things together and spending time together that's proof of the relationship," says Dr. Tannen.

What results from this difference in perspective is that "a lot of women complain about a lack of communication in their relationships," says Dr. Tannen. Or worse—"Women with husbands who don't talk to them may think that they're married to the wrong man," and may even try to get out of the marriage.

But a woman who comes to this conclusion may be wrong. "She should realize that many men are not talkers at home," says Dr. Tannen. If you are married to the strong, silent type, Dr. Tannen suggests that you discuss with him this problem of cross-cultural communication. "He'll be much more willing to make adjustments if he realizes it's a cultural difference, rather than thinking he's being accused of a personal failure."

And what must *men* do to help cross the cultural boundary? They, says Dr. Tannen, "might learn to say 'How was your day?'—and listen to the answer."

Her second option is to be aggressive: "Paul! You lousy stinking rotten lazy slob. I'm sick and tired of you doing nothing around here but watching TV and drinking beer. You get

Aggressive behavior breaks down communication.

over here this minute and take out the garbage and do the dishes—or else!"

Or, Helen can act assertively: "Paul, Honey, I'd really appreciate it if you'd take out the garbage and do the dishes."

You can see that assertive behavior will promote a healthy relationship, while unassertive or aggressive behavior will only turn minor tussles into major scuffles.

■ Flattery Can Get You (Almost) Anywhere

Helen called Paul "Honey." Such sweet expressions nourish relationships and should not be reserved for only special occasions (like trying to get your mate to do the dishes). People like to be liked. So if you like someone, why not show it?

Dr. Bunker suggests voicing your appreciation of your friends, to them, often. Tell them "You look really nice," or "That was really thoughtful of you," or "I always enjoy talking to you." "It's important to show how you feel," says Dr. Bunker. "Relationships tend to go better when you're appreciating both yourself and your partner."

It's important to al- ways express your appreciation.

Communicating beyond Words

Earlier we discussed eye contact. What we do with our peepers is certainly not the only way we communicate beyond words. For example, the tone you use when you speak, the way you hold your body, and the distance you stand from someone all "say" something about what you're feeling. These factors can play an even larger role in determining the quality of a conversation, or a relationship, than do your words.

■ How *You* Say It Is Important, Too

Consider this sentence: "I didn't say she socked her husband." What does that mean? The truth is, without hearing it spoken, you can't know. It may mean, "I didn't say *she* socked her husband." Or it may mean, "I didn't say she socked *her* husband." Or with the emphasis put on any other word in the sentence, we can deliver seven quite different messages!

Where you put your emphasis can change the meaning of a message significantly.

When communicating with other people you need to be aware not only of the words you pick but also of how you say them, says Dr. McKay, a coauthor of *Messages: The Communications Skills Book*. For instance, suppose that Paul just told Helen that he's off to the ball game. Helen says, "Have a *nice* time," raising her volume and icing her pitch in the middle of the sentence. Does she really wish Paul a nice time?

If she doesn't want Paul to go to the game, she should say so, instead of sending Paul a vague and partially hidden message. Dr. McKay calls these *metamessages*. Be aware if and when you are sending them to others—and challenge others who you feel are sending them to you. Good communication relies on messages that are direct and clear, says Dr. McKay.

Good communication means being direct.

260

Fifty percent of what you're really saying comes from your body language.

There's little that communicates more than a pair of crossed arms.

■ *Watch What Your Body Says*

Perhaps more than 50 percent of the total impact of any message we send comes from our body language, mostly from our facial expressions. Think about it. A smile. A frown. A pair of crossed arms. These things "say" quite a bit. And Dr. McKay says that they are often more believable than verbal communication, so it's important to pay close attention to them—in others as well as yourself.

There's little that communicates more than a pair of crossed arms and legs. The message here is not one of openness and warmth! Other forms of body language may include straddling one's chair (indicating dominance), using one's hand to support the head (suggesting boredom), and rubbing the back of one's neck (hey, I'm getting frustrated).

Since body signals can be as varied as words, the key to using them is looking for "clusters of signals that have more or less the same meaning," says Dr. McKay. Take note of anything that falls outside of the cluster. For example, the expressions on Helen's face may have indicated that she was in a good mood until Paul announced he was going to the ball game. At that point, she rolled her eyes and tightened her lips, indicating to Paul that something was wrong—even before she spoke.

■ *Keep in Tune with Others*

A subtle aspect of communication, but one that is more important than we think, is the rhythm or tempo of conversation, says John Gumperz, Ph.D., a professor of anthropology and a sociolinguist at the University of California at Berkeley. Having a conversation with someone is "like playing an instrument in an ensemble," he says. That is, in good conversation, you modulate your activity in accordance with what others are doing.

Just like a good violinist, a good conversationalist picks up right where his partner leaves off. The two are in sync. One person is speaking, and the other says uh-huh, or gestures, at just the right moments. In a bad conversation, thoughts are interrupted, speech is choppy, and two people are often talking at the same time. "We sense when a conversation is good and when it isn't," says Dr. Gumperz.

> A good conversationalist picks right up where another has left off.

And we can also do something about it. "Pay attention to the tempo," says Dr. Gumperz. "You can speed it up or slow it down." By adjusting, you and your conversation partner might reach a new level of understanding.

> Notice the tempo of your conversations.

■ Ya'll from New York—Listen Up!

Talking at 80 miles an hour is normal in New York, but in Nebraska, you're likely to get a ticket for poor communication. And it's not only the speed of speech that separates Americans into two (often antagonistic) conversational-style camps. It's much more, says Deborah Tannen, Ph.D. a professor of linguistics at Georgetown University, and author of *That's Not What I Meant!: How Conversational Style Makes or Breaks Relationships*.

People in the East tend to speak loud and fast, with lots of sarcasm.

According to Dr. Tannen, some Americans use a "high-involvement style" of conversing. These people often were born and bred in New York and other Eastern cities. They tend to speak fast and loud, use short pauses, lots of sarcasm, extreme intonation, and a fair amount of hand gesturing. Others, typically raised in the Midwest and South, have what Dr. Tannen calls a "high-considerateness style." These people talk slower, take longer pauses, and are generally less flamboyant in their body language.

There is often miscommunication when two people using different conversational styles try to relate. Worse yet, "you don't always know there's a miscommunication, you just develop a negative impression of the person," says Dr. Tannen. High-involvement people can see high-considerateness people as withdrawn, uncooperative, stupid, and sullen. High-considerateness people can see high-involvement people as pushy, aggressive, self-centered, and overbearing.

Miscommunication often occurs among people from different parts of the country.

What's the answer? "Become aware of these differences," says Dr. Tannen. If you're from the heart of Mississippi talking to someone from the heart of the Bronx, don't assume he's being rude if he cuts you off. He may think he's doing you a favor by jumping in because he assumes you have nothing to say. And if you're from Manhattan, New York, and talking to someone from Manhattan, Kansas, don't assume that he's being cold just because his speech seems undramatic—he's just being polite, Kansas-style!

■ *Develop the Art of Mirroring* 263

If you really want to be liked, you'll be sensitive not only to someone else's speech patterns but also to how he sits or stands and even what he likes to wear. Then you'll try to imitate or "mirror" that person. "Human beings crave to be with people who seem like themselves," says Michael W. Mercer, Ph.D., an industrial psychologist and president of The Mercer Group, Inc., in Chicago.

Dr. Mercer does not advocate that you totally abandon your personality and become just like the person you are with—just do it to a degree. If someone is talking to you leaning forward at 45 degrees—you lean forward at 45 degrees. If someone you're with loosens his tie—you loosen your tie. If he crosses his legs—do it! These small gestures will subconsciously make your acquaintance feel, "Hey, this guy's a lot like me," and, chances are, he'll like you for it.

If you doubt the effectiveness of the mirroring technique, look around you for someone who is constantly surrounded by friends. "People who get along well with people tend to act a little different with each person they're with—they are adaptable and flexible," says Dr. Mercer.

People crave being with others who seem to mirror themselves.

Act a little different with each person.

Intimates and Other Strangers

Although we're covering some basic communication skills in less than a single chapter,

The Art of Being Vague

Imagine that your Aunt Margaret just came back from the shopping mall wearing the *ugliest, gaudiest, cheapest-looking* dress you've ever seen. She smiles at you, bats her eyelashes, looks down oh-so-admiringly at the pink and green polyester outfit, and asks "don't you just lo-o-ove it!?"

What do you say?

You've undoubtedly been in a situation where someone asks for your opinion, and you feel that you only have two choices: You can tell the truth—and hurt or anger the other person. Or, you can lie. Since either option makes you feel uncomfortable, all you want to do is bury your head in the sand.

Well, lift up your head and consider a third option! Tell Aunt Margaret, "My, that's a very interesting dress!" What you're doing here is being "artfully vague," and it's often the best way out of these sticky situations, says psychologist Michael W. Mercer, Ph.D., author of *How Winners Do It: High-Impact People Skills for Your Career Success.*

"Being artfully vague means that you don't agree or disagree, but you let the other person interpret what he will," says Dr. Mercer. So if someone presents a point of view that you find totally lacking in intelligence and sensitivity, don't say "that's the stupidest idea I've ever heard" (which is exactly what you're thinking)—say "That's quite an idea!" suggests Dr. Mercer.

Even the most intimate couple can end up in a conversation knot.

don't be fooled; successful communication is difficult work. Even two highly intelligent, sensitive people who love each other deeply can sometimes wind up in seemingly hopeless communication knots.

If someone tries to see if you share their narrow point of view on a political or religious subject, rather than get in a heated and unpleasant debate, Dr. Mercer recommends the following line: "You know, I was listening very carefully to what you were saying, and it's something I think about *very* intensely at times." (Sure you do . . . for about half a second a year.)

Author Robert Thornton gives dozens of examples of artful vagueness in his snappy little book, *Lexicon of Intentionally Ambiguous Recommendations (LIAR)*.

Problem: You've been asked to write a letter of recommendation for a former employee who can't manage his own sock drawer. You don't want to lie, but you feel compelled to give the guy a break. What do you do? Simple, says Thornton. Write: "You will be very fortunate to get this person to work for you." Or "All in all, I cannot recommend this person too highly." Or "You won't find many people like her." Leave it up to the recipient to interpret as he wills!

In conversations about topics where contentious comments are likely to come up—that is, politics, religion, and money—it usually proves best to avoid the topics in the first place, says Dr. Mercer. But, of course, you'll still have to deal with Aunt Margaret's dress! ———■

In his book *Knots*, well-known psychiatrist R. D. Laing gives such an example:

JILL: I'm upset you are upset.

JACK: I'm not upset.

JILL: I'm upset that you're not upset that I'm upset you're upset.

JACK: I'm upset that you're upset that I'm not upset that you're upset that I'm upset when I'm not.

What are poor Jack and Jill to do?

■ Communicate about Your Communication

Chances are, Jack and Jill have wound up in knots before. Now may be the time for them to sit down and discuss their communication styles, and why they aren't connecting. What is getting in the way? How can they communicate better?

Troubles can be ironed out.

Often, what brings up troubles between intimate friends is the notion by one or both parties that the other is less committed to the relationship. If you feel this is going on in your relationship, bring it out into the open. Approach your partner and say, for instance, "I feel like this relationship is more important to me than to you." That kind of initiation and assertion can only lead to a deeper relationship, says Dr. Wiggers.

Bring problems out into the light.

■ Make a Commitment

While expressing feelings is extremely important, an intimate relationship requires a certain understanding about the relationship itself. For the relationship to flourish, "there needs to be a commitment between two people," says Michael Emmons, Ph.D., a counseling psychologist in private practice in San Luis Obispo, California, and author of *The Intimate Organism.*

A commitment between intimates can take on many forms. It doesn't have to be a fraternity pin or a diamond ring. "A commitment can be expressed in a large number of ways. It doesn't even have to be verbal," says Dr. Emmons. Perhaps the most important way to express commitment to another is to be there—that is, to be available when a friend is in need. Yes, that may mean that you're sacrificing your time and energy. "Both of you need to sacrifice at times," says Dr. Emmons.

Commitment can come in many forms.

■ *Hang in There*

Learning to communicate is a lifelong pursuit. Sometimes, the lessons will be tough. But like any other skill, only practice makes perfect. So stick with it. "There are always things to learn to become more effective at communicating," says Dr. Bunker. "The more you learn, the more it becomes second nature."

Communication is a lifelong pursuit.

Practice makes communicating easier.

Communication in Special Relationships

Wendy had a miserable day. Alan is standing by the door as she walks in. She brushes him on the cheek, nuzzles her mouth against

How to Survive a Blind Date

Have you ever trembled as you've reached the front door, knowing that on the other side stood your blind date?

Jeff Nagel, a marketing officer from Arlington Heights, Illinois, knows a little bit about blind dates. He went out on 137 of them before the age of 30 and tells all about it in his book *The Blind Date Survival Guide*.

What did Nagel learn over his years in the dating trenches? First, *never* order soup when dining on a first date. "There is no way in the world to eat soup without making that slurping sound," he warns. And don't order lobster, either. "You have to wear a plastic bib with a giant picture of a lobster on it."

Although Nagel's book is humorous, his suggestions are practical. For instance, "Lunch should be your first choice on a blind date. It puts the date at ease, as it is during daylight hours in a situation that is considered 'safe.' More important, however, it allows for a quick exit if the date turns out to be a bore."

If you do wind up with plans for a dinner out, Nagel offers strong advice. "Never, I repeat, *never* let your date choose the restaurant unless you are independently wealthy. Many a person's rent money went into one dinner with a boring date."

If you're wondering just how Nagel wound up on so many blind dates, well, he's not quite sure himself. "I was a single guy living in New York City, and my friends would call me up and leave names and numbers," he says.

But that was then. Today, those friends aren't leaving numbers anymore. Yes, Jeff Nagel, after 137 blind dates, finally found himself a bride. She was *not* a blind date!

his ear, whispers, "Alan, I missed you," and gently tugs his hand in the direction of the couch. Is this a perfectly normal and healthy form of communication?

That all depends *what* door she walked in, and *who* Alan is!

If Alan is Wendy's husband, fine, that's one thing. But what if Alan is the postman? The next-door neighbor? The next-door neighbor's teenage son? Wendy's boss? Obviously, what passes for normal and healthy communication in one set of circumstances may not in another. Communication skills must change depending on circumstances.

Consider relationships between lovers. They are unique. For one thing, there's sex. And bills. And chores. And sometimes children. Put them all together, and communication between loving partners can sometimes be sticky business.

Love is a many complicated thing.

■ Beware of Money and Sex

Money and sex are not only the major themes of many of today's rock 'n' roll songs, they are also the most common reasons for spats in couple relationships, says Dr. Jaffe. Money and sex are problem areas for many because they tend to represent a lot of other things "like love and power," says Dr. Jaffe.

Money and sex are analogous to love and power.

For instance, withholding either sex or money is a way that one member of a couple may try to exercise power over the other. What you need to do if you're feeling angered by your partner's treatment of money or sex is to bring the issue up for discussion—preferably at a moment when you're not feeling so angry. Talk about your feelings. Say, for instance, "When you don't have sex with me, I feel like you don't love me."

Be aware that "feelings of anger come up because you've been hurt or you're afraid of being hurt," says Dr. Jaffe. Get in touch with the fear behind the anger before you express it to your partner, he suggests. Remember, in order to communicate your feelings clearly to someone else, you must first understand those feelings yourself.

Know yourself in order to communicate better.

■ Start with the Positive

Whatever the problem is between you and your partner, the way to handle it is calmly. When bringing up a problem, always try to start by saying something positive. It will make your partner more receptive to what you are about to say.

Let's suppose that hubbie Paul isn't doing the dishes. Wife Helen may open the conversation by saying, "Paul, I love you and you're a wonderful husband, but there is something that's been bothering me. . . ." That's the best way of getting into it, says Dr. Fay. The nitty-gritty can follow.

■ Don't Hash Over What Was

You can't change what's already happened. Don't dwell on it.

In dealing with dishes, or any other problem in a relationship, "you don't want to bring up past problems—instead, request changes for the future," says Dr. Fay. That is, Helen should *not* reprimand Paul for not having done the dishes for 20 years (after all, there's nothing he can do to change that). Instead, Helen should tell Paul what she wants in the future, namely, "Paul, from now on I'd appreciate it if you'd help me out with the dishes."

■ Consider Professional Help

Some relationships unfortunately get to the point where one or both partners become so filled with rage that hurting the other person actually becomes more important than solving a particular issue. Ask yourself if this is the case in your situation. If it is, it's probably time for you and your mate to seek professional counseling, says Dr. Jaffe.

Seeking professional help shouldn't be put off forever.

■ Declutter Your Relationship

A common source of hostility in otherwise peaceful households is the problem of sloppiness. It's no problem, of course, if both partners are the Oscar Madison type (the slob in Neil Simon's story about two battling bachelor roommates). But when only one is an Oscar, and the other is a Felix Unger type, then you have a problem, says Selwyn Mills, Ph.D., a psychotherapist in private practice in Great Neck, Long Island, and coauthor of *The Odd Couple Syndrome: Resolving the Neat/Sloppy Dilemma.*

Dr. Mills contends that the general population breaks down fairly evenly—50:50—into

272

The population is 50 percent neatnik, 50 percent slob.

Nagging won't work.

Regularly remind yourself of what you find attractive in your mate.

neatniks and slobs. That means your chances of winding up as an "odd couple" are pretty good. How do you keep dirty socks and old magazines from destroying a relationship? "You must realize it's not the intention of the other person to drive you crazy," says Dr. Mills. An Oscar Madison type just doesn't have the same *need* for neatness and order as the Felix Unger type.

Whatever the reason for your differences, "attacking the other person or continual nagging won't work," says Dr. Mills. Instead, talk about the problem and try to depersonalize it. If you're the Felix type, tell Oscar, "the clutter is a problem for me," rather than, "you're a pig." Then try to think of something nice that you can do for Oscar in exchange for his agreement to stop dropping socks on the sofa.

■ *Cultivate Your Attractiveness*

Dealing with the day-to-day hassles of life can sometimes make lovers forget they're lovers. It's important to a relationship that each partner recall and cultivate what makes him attractive to the other. "Attraction needs to be kept alive and vital. It needs rebuilding if it starts to sag," says Dr. Emmons.

That means you should regularly remind yourself of what you find attractive in your mate—and what makes you attractive to him. If you know he loves you for your intelligence, your wit, your sense of humor, and your affection, these are qualities you should try to cultivate, says Dr. Emmons.

All in the Family

273

Wouldn't it be nice if family relations were just like they were on the old sitcoms? June and Ward, Ozzie and Harriet, and Lucy and Ricky never had any problems that couldn't be solved in half an hour. Unfortunately, in real life, resolving family problems "sometimes isn't just a matter of communicating better—it's a matter of communicating," says Timothy Rot, Psy.D., a family therapist with the Florida Couples and Family Institute in West Palm Beach.

Part of the problem is that "family relationships are our longest-lived relationships," says Dr. Jaffe. That longevity means that any unresolved anger from the past has had lots of time to snowball, as it often does. How can we melt familial snowballs?

Lack of communication in families is common.

■ See Your Parents as Human Beings

Relationships between parents and their grown children aren't as bad as many people make them out to be. Sure, lots of us roll our eyes when asked how our weekend with the folks was, but the fact is, we're usually just kidding. According to at least one study, at the University of Southern California, over *90 percent* of adults *like* their parents!

"Particularly the mother-daughter relationship tends to be a remarkably close one," says Lillian Troll, Ph.D., adjunct professor of human development at the University of California in San Francisco and past president of

Relationships with parents are among the most important in your life.

274

Parents represent un-
achieved goals.

Parents *are* human.

the Adult Development and Aging Division of the American Psychological Association.

Part of what may make the relationship between you and your parents tough at times is that "your parents represent your goals—so if you haven't achieved them, it may be hard to face that reminder," says Dr. Troll. Parents, she adds, are also apt to push their expectations, which can make things uncomfortable.

Easing conflicts with your parents is much like easing conflicts with anyone else—"try to bring out and talk about sticky issues," says Dr. Troll. Of course, your parents *aren't* just anyone else, but they are human beings, and it's necessary for you to see them as such. Part of maturity, says Dr. Troll, is being able to see your parents as human.

■ Be Tough with Mom and Dad

Seeing your parents as human means you can be—should be—assertive with them. If they shove their expectations onto you, say no! Stand up! "Parents' greatest concern is to feel that they did right raising their children—if the children stand up to them as adults, it gives them satisfaction," says Dr. Troll, who is also a professor emeritus at Rutgers University.

■ Put Sibling Rivalries behind You

As years go by, most of us come to appreciate deeply those whom we once considered "brat" sisters or brothers. Sibling relationships among adults are often among the most intimate and rewarding. Sometimes, however, the same rivalries that existed back when you were in pigtails stick around.

Sibling relationships are among the most rewarding.

What's happening in these situations may be that the siblings, in each other's presence, are reverting back to their roles as children, says Renee A. Cohen, Ph.D., a clinical psychologist in private practice in West Los Angeles and an expert on family and child relationships. One sibling may become "the clumsy one" and another "the bratty one," just as they were back in the old days.

If you find yourself falling back into your old role, you need to catch yourself. "Don't allow yourself to get caught in an old mold," says Dr. Cohen. Instead, remind yourself that you are an adult, that much has changed in 25 years, and that the child who was once seen as clumsy is now a great tennis player, an expert ice skater, and a hot modern dancer! And don't only remind yourself—remind the rest of your family. "If they try to typecast you or call you by your old label, correct them," says Dr. Cohen. "Do not accept the label anymore."

Do not accept labels your family pins on you.

Old labels die hard.

■ Put the Blame Where It Belongs

Be aware that parents can sometimes instigate sibling rivalries. If you have a brother or sister, you've probably heard from your parents at one point or another, "Why can't you be more like your sister, Deb, who just got a terrific job and blah blah blah. . . ."

Parents sometimes do this in a misguided effort to push their children to succeed, says

Even the happiest
families argue.

Dr. Cohen. Rather than get angry at your *sister*, tell your parents to stop comparing the two of you. "Tell them 'I'd prefer to be acknowledged for the unique individual that I am,' " says Dr. Cohen.

■ White-Flag the Chore Wars

There are no documented records of the Swiss Family Robinson having fought over who was going to crack open the coconuts, but rest assured, it happened! When there's garbage to be taken out, the dog to be walked, grass to be mowed, dishes to be washed, or coconuts to be cracked open, there's need for family communication. Without good communication, these everyday tasks can result in full-blown chore wars.

The best road to peace is to sit down and talk about who needs to do what. "Or better yet, talk about who *wants* to do what," says Dr. Rot. Typically, he says, families break up chores according to long-standing tradition. Dad, because he's a man, is supposed to care for the outside of the house. Mom, because she's a woman, is supposed to care for the inside of the home (and certainly everything in the kitchen). The kids, because they're kids, are supposed to walk the dog and take out the garbage.

Feel free to break
from tradition.

But it doesn't have to be that way! "If you all talk about it, you may find that some chores are easier for some to do than others. For instance, it may be relaxing for the adult coming home from work to walk the dog, so the child can do something else," says Dr. Rot.

The Business Side of Communication

It shouldn't come as a surprise that in companies where the lines of communication are open, the bottom lines are strong. Successful businesses depend on efficient communication. Bosses need to communicate with their staffs, staff members need to communicate with each other, and sales reps need to communicate with customers.

Successful business depends on efficient communication.

Business relationships differ from personal ones (how often do you tell your boss "let's kiss and make up?"), but there are certainly many similarities. "The basis for most workplace communication is the development of rapport, comfort, and trust," says Dr. Mercer, author of *How Winners Do It: High-Impact People Skills for Your Career Success.*

Whether you're the president of a Fortune 500 company, a flea market hawker, or a homeowner who needs to negotiate with plumbers and repairmen, a few special skills for negotiating, influencing, and persuading might make your dealings run a little smoother.

■ Win a Friend

As implied in the title of Dale Carnegie's 1936 classic, *How to Win Friends and Influence People,* making friends and influencing people go hand in hand. "We're all much more likely to be persuaded by someone we like," says Dr. Mercer. So the key to closing a business deal is establishing a friendship, not necessarily a close one, but a friendship.

We're most likely to be persuaded by someone we like.

We've already covered lots of techniques for this: mirroring, using compliments, expressing care with your tone of voice and body language. But you need to use these techniques, says Dr. Mercer. "Some people can persuade by virtue of their position or a title, but they find over time that this is only moderately effective," he says.

Say, for instance, that you are the head of a large division in a major corporation. You'd find that you could bully most employees into toeing the line with intimidation and threats. But toeing the line is all those employee would do—nothing more, nothing less. But if you want real energy, creativity, and maximum productivity from your staff, you should try developing rapport!

Rapport is essential to productivity.

■ *Be Different with Different People*

It's fine to follow the Golden Rule (by doing unto others as you would have them do unto you), but in a business environment you might want to consider "the Platinum Rule," says Dr. Mercer. The Platinum Rule, he says, is "to do unto others as they would like to be done unto."

Treat co-workers according to their work style.

Sure, *everyone* wants to be treated with kindness and consideration, but beyond that, each of us brings to the work environment certain hopes and expectations about the way we'll be treated. Most people fall into four categories (with some overlap), says Dr. Mercer. If you can recognize which category a colleague of yours falls into, and treat him accordingly, your working relationship should flourish. (It doesn't matter, by the way, whether this colleague is higher or lower on the totem pole than you—this technique will work regardless.)

Here are Dr. Mercer's four categories.

Result-focused individuals "like to know what time it is, but don't care how you built the clock," says Dr. Mercer. These folks feel most comfortable when you simply tell them what you did or what needs to get done—"and then leave and let them do it." They don't like chit-chat or painstaking detail.

Detail-focused individuals "have minimal interest in what time it is; they want to know how you built the clock," says Dr. Mercer. When you approach these folks, come with lots of facts and figures. Be very specific about what needs to be done and why—that's what works here.

Friendly-focused individuals typically settle in and become either result- or detail-focused, but they find it hard to launch into the work without first sharing a few friendly words about the family or about the weekend. Without a bit of chit-chat, they may feel insulted or unappreciated.

Partying-focused individuals can get the work done, but they feel that work should be fun. They like to laugh—a lot. Approach these colleagues prepared to tell a few jokes or share a cartoon.

"People who get along well with people tend to act a little different with each person they interact with—they're adaptable and flexible," says Dr. Mercer. He suggests you apply "the Platinum Rule" both inside and outside of the workplace.

> Some like to chit-chat, some like jokes, some just want the facts.

> It pays to be flexible.

■ *Get Someone to Say Yes*

It has been said that we are all creatures of habit. It's true, says Dr. Mercer. So if you want someone to say yes to your proposal, first get them in the habit of saying yes to you. "The more you get someone into the habit of saying yes, the more likely he will be to say yes when you really want," says Dr. Mercer.

How do you get someone in the habit of saying yes? "By asking innocuous questions," says Dr. Mercer. For example, say your goal is to have Mr. Jones purchase a car from you. The conversation might go something like this:

Innocuous questions can get you the answer you want.

> YOU: Gosh, you've been looking at this car for 10 minutes now, huh?
>
> MR. JONES: Yeah.
>
> YOU: That's a beautiful interior, isn't it?
>
> MR. JONES: Yes, it sure is.
>
> YOU: But I'll bet that the price tag is an issue for you, am I right?
>
> MR. JONES: (laugh) Yeah, I'm afraid that it is.
>
> YOU: Would you like to look at the financing possibilities with me to see if something can be worked out?
>
> MR. JONES: Yeah—sure.

All right, not all car sales are made this easily, but Dr. Mercer promises that you'll increase your odds of getting someone to say yes by using this tried-and-true technique.

Crossing Cultural Borders

"Ladies and gentlemen, please make sure that your seats are upright and your seat belts are securely fastened. We are about to make our descent into Kangaloogu International Airport."

A perfect landing. You step out of the plane onto the sizzling blacktop and head immediately for the restroom, where you change into something cooler. You next head for the money kiosk, where you change 100 U.S. dollars into 45,230 Kangaloogian francs. Anything else you need to change before leaving the airport? You bet there is: your communication skills.

This last section is a sort of caveat emptor. Nearly *everything* you've read till now is subject to change when you cross cultural borders . . . so let the traveler beware!

■ Leave Your Local Customs at Home

Roger E. Axtell, a former vice-president with the Parker Pen Company and author of *Do's and Taboos around the World,* spent 22 years living and traveling abroad. He recalls one of his earlier and most shocking cross-cultural experiences occurring in Saudi Arabia: "I was walking down the street with a Saudi business colleague I had recently met, when all of a sudden he reached over and held my hand. I said to myself, 'This guy's trying to tell

Rules of communication change when you cross the border.

Cross-cultural experiences can be shocking.

Cross-cultural communication is often tricky business.

me something.' I started to perspire." As it turns out, "all the colleague was trying to do was express friendship and respect," says Axtell.

On another trip, Axtell says he extended his hand to greet an Argentine colleague, but the South American thought that a firm hug would be more appropriate. So, "we wound up smashing noses," says Axtell.

Such problems are legendary among frequent travelers. At times these miscommunications may be unavoidable, but you can ease your way into another culture by dropping some of your old habits at the airport.

Keep your eyes open.

"Watch. Keep your eyes open. See how people eat, and how they greet. Listen. Be sensitive that there are differences," says Robert Moran, Ph.D., a professor of international studies, and director of the program in cross-cultural communication at the American Graduate School of International Management, in Glendale, Arizona.

■ *Learn the Local Body Language*

In another culture, you risk insulting someone with your foreign communication style, and you risk being insulted by someone else's. Avoid both. Remember that when meeting with people of other nationalities, you may not only be speaking different languages, you are also using different body languages!

Other countries have different body language, too.

For instance, America's "A-OK" sign (thumb touching index finger) "is considered the most obscene gesture you can make in about 40 countries," says Dr. Moran, who is also the author of *Managing Culture Differences*. Patting a child on the head is a sacrilege in Malaysia, because the top of the head "is considered the seat of the soul" in that country. And to beckon to someone with your finger would be highly disrespectful in many cultures (where the gesture is reserved for calling animals).

Body distance can vary greatly among cultures. In the United States, we generally stand about 30 inches from someone we're talking casually with; in Japan, it's more like 40 inches, and in the Middle East, "it's so close your eyes have trouble focusing," says Dr. Moran. Maybe that's why "you shouldn't be insulted if a Middle Easterner doesn't look you in the eye." People from that part of the world usually don't. It's just a different communication style.

283

Middle Easterners stand *real* close.

- ## Leave Your Idioms Behind

You're lucky if you're a native English speaker. English is more widely spoken in international business than any other language. But have pity on those trying to communicate with you in a language not their own!

Speak slowly and clearly, of course. But beyond that, beware of idioms and cultural allusions that are almost certainly not going to be understood by anyone who was brought up outside of North America. Tell your Chinese or Soviet colleague that entrusting you with his money is "as safe as Fort Knox," or that something is "as funny as a rubber crutch," and

Idioms can cause real confusion.

you're probably not going to be creating anything but confusion, says Axtell. But if you *really* want to create confusion—look up to the sky and say, "It's raining cats and dogs!"

■ *Focus on What You Have in Common*

Differences in communication styles among different cultures include many aspects—including "language, hand gestures, gift-giving, and eating habits," says Axtell. But, he says, there's one thing to always keep in mind: "All of this is the veneer to a culture—the beautiful thing is that once you cut through that veneer, you'll find that we're all more alike than we are different."

The Universal Signal

In closing, a final word from the last page of Roger Axtell's *Do's and Taboos:*

"There is one universal action, one signal, one form of communication that is used and understood by every culture and in every country, no matter how remote.

"It can help you with every relationship—business or personal—and become the single most useful form of communication.

A smile is understood in every port of call.

It is . . . the smile."

So, like, next time you've got nothing to, like, you know, say . . . try a simple smile. It'll serve you better than "ugh!" ────────■

A large part of successful communication is mastery of one's own language. How well is your mastery of English? (Did you catch the mistake in that sentence?) Below are a couple more ways in which you can test your knowledge of the world of words.

A Stone's Throw

The following multisyllabic pronouncement is a badly garbled popular proverb. See if you can translate it into simple, common English.

Individuals residing in habitations composed of dried vegetable matter are seriously advised to consider the inadvisability of having seats of power kept for safekeeping in a repository in said domicile.

Help Wanted

The same five letters, rearranged to make two different words, can fill in the blanks below. Try to complete the sentences.

"I had to fire that nincompoop," said the boss. "Our company _ _ _ _ _ somebody a lot less _ _ _ _ _ ."

To find the answers, see Solution #9 on page 457.

Intuition

Tools That Tap Your Inner Voice

Have you ever had a hunch that proved right? A gut feeling about something that turned out to be exactly on target? Unexplained vibes about someone you just met? Have you ever had . . . *intuition?*

For Nancy King, it was the night she decided not to get into her friend Linda's car but to seek another ride home. She had no specific reason for her decision, merely this "weird feeling." Nancy later learned that Linda's car was hit and badly damaged by a drunk driver that night. So what *is* intuition, exactly?

"Intuition is a mind process that allows us access to information apart from the usual channels of reasoning, memory, or sensing," says William Kautz, Sc.D., founder and director of The Center for Applied Intuition in San Francisco. In other words, intuition can be what some people call extrasensory perception—

287

Intuition bypasses normal mental processes.

ESP. Everyone has it, says Dr. Kautz. It's a natural human process, but some of us are more skilled at using it than others.

For Caitlin Grandinetti, intuition came on her vacation trip to New Mexico, when a hike through Cibola National Forest turned into a near nightmare. She found herself hopelessly lost, with the sun about to set, when, she says, she suddenly heard a "little voice." It told her to turn right, and then left, and then right, until finally, just before sunset, she found herself standing by the main road, safely out of the forest.

According to Shakti Gawain, author of *Living in the Light* and several other books on the mind, intuition is a connection "to the higher power of the universe." Our intuitive minds, she says, are deep storehouses of knowledge and wisdom, containing "an infinite supply of information."

For Eve Buchay, intuition comes often. "Many times I've had a feeling that my friend Antoinette was going to visit me, and she did," says Eve.

Intuition comes from experience.

Intuition is the ability to unconsciously tap our knowledge base. It comes from experience, aided by environmental cues that call forth that experience, says Nobel laureate Herbert Simon, Ph.D., a professor at Carnegie Mellon University in Pittsburgh. A seasoned physician who can intuitively look at a patient and tell what's wrong is pulling upon years of experience, sparked by what he sees, hears, and possibly smells. He doesn't need to go through a lengthy examination of the patient because he's done it so many times before with other patients.

Two Schools of Thought

Where did Nancy's "weird feeling," Caitlin's "little voice," and Eve's insight really come from? Some experts, like Shakti Gawain, say that it's a mystical and magical connection between the brain and beyond. Others say otherwise.

Dr. Simon, for instance, agrees that intuition surely does exist, but it is not anything mystical. Rather, the human brain is "like a big indexed encyclopedia," with masses of stored information from our past. Intuition is the "aha!" feeling you get when you've just tapped into this encyclopedia. But he doesn't lend much credence to talk of ESP or "higher powers of the universe." Neither do some other experts.

> You can learn to use your intuition more effectively.

As they all see it, however, intuition—no matter how you define it—is a very powerful tool. And regardless of which school of thought you adhere to, there are ways in which you can tune in to it, sharpen it, and polish it. On the following pages, experts from both of what might be called the "universal" and the "secular" schools of thought will tell you how. And you'll hear other stories of exemplary intuition.

You're Only As Intuitive As You Feel

"Every day I use my intuition," says Dennis Bolda, a veteran detective with the Chicago Police Force. He recalls a case in which a woman was grabbed by two men in the parking lot of a grocery store. They took her in her car to an abandoned railroad site, where they robbed her and raped her.

"I had a feeling that the guys who did it lived between the grocery store and the railroad. So I pulled out a map and located the midway point." He drove to that point and spotted the victim's car; near the car were her two abductors. They were seized, tried, and sentenced to 25 years in prison.

One cop's intuition led him right to an abductor.

■ Believe in Your Intuition

A police officer lacking Detective Bolda's powers of intuition might have had the same hunch to pick up a map and check the midway point, but he then would have dismissed the idea as silly. Whether or not you believe in intuition largely determines how well it works for you, says Jerry Lynch, Ed.D., author of *Living Beyond Limits* and founder of the Beyond Limits Center for Excellence in Santa Cruz, California.

You must be able to trust your own mind.

"Intuition comes about when you trust your mind. If you don't believe in it, you won't look for it. If you don't look for it, you won't find it," he says. Detective Bolda concurs: "I've always had good intuition, even when I was a kid. I think that's what makes for a good detective."

■ Keep Your "Buts" Out of It

Intuition is "feeling knowledge," says Dr. Lynch. We're all born with it, but as we grow we're taught to nullify our "inner voice" with layers of afterthought. For instance, our intuition says, "I want to quit this program." And then something clicks in to make us add "*but* people will get down on me."

Intuition is "feeling knowledge."

This "something" that clicks in, this afterthought, is often the voice of fear, says Dr. Lynch. "Believing in your intuition can be frightening—and this fear is a major block to using it." He suggests that you get in touch with this fear, and moreover, "try to stay to the left of your 'buts' "—that's where your intuition lies.

Fertile Surroundings, Fertile Thoughts

Jeff Davidson, a certified management consultant in the Washington, D.C. area, has been consulting entrepreneurs for 15 years. In that time, he's had a lot of businesspeople run ideas by him, some good, some not so good. He finds the best ideas and the sharpest intuition seem to come in certain environments, he says. Some people have told him they get their ideas sitting by babbling brooks, others get bursts of intuition staring into a candle, and yet others think best in a hot bath. Everyone, says Davidson, has such an environment. The key is finding it.

Intuition occurs in the strangest places.

■ Find a Soft Place

How do you know what environment is right for you? "Remember where you had your
(continued on page 294)

How Good Is Your Intuition?

Not all of us have the same intuitive abilities. Take the following quick test to find out how good a hunch-maker you are. Remember though, your answer will represent only your *present* level of intuitive powers, says Weston Agor, Ph.D., developer of the test. By following the advice throughout this chapter you can boost your score over time.

1. When working on a project, do you prefer to:
   (a) Be told what the problem is but be left free to decide how to solve it?
   (b) Get very clear instructions about how to go about solving the problem before you start?

2. When working on a project, do you prefer to work with colleagues who are:
   (a) Realistic?
   (b) Imaginative?

3. Do you most admire people who are:
   (a) Creative?
   (b) Careful?

4. Do the friends you choose tend to be:
   (a) Serious and hard working?
   (b) Exciting and often emotional?

5. When you ask a colleague for advice on a problem you have, do you:
   (a) Seldom or never get upset if he/she questions your basic assumptions?
   (b) Often get upset if he/she questions your basic assumptions?

6. When you start your day, do you:
   (a) Seldom make or follow a specific plan?
   (b) Usually make a plan first to follow?

7. When working with numbers, do you find that you:
   (a) Seldom or never make factual errors?
   (b) Often make factual errors?

8. Do you find that you:
   (a) Seldom daydream during the day and really don't enjoy doing so when you do it?
   (b) Frequently daydream during the day and enjoy doing so?

9. When working on a problem do you:
   (a) Prefer to follow the instructions or rules when they are given to you?
   (b) Often enjoy circumventing the instructions or rules when they are given to you?

10. When you are trying to put something together, do you prefer to have:
   (a) Step-by-step written instructions on how to assemble the item?
   (b) A picture of how the item is supposed to look once assembled?

11. Do you find that the person who irritates you the *most* is the one who appears to be:
   (a) Disorganized?
   (b) Organized?

12. When an unexpected crisis comes up that you have to deal with, do you:
   (a) Feel anxious about the situation?
   (b) Feel excited by the challenge of the situation?

How to Score

Step 1. Total the number of (a) responses you have circled for questions 1, 3, 5, 6, and 11.

Step 2. Total the number of (b) responses you have circled for questions 2, 4, 7, 8, 9, 10, and 12.

Step 3. Add the totals from steps 1 and 2.

A score of 10 to 12 means you are an intuition superstar, in the top 10 percent of all Americans—congratulations! A

(continued)

How Good Is Your Intuition?—*Continued*

score of 8 points or higher indicates that you are a highly intuitive person. A score of 3 or lower indicates that you are probably the kind of person who is good with details, thinks logically, and can face difficulties realistically, but your intuition is on the, well, slow side. A score somewhere in the middle indicates that you generally rely both on your intuition and on more formal logic to make decisions.

■

last inspiration—and go there," Davidson suggests as a good first step.

Dr. Lynch, who works as a consultant training the staffs of such companies as AT&T to get more in touch with their intuition, has found that intuition flourishes in environments that are comfortable and relaxed. Describing the kind of environment *he* personally finds most conducive to intuitive thought, Dr. Lynch says, "I like soft music (acid rock doesn't lend itself to intuitive thinking), nice dim lighting (not glaring tubes overhead), soft rugs, soft pictures, and a soft place to sit."

Inspiration comes in the right environment.

■ *Clear Your Mind of Clutter*

The word "vacation" comes from the same root as the word "vacate," says Dr. Lynch. And it's when you vacate your mind, or remove the clutter, that intuition can best work its magic, he says. You can't run to the Caribbean each and every time you feel your mind getting "cluttered," but you can at least take a break from what you're doing. Exercise, such as jogging, or various relaxation techniques can help clear the mind tremendously, says Dr. Lynch.

Exercise can clear the mind to intuit better.

Intuition Comes to Some Easier Than Others

In picking stocks for one of his multi-million–dollar mutual fund portfolios, Leonard Heine, Jr., president and chairman of the Management Asset Corporation, says he sometimes starts with "a feeling" about a particular company. His feelings often pay off in big bucks. But Heine asserts that there is a lot that goes on behind his feelings. When he picks a winner, says Heine, "people say 'isn't that wonderful—how do you do it?' I do it because I've been in the market for years. If something feels right to me, there are a lot of factors coming together."

Intuition may be the tip of an iceberg of knowledge.

■ Rely on Your Experience

If you work hard and apply yourself, you will increase your ability to make sharp intuitive decisions, says Carnegie Mellon's Dr. Simon. It doesn't matter whether you're a stock fund manager, a doctor, a lawyer, or an Indian chief.

He quotes Louis Pasteur, the famous French chemist, as saying, "Accidents happen

Wise intuitive decisions are backed by years of knowledge.

to prepared minds.'' Be forewarned, however, that those who make the sharpest, most regular intuitive decisions often have ten or more years of intense devotion to a particular subject, says Dr. Simon. Leonard Heine, for instance, has been wheeling and dealing stocks for over 38 years, and Dennis Bolda has been a detective with the Chicago police for nearly 20 years.

■ *Make a Study of Life*

"Intuition is something that we can hone by exposure, by experience, and by going through the school of hard knocks,'' says Gerald S. Held, a Justice of the Supreme Court of the State of New York. Having good intuition about people is tied to being able to pick up on subtle body language, he says.

Look for subtle body language.

"There are nuances, the inflection of voice, the slowness of speech, the way someone holds his hands, that I take into account when I hear someone tell a story and I need to figure out if he's telling the truth,'' says Judge Held. If you pay careful attention to people as you go through life, your intuition about them will get stronger and stronger, he says.

It Has Changed the Course of History

The Battle of Gettysburg, as you know from history class, was the battle that changed the tide of the American Civil War. What you might not know is how close the tide came to going the other way.

According to U.S. Army Major David Fitzpatrick, an instructor of military history at the U.S. Military Academy at West Point, what probably made all the difference at Gettysburg was a hunch by Union General John Burford that Confederate forces would first attack at dawn. Based on nothing but a hunch, he moved his cavalry division into place before dawn and was able to take the punch out of the Confederate Army's initial attack.

Victory at Gettysburg was based on a hunch.

"There are no formulas for victory. What makes for a great general is the ability to react not only to what he sees but also to what he senses," says Major Fitzpatrick. In other words, to use intuition. "Alexander, Napoleon, Ulysses S. Grant—they all had it," he says.

■ Broaden Your Horizons

What makes for intuition on the battlefield—or in life? Major Fitzpatrick says it's largely "a good broad knowledge." That explains why he has his students read historical novels as part of their education at West Point.

Philip Goldberg, author of *The Intuitive Edge*, says, "By bringing your mind a broad base of information and a wide variety of impressions, you give your unconscious more raw material to work with." He suggests that you read, travel, and talk to people whose interests are different from your own.

Familiarity with different mindsets is important.

■ Open Your Mind

Being broad-minded also means being open-minded, says Dr. Lynch. Remaining open to your own thoughts *and* the thoughts of others is crucial to developing an intuitive mind. "Like an umbrella," says Dr. Lynch, "the mind works best when it's open." Goldberg says that "rigid concepts can give you a kind of hardening of the mental arteries that can stifle the flow of creative ideas."

It's a Little Like Swimming

It takes no practice to splash around in water, but it does take practice to be a good swimmer. Intuition is a bit like swimming, says Dr. Kautz. "Everybody has the capability of being a swimmer, but if you didn't grow up around water, you may not know how to swim." Similarly, the successful use of intuition requires using it, over and over.

It takes practice to
make good hunches.

■ Practice, Practice, Practice

Dr. Kautz suggests that you seize any opportunity you can to practice your intuition. When the phone rings, for instance, try to guess who it is. Before you open your mailbox, tell yourself what is waiting for you within. When you're about to meet someone for the first time, ask yourself what he is going to look like.

Pick things that are
significant.

"You want to pick things that are significant, but not compelling," says Dr. Kautz. That is, try to pick something more significant than flipping a dime but less compelling than sinking your entire weekly paycheck on a lottery number.

■ *Keep a Journal*

Many swimmers and other fitness enthusiasts keep journals so they can track their efforts and progress. What about keeping an intuition journal? Weston Agor, Ph.D., a professor of public administration at the University of Texas at El Paso, and president of ENFP Enterprises, a management consulting firm specializing in intuitive management skills, recommends just that.

Journal keeping will give you insight into your intuition.

By keeping such a journal, you may identify the best kinds of settings for successful intuition, what signs you had that your intuition was on target, and what mistakes you've made in the past while attempting to use your intuition, he says.

■ *Form an Intuition Club*

Just as exercising is often easier in groups, so too is practicing to use your intuition. Form a club with one or several friends or colleagues, suggests Dr. Agor, who is the author of *Intuition in Organizations*. You might all attempt to solve a problem together by forming a circle, focusing on words like *cooperation* and *support,* spending a few minutes relaxing or meditating, writing your suggestions down, and then sharing your ideas and feelings. You'll be amazed at what brilliant ideas can come out of an environment where intuition skills are shared and appreciated, says Dr. Agor.

Try intuition as a team sport.

Meet the Intuition Champs

Want to meet someone with a real knack for making the right hunches? Go find yourself an Asian executive who is wearing a dress.

This may sound bizarre, but Weston Agor, Ph.D., of the University of Texas at El Paso, has some good evidence. For, when he gave an intuition test (see "How Good Is Your Intuition?" on page 292 for an adapted version) to several thousand executives and government officials, he found significant differences among the scores of different groups.

One of the clearest differences in intuitive ability shows up in different levels of employment. "The use of intuition appears to be a skill that is more prevalent as one moves up the management ladder," says Dr. Agor. He theorizes that the difference is due to a process of natural selection. "I think intuition is necessary for getting to the top," he says.

The study also found that Asians score somewhat higher in intuitive abilities than do non-Asians. Dr. Agor believes that this is a result of cultural conditioning. Those brought up in Asian families are taught "to emphasize and practice the East-

Into the Deepness of Your Mind

J. Cheng is a 134-year-old Taoist wise man. He is kind and humorous, honest and insightful. He lives a simple life. When Dr. Lynch has problems or questions concerning his life, J. Cheng comes immediately to give him counsel and wise advice. Sometimes he and Dr. Lynch laugh and play together like two children.

ern world's approach to life, which encourages the development of intuitive brain skills," he says.

And last, validating the old adage about "women's intuition," the study found that women scored about 10 percent higher than men. Dr. Agor says that the difference here is also likely due to upbringing. "Boys are taught to act tough and suppress feelings, while girls are taught to act nurturing." Boys who bottle up emotions become adults with stunted intuitive powers, he says.

But the intuition sex gap could go beyond upbringing. Scientists have discovered that a portion of the corpus callosum, the bundle of nerves that bridges the two halves of the brain, is larger in women than in men. Could this difference give women a slight intuitive edge? Dr. Agor says it's possible.

Of course, what critic George Jean Nathan once said about women's intuition may also be true: "What passes for women's intuition is often nothing more than man's transparency." ■

J. Cheng, of course, is a figment of Dr. Lynch's active imagination. But far from being a mere flight of fancy, the old wise man serves a very practical purpose. He allows Dr. Lynch to get in touch with his intuition.

It helps to have an active imagination.

■ **Follow Your "Spirit Guide"**

Dr. Lynch calls J. Cheng his "spirit guide" or "spiritual teacher." When J. Cheng speaks,

Listen to your inner
voice.

it is actually Dr. Lynch's inner voice, or intuition, speaking. "Your inner self is always trying to communicate with you," he says. By taking it "outside of yourself," you allow it to speak most clearly.

"Your teacher could be totally fictitious, a figment of your imagination, or a real person, a friend or perhaps someone famous that you may not know personally but you admire," says Dr. Lynch. He suggests that whenever you need answers in your life, listen to your intuition—let it come in the form of your guide.

■ *Listen to Your Dreams*

"Dreams," says Dr. Lynch, "are an extension of your intuition. They are a vehicle for discovering your innermost thoughts." He suggests keeping a notebook next to your bed to jot down any ideas that come to you in the middle of the night. They may be the best ideas you'll ever have.

There is clear ac-
knowledgment of the
power of dreams.

Dr. Agor says that among some of his corporate executive clients, there is a clear acknowledgment of the power of dreams. "The former president of General Motors told me that his executives refer to some of their best decisions as '2:00 A.M. decisions,' " he says.

■ *Meditate to Reach Within*

"Intuition is opening up a channel to the inner mind: meditation is one way of doing that," says Dr. Kautz. Meditation can be learned in a class, but many people succeed on their own, he says.

In *Living in the Light,* Shakti Gawain suggests the following technique: "Sit or lie down in a comfortable position in a quiet place. Close your eyes and relax. Take several slow, deep breaths, relaxing your body more with each breath. Relax your mind and let your thoughts drift, but don't hold onto any thought. Imagine that your mind becomes as quiet as a peaceful lake."

From this point, Gawain suggests that you focus your awareness into a deep place in your body, where you feel your "gut feelings." It's here, she says, that you can most easily contact your intuition.

Focus your awareness on your gut feelings.

An Intuition You Can Trust

"Your intuition is always 100 percent correct, but it takes time to learn to *hear* it correctly," says Gawain.

Management consultant Davidson warns that entrepreneurs often appear to have wax in their ears. "The woods are full of people who said 'I knew my intuition was right'—but they were wrong," he says. Wall Street's Heine similarly warns: "Hunch-players typically go bankrupt." So how do you know when your inner voice is steering you wrong?

■ Learn the True Voice of Intuition

Dr. Kautz theorizes that there are two kinds of inner voices, one comes from what he calls the "subconscious," the other from the "superconscious."

There are two kinds of inner voices.

304

Recording your insights is worth the trouble.

The superconscious is where our intuition comes from. The subconscious is a dangerous zone filled with emotional booby-traps that can send us incorrect messages. Only with practice, he says, can you learn to tell the difference between a true message and a false one. Author Goldberg suggests that keeping your intuition journal is one of the best ways to learn to tell the difference between good, solid intuition and shoddy, emotion-strewn hunches.

■ Run Your Thoughts By Your Opposites

Consultant Jeff Davidson says that successful entrepreneurs and the types that wind up in bankruptcy court both start their business paths with what they thought were great ideas. The difference between the two groups is that the successes followed up their ideas with lots of homework.

Intuition plus research equals success.

"Intuition corroborated with research is a formula for making the most of your intuition," he says. Dr. Agor says that a good way to put your intuition to the test is to "run your ideas by your opposites." That is, if you're the intuitive type, constantly having middle-of-the-night brainstorms, run these brainstorms by a person who thinks analytically before jumping into irreversible action.

By the way, finding your opposite shouldn't be difficult. Dr. Agor says that opposites typically seek each other out—intuitively. What is difficult, however, is learning to really listen to the input of your opposite.

PUZZLE POWER

Below are a couple of brainteasers that you may be able to figure out by applying reason. You may also want to test your intuition by taking a quick shot at the answers. Good luck!

Wise to the Word

You find yourself in a strange land where half the people always tell the truth, and the other half always lie. But you cannot tell which is which by looking at them. You run into two inhabitants of this strange land and you ask the first one, "Is either of you a truthteller?" After she answers, you know the truth. What did she say?

Match Points

The following matchsticks make one triangle. Rearrange five of them to make five triangles.

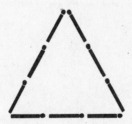

To find the answers, see Solution #10 on page 457.

306

What's the Big Deal?

When all is said and done, just how important is intuition?

Shakti Gawain promises that once you learn to follow your intuition, "Things will just fall into place, and doors will open in a seemingly miraculous way."

Dr. Lynch says, "When I started trusting my intuition—boy!—did I see big payoffs." He warns that when you first start to follow your intuition, you'll likely encounter a fair amount of criticism from people who'll say, "that's silly." But, he adds, "get past that, and the increased feeling of power you'll get is *wonderful*."

And—who knows? You may be on your way to becoming an ace stock-picker, a top-notch homicide detective, a fantastically successful entrepreneur, a great general, or simply a better, more powerful you!   ■

Using your intuition can open doors for you.

Mental Energy

Feel the Flow of Enthusiasm

Call it drive, vigor, enthusiasm, or get-up-and-go. Call it zest, gusto, razzmatazz, or just plain *oomph*. It's what gives you ambition, puts a sparkle in your eye, and fills your day with spirit and glow. It's what makes you jump out of bed in the morning, fill your lungs with air, and charge out the front door ready to take on the entire world.

We're talking about the greatest form of energy on earth. It doesn't come from oil, coal, or natural gas. It comes from your mind.

When the energy is flowing, *really* flowing, nothing, but nothing, can stop you. You feel powerful, brilliant, and tremendously alive. You feel like King Kong with a Ph.D. But, when the energy stops flowing—ugh. You feel like Dr. Kong *after* he fell from the Empire State Building.

If you're like most people, your energy flow can get a little erratic from time to time, and you'd like to do something about it.

308

When mental energy is flowing, nothing can stop you.

You'd like to boost the wattage and assure yourself of a steady, never-ending supply of power. Well? Don't just lie there like a big ape sprawled out on a Manhattan sidewalk! Read on!

The Brain in the Energetic Lane

If King Kong hadn't been shot down by buzzing planes, he likely would have wound up facedown on the sidewalk anyway. After all, the only thing Kong did, day in and day out, was beat his hairy chest and furrow his massive brow. Just what kind of life is that? "Ritualization leads to boredom, and boredom leads to fatigue," says Ernest Dichter, Ph.D., a well-known expert on motivation.

Boredom leads to mental fatigue.

■ Dig Out the Root of Your Rut

Greater energy comes from "having the courage to do things differently from the day before," says Dr. Dichter. "Make yourself aware that you're in a rut and don't blame anyone else—you got yourself into it, you can get yourself out." That doesn't mean you should do something drastic like change your spouse, career, or address. Making much smaller changes in your life is generally all you need.

Try dressing differently, redecorating your house, or making love in a different position, suggests the 83-year-old Dr. Dichter. Professing he has as much mental energy as ever, the senior psychologist attributes his vim to following his own advice. He's recently been studying Russian and Chinese and reading a book about baseball (Dr. Dichter was raised in Austria, where baseball wasn't played).

■ Play Hooky Once in a While

Sometimes the kind of change you need is a respite from the hustle-bustle. Whether it's from the office, the kids, or the coal mine, we're talking escape. "I sometimes prescribe a day off in the same way a doctor would prescribe an aspirin for a sore knee," says Allan J. Schwartz, Ph.D., clinical psychologist and chief of the University of Rochester's Mental Health Unit. Dr. Schwartz sees lots of cases of mental fizz-out. He counsels medical school interns who work endless demanding shifts.

Everybody needs his own form of mental escape.

What's the best thing to do with your "escape" time? "Go with what feels right for you," says Dr. Schwartz. Some people feel wonderful after a day or two lying on the beach, others thrill in taking hikes or going sailing. "Just because someone else says something was wonderful for them doesn't mean it's right for you. You have to allow for individual differences and pick what is most enlivening and refreshing to you," says Dr. Schwartz.

■ Oweeee! Get a Little Risky

Vacation time, of course, is a limited commodity. So what can you do the rest of the time to boost your mental reserves? Part of the answer is to take more risk in your life, says

The best students are those who take the most academic risks.

Margaret M. Clifford, Ph.D., professor of educational psychology at the University of Iowa. "Moderate risk is what seems to most interest and motivate an individual," she says.

In studies with children and teenagers, Dr. Clifford has found that those who take the most risk in choosing and solving academic problems tend to be better and more satisfied students. Those who stick with solving only easy problems tend to grow bored and fatigued.

In life beyond the classroom, the same applies, says Dr. Clifford. To add energy to your life, you can ask for more responsibility at work, get involved in athletics, try new recipes, sign up for evening classes, play chess, overhaul a car—"anything you enjoy doing that involves an element of risk," she says. Once you've mastered an activity, and you feel boredom creeping in, it's time to seek a fresh challenge.

■ *Journey to Points Unknown*

Experience the thrill of a spur-of-the-moment vacation.

Perhaps you're wondering if you can combine escape time with risk for a double jolt of mind recharging. Yes, you can! Follow the advice of Stanley Moss, Ph.D., professor of psychology at the University of Massachusetts in Amherst. His idea: Arrange a week off from work, and don't make *any* plans in advance! "When I vacation, much of the thrill is doing it on the spur of the moment. That may sound strange and counterproductive—and in many ways it is—but it does add *a lot* to the excitement," says Dr. Moss, who recently jumped into his car and drove 3,000 miles to California.

Energy Is a State of Mind

Getting out of your rut and injecting risk into your life may free you from fatigue. But you want more than that. You want superhigh energy. Your next step in this pursuit is to examine your state of mind. "Clearly, positive thoughts create positive energy," says Richard N. Podell, M.D., clinical associate professor at Robert Wood Johnson Medical School in New Jersey.

Positive thoughts create positive energy.

Certainly the main character of the children's classic *The Little Engine That Could* knew the importance of positive thoughts: "I think I can—I think I can—I think I can—I think I can," the Little Blue Engine repeated over and over as she puffed her way up the mountain.

■ *Belief in Yourself Is the Sparkplug of Your Mind*

"I thought I could. I thought I could. I thought I could," the smiling Blue Engine seemed to say as she puffed her way down the hill. Perhaps it was *because* she believed in herself that she had the energy to succeed.

Belief in your ability is to mental energy what sparkplugs are to an engine. "Many people are too critical of themselves, and that is what saps their energy," says Richard Ryan, Ph.D., director of clinical training and associate professor at the University of Rochester.

Dr. Ryan espouses the theory that all of us come into this world teeming with energy. It's only when we start dealing with other people,

Greater energy comes with greater control.

312

All of us have the capacity for unlimited mental energy.

and start feeling controlled and coerced by other people, that our "sparkplugs" start to miss and our natural energy drains from our "engine" like oil into a gutter.

The remedy? "Recognize who the task-master is. *You* control your own life. Seek autonomy and challenge. And take a less critical stance," says Dr. Ryan.

■ Have a Chat with Yourself

Just like the Little Blue Engine did, there's nothing wrong with giving yourself a good pep talk now and then. In fact, there's nothing wrong with looking into a mirror, clasping your hands together and screaming, "Yes! Yes! Yes!" So advocates Stan Kellner, frequent speaker on motivation, founder and owner of Yes I Can Sports Camps in East Setauket, New York, and a former Long Island high school basketball coach whose teams racked up 166 wins and only 30 losses.

Look in the mirror and say, "Yes, I can."

To attain higher levels of energy and confidence "you need to change your personal dialogue," says Kellner. Looking into a mirror and clasping your hands is a great way to "anchor a feeling," he says. That's why it helps to perform this little ritual when trying to sink positive feelings into your head. Do it as often as you need to, says Kellner, until you feel energized and brimming with confidence.

■ Visualize Achieving What You Want

There's no way to know whether the Little Blue Engine visualized herself reaching the top of the mountain, but it's a technique that might work for you. "Realize that you have a success mechanism. It works by pictures. And you control those pictures," says Kellner.

In other words, *seeing* what it is you want will help you attain the energy to get it. Chugging your way up to the top of a mountain? *Visualize* yourself at the top of the mountain. Trying to land a basketball in a hoop? *See* yourself sinking the shot. Want to write the Great American Novel? "You have to see yourself as a writer, think you are a writer, before you are one," says Kellner.

> Visualize yourself at the top of the mountain you want to climb.

■ Put Your Hopes and Dreams Where You Can See Them

Paul Basist, president of Target Plastics, Inc., visualizes his goals—he also pins them up on his bulletin board! The 29-year-old Long Islander went into business for himself right out of high school and today runs a company that serves thousands of clients around the world. Friends and acquaintances describe Basist's energy level as "atomic."

What's his secret? "I make a vision out of my goals and I look at them all the time," he says. Surrounding his office desk, Basist has four bulletin boards. On them, he posts magazine clippings portraying his dreams. "Right now on the wall I have a picture of a house, very stately, up on the north shore of Long Island, and I have a picture of a new BMW M-3. My goal is to have these things," he says. If he can't get them right away, he'll keep the pictures up. "If at first I don't make good—I

> One achiever became inspired by posting pictures of his material dreams.

don't rip the pictures down. I leave them up to constantly remind me what I'm working for," says Basist.

A Deeper Sense of Self

Perhaps all high-energy people, such as Basist and Kellner, use techniques like visualizations to shift their mind into high gear, but their energy reserves also appear to come from a place deep within. They seem to have a high-energy attitude, a high-energy personality, and a high-energy way of looking at the world.

■ You Can Find Joy in Any Task

Peggy Jo Kienast became a celebrity when, in 1970, she found herself the surprised mother of quintuplets. To most of us, even thinking of raising *one* child is enough to make us feel exhausted. Kienast, who already had two infants, gave birth to five all at once. *And,* she never used a disposable diaper! How did she manage to keep up her energy level?

Worrying wastes mental energy.

"You don't overplan. There's no point wasting vital energy worrying about things that may or may not happen. Worry creates stress and fatigue," says Kienast. Her most important advice, however, is to try to handle responsibilities with a sense of joy. It was the joy of raising quints, more than anything, that kept her going through the early years—and the later ones, which she says were far more stressful. (Can you imagine five teenagers getting their drivers' licenses all at once?) "I think my energy came from getting such a kick out of it all," says Kienast.

■ Get Yourself into a Flow

Regardless of whether you're trying to raise quintuplets, write a book, win a talent show, or build a better mousetrap, whenever you're in need of more energy, totally absorb yourself in what you're doing. So advises Mihaly Csikszentmihalyi, Ph.D., professor of psychology and education at the University of Chicago, and author of *Flow: The Psychology of Optimal Experience.*

Dive deeply into whatever you're doing.

Dr. Csikszentmihalyi says he came to his conclusion while studying artists. "I became curious as to how a sculptor could spend so many hours absorbed in his work, and then when the sculpture was complete, just shove it aside and start another. I came to see that it was the process itself that was so rewarding," he says. Similarly, Dr. Csikszentmihalyi says he found the same kind of intensity and high-energy involvement among athletes, chess players, composers, and mountain climbers.

How can you instill the same kind of energetic passion into your life? "Transform all your activities into goal-directed, achievement-oriented activities," says Dr. Csikszentmihalyi. Even if you're doing something as mundane as ironing a shirt, try to absorb yourself in the process. Ask yourself, "Can I do it better by doing the arms first? . . . Or by folding it this way?" Such engulfment in what you are doing, such a flow state, will keep your energy levels high.

Make your activities goal-directed.

Sh-h-h-h-h. Mind at Work

Outside distractions will interrupt mental energy flow.

What might hinder you from getting into a flow state? "The *un*energetic mind is characterized by distraction, an inability to focus and concentrate," says John Harvey, Ph.D., director of psychological services at Allied Services Rehabilitation Institute in Scranton, Pennsylvania, and teacher at the Himalayan Institute in Honesdale, Pennsylvania. Distraction, says Dr. Harvey, comes in two forms: external (radios, televisions, shouting neighbors) and internal (concerns, worries, objections, duties).

The mind is like a muscle, says Dr. Harvey. Just as a muscle needs both activation *and* relaxation in order to perform, so too does the mind. But the kind of relaxation Dr. Harvey advocates doesn't involve pillows and blankets. "The key is to *consciously* rest your mind," he says.

■ Take Ten to Meditate

Meditation will restore the mind naturally and build reserves.

Some people think of this kind of relaxation as meditation, and that's fine, says Dr. Harvey. But he emphasizes that you don't have to sit cross-legged like an Indian guru unless you want to. As an alternative, you can sit in a chair with your hands on your knees, close your eyes, breathe evenly and slowly (from the belly), and relax your entire body from toes to head. Then (the essential part), "give the mind only *one* thing to focus on" says Dr. Harvey. Try focusing in on your breath, but you can also use a saying, a prayer, or a favorite place, he suggests. "Do that for 10 minutes, a couple of times a day, and the mind will restore itself naturally and build up its energy reserves."

■ Show Others the Sign: Do Not Disturb

What about all those physical distractions? Ironically, one of the toughest places to get any work done is in the workplace. Phones ring, papers whiz by, and people with coffee mugs in hand mill about looking for a chat. The best way to keep from getting mentally sapped is to get yourself into the kind of flow state described earlier. But how, with all these interruptions?

If you have your own office, the key may be in its design, says Michael Brill, professor of architecture at the State University of New York and president of the Buffalo Organization for Social and Technological Innovation. "You need a work station where everybody knows you're not to be disturbed," he says. Creating that work station may mean facing away from the door, lighting a particular light, putting a red square on your door, or closing the door. However you decide to indicate that you are in "flow," make sure your colleagues understand that all but urgent business should wait, says Brill.

Create a work station compatible with your mental energy needs.

■ Take Time to Reflect

By the way, what kind of work do you do? Do you work? How's your love life? Have you written any poems lately? Excuse the personal questions, but these concern your energy level.

318

Everybody has something that makes thinking flow.

"Every human being has something that really makes him tick. When he finds that, things open up, life opens up," says Charles Ingrasci, director of corporate affairs for Lifespring, a company offering courses nationwide in personal development.

"The next question then becomes not how to get more energy, but how to use what you have. Zest comes from an inner sense of direction," says Ingrasci. To get more zest, "sit down and take the time to reflect on what your highest ideals and aspirations are in life. Ask yourself what you would like to someday be remembered for. Consider family, career, love life, and community. Then do something each day to accomplish your vision," he says.

■ Locate Your "Heartpath"

Tom Pinkson, Ph.D., therapist and business consultant, helps people find their vision by taking groups into the California mountains for several days of fasting, meditation, and communing with nature. "You're here not by accident—there's purpose in your life," he says. A solitary retreat into the wilderness follows the tradition of native American Indian culture, in which adolescents were encouraged to do the same in order to find their purpose in life.

Solitary reflection can do wonders for the mind.

Those who are able to get a feeling of zest are those who have found their "heartpath," which Dr. Pinson says is "a sense of a larger mission in life." To start on the road toward finding your heartpath, "you must look at who you are, and what is not being honored by how

Circadian Rhythms: They Keep You Ticking

Your body is pulsating with life. In the space of a minute your heart pumps ⅕ quart of blood. Your eye blinks 24 times. You breathe 12 times. Every body function moves to its own natural rhythm, known together as circadian rhythms. But what keeps everything running on time?

The coordinator is believed to be a "master clock" located in a small group of nerve cells within your brain's hypothalamus. The clock was "set" by your mother's master clock sometime during her seventh month of pregnancy, and sunlight hitting the retina keeps it in sync by transmitting signals directly to your hypothalamus.

One of your master clock's key functions is to set the daily rhythm that determines when you sleep, when you wake, and when you feel most energetic. According to Kenneth Groh, Ph.D., an assistant biologist in the biological and medical research division at Argonne National Laboratory, your master clock receives its wake-up call each morning when your eyes begin to perceive daylight and relay this information back through your optic nerves. It then stimulates a chemical path—the catecholamine pathway—that gets you moving.

"This pathway tells the adrenal glands to pump epinephrine (also known as adrenaline) out into the bloodstream so that you—like your primitive ancestors—can go out and kill your dinosaur," says Dr. Groh. Adrenaline and other natural wake-up chemicals speed up your heart rate and release stored sugars into your bloodstream to give you the steady supply of energy you'll need throughout the day.

Alertness generally peaks around noon, the most active part of the daytime phase. Then, in early afternoon, your alertness suddenly sinks. In an hour or two, it perks up again and continues until evening when a different chemical pathway kicks in to slow you down for bed. ■

320

Examine your mission
in life.

you are living. You must look at what you are doing every day," he says. If you're not sure that you can do that on your own, look up Dr. Pinkson in Mill Valley, near San Francisco, and take one of his trips into the mountains!

The Will to Succeed

Life, as you well know, is full of challenges, big and small. To deal with these challenges, sometimes you need a particular kind of mental energy, a kind we generally refer to as willpower or motivation. Anyone who's ever had to lose weight, break a nasty habit like smoking, or force themselves to do something tough, like sell door-to-door, knows the effort it takes. Here's what it takes to power your mind.

■ Motivation Must Come from Within

For many dieters, the ultimate test of willpower comes when some thick, dark chunk of chocolate cake or a creamy, sweet, vanilla ice-cream sundae beckons in their direction: "Eat me-e-e-e.... Eat me-e-e-e!" As many of us know, gritting our teeth and saying "no!" doesn't always work. That's because successful weight control isn't *just* gung-ho willpower that we turn on when needed. Successful weight control—and success at *anything*—relies on long-term motivation.

Motivation is more
successful than will-
power.

"Motivation is less harsh than willpower," says Ronna Kabatznick, Ph.D., psychological consultant to Weight Watchers International.

Motivation is the capacity to judge how to handle a situation and stay inspired. Motivation is not an in-the-moment condition."

There are two kinds of motivation: effective and not-so-effective. The kind of motivation that leads many to diet is the *extrinsic* kind—"I need to lose 20 pounds for my daughter's wedding." This kind of motivation has one serious flaw: once the wedding is over, so is the diet. The more lasting kind of motivation is the *intrinsic* variety.

"Intrinsic motivation is doing something for *yourself,* not for anything or anybody else," says Dr. Kabatznick.

> There are two kinds of motivation, and one is clearly superior.

■ *Willpower Requires Thinking Ahead*

Garland DeNelsky, Ph.D., head of the Cleveland Clinic Foundation's Smoking Cessation Program, agrees with Dr. Kabatznick. "People who use only willpower, as in 'gutsing' it out, are less successful than people who have several active coping strategies," he says.

Part of coping means getting yourself into the kind of environment where gutsing it out won't be necessary. "One overlooked aspect of willpower is that people who succumb usually do so in situations where it's hard not to succumb," says Dr. DeNelsky. For example, if you're trying to quit smoking, at least in the initial stages of breaking the addiction, "you need to get away from cigarettes, get rid of all your cigarettes, and stay away from smokers," he says.

> Willpower requires that you be in charge of the situation.

"Arranging the situation" is very much a part of effective willpower.

■ *Confidence Is the Key Motivator*

Pete Pfitzinger, one of the top marathon runners in America, will tell you that running is as much mental conditioning as it is physical conditioning. "The Great American Sports Myth tells us to give 110 percent. There's no such thing. All you can give is 100 percent," he says.

In other words, reasonable goals are part of the recipe for success. When training for the 1988 Olympics, Pfitzinger set up small, intermittent challenges for himself throughout his 15 weeks of intensive training. By the time the big day rolled around, he felt confident and relaxed. And it showed. Pfitzinger ran the 26.2 miles faster than any other American in the race, just as he had in the 1984 Olympics.

Be confident and set reasonable goals.

"You need to stay calm in order to achieve your best," says Pfitzinger. He recounts that the only time he really blew a race (the Boston Marathon of 1986) was because he "just got carried away and too excited." Confidence, he says, is the key to staying calm. "But you can't lie to yourself. You know if you can do it," says Pfitzinger.

Don't try to lie to yourself.

■ *Keep Your Mind on That Pot of Gold*

Shedding pounds, quitting smoking, and running races are not the only situations in life that require getting mentally keyed up. Imagine starting your own business and having to drum up a customer base by knocking on strange office doors. For years, entrepreneur Paul Basist did just that, slowly building up his plastics business by soliciting busy New Yorkers who didn't always treat him with courtesy. How did he deal with the rejection and keep coming back?

Dealing with rejection is part of the game.

"It's a numbers game," says Basist. "If someone wants to scorn me, that's fine, because I know that here in the New York metropolitan area I can walk to an endless number of doors. Yeah, 80 percent will say no, but another 20 percent will say yes. Knowing this, I *like* rejection! Because I know that out of every 100 people, 80 will say no—but 20 will say yes!

"It's like having a pot of gold in the deep Amazon forest with poisonous snakes all around. You walk through gallantly, and you pet that snake on the head and say 'nice boy'— because you got your eyes on that pot of gold!"

Of Body and of Mind

"Energy is not merely mental or merely physical. The mind and the body are closely interrelated," says Richard N. Podell, M.D., author of *Doctor, Why Am I So Tired?* If you're not getting proper sleep, if your diet consists of mainly pork rinds and licorice sticks, and the only exercise you get is manipulating twist ties, then your body—and your mind—are likely to prance off together into the sunset and flop over the horizon. These last several pointers are therefore dedicated to the happy and energetic marriage of body and mind.

If the body suffers, the mind suffers too.

■ *It's 11 O'Clock—Do You Know Where Your Pillow Is?*

"The optimum amount of sleep differs for every individual, ranging anywhere from 4 to 9½ hours," says Ralph LaForge, program coordinator for the Health Promotion Certificate Program at the University of California in San Diego. There are three main determinants of how much sleep an individual needs, says LaForge. First is your genetic disposition, or "how your central nervous system is wired." Second is the degree of stress in your life. And third is the amount of physical exertion you put out during the day.

How do you know if you're getting enough sleep? Dr. Podell suggests that excessive grogginess in the morning, sleeping long hours on weekends to "catch up," and nodding off during afternoon meetings or social events are all signs that you may not be getting enough. He suggests adding 45 minutes to your nightly sleep time for two weeks to see if you feel better. Or try afternoon siestas.

Sleep needs are partially determined by genetics.

■ *Eat Right, Feel Right*

If your energy seems to fade in the late afternoon, especially on days you've had a big lunch, know that what you're experiencing is normal. But you can reduce fatigue by eating right.

Make sure you get all the nutrients you need by eating a wide variety of foods. One simple yet effective way of ensuring a good va-

Attack the midday slump.

riety of vitamins is to make your plate as colorful as possible, says LaForge. Shop for fruits and vegetables from all parts of the color spectrum—include reds, greens, and yellows.

Eat a colorful variety of foods.

Fatty foods drain energy and should be kept to a minimum: no more than 30 percent of your caloric intake should come from fat, says LaForge. (A detailed nutritional program for brainpower can be found beginning on page 41.)

■ *Expend Energy to Get Energy*

There's no question that exercise builds mental as well as physical muscle. Exercise can help relieve stress, dispel depression, and improve self-image. Aerobic exercise also pumps oxygen into the body, helping to metabolize food energy more efficiently.

Dr. Podell says that half an hour of brisk walking daily has made a great difference in the energy levels of many of his patients.

For maximum zip, LaForge recommends an exercise program that not only gets the heart pumping but also strengthens muscles and stretches them out. He recommends that in addition to your regular aerobic exercise, you perform strengthening exercises like bent-knee sit-ups. And at least three days a week, you should spend 15 to 20 minutes doing yoga-type stretching exercises.

Add yoga stretches to your aerobic exercise program.

"Find a quiet place, relax the mind, and gradually stretch those muscles that are tightest," says LaForge. This gentle form of fitness is particularly energizing to those who work in high-stress environments.

326

■ *Live a Rhythmic Life*

While you're reconsidering your eating, sleeping, and exercise habits, consider for a moment how they fit into your daily schedule. Speaking of which, do you have a schedule? Your body and mind like regularity, says La-Forge. You have an internal clock that regulates such things as hormone levels, body temperature, blood pressure—and energy levels. You help that clock to work its best when you eat, sleep, and exercise in natural and regular cycles, says LaForge.

You don't have to run your life with the regularity of a military parade, but do try not to skip meals, and get up at roughly the same hour every morning, says LaForge. Your body cycle also benefits if you give the mind a break from work every 90 minutes or so. LaForge recommends that you get up from your office desk for at least 5 minutes every hour and a half. A brief brisk walk outside in the sunlight is about the most energizing way to spend your break.

Give your mind a break every 90 minutes.

■ *Pause before That Next Sip*

The caffeine in coffee likewise can give you a boost. But over the long run, too much caffeine can make you nervous and jittery and may interfere with your sleep, which can wreak havoc on your energy level. Some people are more sensitive to caffeine than others. If you're a heavy coffee drinker, and you've been tired lately, the two may be connected, particularly if you've been having frequent headaches and

Too much coffee can wreak havoc on your energy level.

PUZZLE POWER

No easy answers on this page! No, you're going to have to harness your mental energy and dive in. If you get these puzzles figured out, your mental energy must be soaring.

Don't Surrender

The spy was captured easily, and his message proved to be so simple that the lieutentant saw its importance immediately. Here it is. What does it say?

Alice: Tom told Ann Carter Killy and Ted, David Atwood was not moving out now. David awaiting you.

Pile of Money

It's nice in real life, but it's much easier on paper. Go from POOR to RICH in seven steps, changing one letter each time and making a different English word each time.

```
P   O   O   R
_   _   _   _
_   _   _   _
_   _   _   _
_   _   _   _
_   _   _   _
R   I   C   H
```

To find the answers, see Solution #11 on page 457.

328

the thought of a day without coffee makes you shudder with fear, says Dr. Podell.

If you suspect caffeine is draining your energy, try slowly tapering off until you can go without caffeine for at least three weeks. If caffeine withdrawal causes headaches, your doctor can probably help. It's possible that once you break the coffee habit, you'll find your mind percolating with newfound energy.

———▪

The Tranquil Mind

Mental Renewal through Personal Peace

Today is going to be a zoo. There are yellow stickies fluttering from the dashboard of your car reminding you to pick up the dry cleaning, the dog, and your kid. There are message slips propped up beside your phone asking you to call your boss, your mother, and your doctor. And there are postcards stuck to your refrigerator with magnets reminding you to make appointments with the dentist, the vet, and the bank.

You scramble to do, be, and have everything for everyone. But your mind is whirling in a thousand different directions with a thousand different instructions. And as you plop the dog in the back seat of the car next to your kid and dive into the day, you

We instinctively crave moments to escape mentally.

worry that you'd sell at least one of them for just 5 minutes of personal peace.

Ah, personal peace. It feels so good in so many different ways. For some, it's those few, quiet moments when you can stand alone on a beach or a mountain trail, put your face in the wind, and feel as one with nature. Or it's that inner feeling of tranquillity and stillness you've found through total thought control to escape on a moment's notice from a world swirling around you at hurricane force. Or maybe it's just that brief, single moment in which you gaze out a window without anything that resembles a thought passing through your mind.

For others, it's that long, drifting moment before sleep when mind and body float from the happy realization that another good day's work is finally done. And for still others, it's those soft, soothing moments when you walk into the peaceful stillness of a chapel and realize that you're never truly alone. It's peace so peaceful that all you can hear is silence.

Most of us instinctively crave moments such as these whenever life starts feeling like a yoke. But what many of us don't realize is that they are also moments that our brain *needs*.

The Tranquillity Zone

Learning to silence the mind can make you smarter.

Tranquillity is to the brain what sleep is to the body. It needs it to thrive. Studies indicate that when people regularly relax and give their mind a few moments of tranquillity, they can actually think better and remember more.

Learning to silence your mind can even make you smarter. In one study, for example, a group of Iowa researchers divided 100 men and women into two groups. One group meditated twice a day over a two-year period, the other group did not. The result? The group that regularly gave their mind a break actually increased their IQ by an average of five points each! The group that kept their mind constantly in gear showed no change at all.

In another study, researchers at Stanford University Medical Center divided 39 people between the ages of 62 and 83 into two groups. One group was taught how to use a relaxation technique to quiet their mind, the other was not. The result of this experiment? The group that was able to create a tranquil mind through relaxation increased their ability to remember by 25 *percent*. And, again, the group that kept their mind in gear showed no improvement.

331

Meditators showed increased IQ.

Relaxation increased memory by 25 percent.

The Quick Fix

How often do you find *your* mind racing around in a dozen different directions? Probably too often in today's fast-facts, fast-fax world.

Fortunately, there are a variety of ways to put the brakes on those speeding neurons. Some are supported by a mountain of scientific data. Others make the grade merely by virtue of having withstood the test of time. Some are quick and easy to follow; others are more complex and take time and practice. Try the fast routes—such as the following—when your whirling mind is in quick need of a steadying oar. Try the more complex routes—those that involve muscle relaxation, body focusing, meditation, or gentle movement—when you have the time and space to settle down.

■ Instantly Calm Your Mind

Once you've learned how to do it, a technique called the instant-calming sequence (ICS) can create a tranquil mind in less than a second, says its developer, Robert K. Cooper, Ph.D., president of Advanced Excellence Systems in Bemidji, Minnesota.

ICS calms the mind in less than a second.

And ICS can be used anytime and anywhere to help you handle unexpected bad news, to help you make critical decisions, to keep you calm in the face of an argument, to help you relax in traffic jams, even to help you ward off nagging feelings of worry or guilt. Here's how to do it.

First, train yourself to continue breathing normally. "Most of us halt our breathing for several seconds or more during the first moments of a stressful situation," Dr. Cooper says. This reduces oxygen to the brain and can push us toward feelings such as anxiety, panic, anger, frustration, and loss of control.

Practice controlled breathing in times of stress.

Then put a smile on your face. Some scientists speculate that a positive facial expression, no matter what your mental state, may increase blood flow to the brain and transmit nerve impulses to a key emotional center there that can help prevent feelings of distress and keep you in better control of challenging or difficult situations. "Even the slightest smile may help prevent the nervous system from over-reacting to negative stress," Dr. Cooper says.

And don't forget to stand or sit upright as you start the ICS technique. Many of us collapse into a slouching position when hit with a stressful situation, Dr. Cooper says. This not only restricts breathing and reduces blood flow to the brain, it adds needless muscle tension and can magnify feelings of helplessness. "Keep your posture buoyant when stress strikes," Dr. Cooper says.

Now take a quick tension inventory. With one fast mental sweep, try to notice any area of your body that may be tightening—from your scalp clear down to your toes—and imagine the tension being released as if you were standing under a soothing waterfall.

Imagine standing under a soothing waterfall.

Too often, when faced with a stressful situation, we react emotionally, blaming ourselves or others or bemoaning the hand we've been dealt. When we do this, however, we lose our ability to control the situation and improve the outcome. What's better? Simply acknowledge and accept what's happening. Then you will be much better prepared to choose a wiser response.

Acknowledge and accept instead of blaming yourself.

"That's the key to the ICS," says Dr. Cooper. "Learning to insert that calm, clear-mindedness in precisely the right place at the very beginning of each stress scene."

■ *Use Your Mind's Eye*

Another quick way to calm your mind is to use your mind's eye. Gerald Epstein, M.D., author of *Healing Visualizations*, offers this exercise for reducing anxiety and increasing tranquillity.

Close your eyes and take three deep breaths. Imagine yourself at the ocean under a clear blue sky with all the mental turbulence and anxiety you feel rolled together inside you in the form of a stone. Let the wind and water erode the stone, washing and blowing it away. When the stone is gone, your anxiety will be gone as well and your mind will be clear and calm.

■ *Retreat to Your Private Oasis*

"I get in that tub and my troubles melt," says one working mother. "It's my daily oasis." That may sound poetic, but it has some science on its side. Warm baths work by relaxing the muscles but also perhaps by slightly heating the brain, which can be calming, experts say. Notice the word "warm," however. If water is too hot it can shock the system, causing muscles to constrict. Water between 100° and 102°F (that's comfortably warm to the touch) is best. Soak for no more than 15 minutes.

Warm baths slightly heat the brain, which can produce calm.

You can mellow out even more from a bath if you consciously encourage individual parts of your body to relax, says Carole B. Lewis, Ph.D., of George Washington University and the University of Pittsburgh. Let your hand float gently on the water, then allow that feeling of relaxation to flow to your elbow, then to your upper arm and shoulder and finally to your head. Let the soothing sensation flow to any area of your body that might feel tense.

Let your hand float gently on the water.

To help make that soothing plunge even more celestial, try buoying your bath with some fragrance. Numerous commercial preparations are available, but you can also concoct your own by making a "tea" from your favorite herbs or flowers. Just add 1 quart of boiling water to 1 cup of leaves or flower buds. Allow to cool, strain the liquid, and add it to your bath water.

■ Envelop Your World in Music

Some experts theorize it's the rhythm, some say it's the "tonal atmospheres" created by music, others say it's just feeling comfortable with whatever you like. And although it's not scientifically proven, few people would disagree that music can work mental magic.

Music not only soothes the mind, it can sedate the body as well. Music that has a tempo slightly slower than your heart rate, says Kansas City music therapist Janalea Hoffman, not only can encourage the heart to slow down to keep in sync but can momentarily lower blood pressure as well. "The average heart beats 60 to 68 times per minute, so I write music with 50 to 60 beats per minute," she says.

Play music with a tempo slightly slower than your heart rate.

This is considerably slower than most popular music being written today, so you'll have to do some shopping around to get tunes that fit the bill. Some classical suggestions: Bach's Brandenburg Concerto No. 4, 2nd movement; Bach's Orchestral Suite No. 2 ("Saraband"); Holst's The Planets ("Venus"); Ravel's Mother Goose Suite, 1st movement.

Classical music rolls over rock.

336

Melody is just as important as rhythm.

Music turns off the mind by turning us loose, says composer and psychologist Steven Halpern, Ph.D., author of *Sound Health.* And melody is just as important as rhythm.

That means if Aerosmith helps you unscramble your mind better than Bach, so be it. That's the thinking of Radford University director of music therapy Joseph Scartelli, Ph.D. "Sitting down and forcing yourself to listen to relaxation music that you don't like may create stress, not alleviate it," he says.

■ Listen to the Wind

Wind chimes can create a soothing environment.

Yes, you may cast your cares to the wind if you have the right set of chimes, says Dr. Halpern. The random melodic "music" created by wind chimes can create a very soothing environment—if that's your cup of tea. But it's important to choose chimes that are in tune with one another so that harmony is created rather than mere noise, Dr. Halpern says. The most soothing sounds of all are produced by aluminum or copper tubular chimes measuring 12 to 18 inches in length, he contends.

■ Give Your Mind a Breath of Fresh Air

What the ears can do, the eyes may do as well—at least in the realm of creating a tranquil mind. The idea is to focus on anything that holds your attention so that you're looking and listening instead of thinking and worrying, explains University of Pennsylvania psychiatrist Aaron Katcher, M.D. Just watching a campfire or fireplace, going bird-watching, taking a walk in the park, or watching fish in an aquarium can unscramble a busy mind. Dr. Katcher says that doing any of these kinds of activities for 15 minutes or so twice a day can have measurable mind-unloading effects.

Do nothing but look and listen for 15 minutes every day.

If you'd really like to give your mind a breath of fresh air, expand your horizons, says stress expert Emmett Miller, M.D., author of *Software for the Mind*. Long-distance views of natural surroundings may be the best eye-pleasers of all because they inspire us with feelings of openness and hope.

Take walks outside whenever possible. Or simply imagine yourself in some breathtakingly open environment, Dr. Miller says. Put yourself on a mountaintop in the Swiss Alps at sunrise. "If you really concentrate on that image, you'll feel a sense of relief," he says.

Muscle-Mind Therapy

When you have the time and space to learn a deeper, more complex method of developing a tranquil mind, you might want to give progressive muscle relaxation (PMR) a try.

PMR is a technique in which each of 16 different muscle groups is first tensed and then relaxed, leaving you with a tranquil mind that can carry you through an entire day.

In one study of clerical workers, for example, women who learned the technique and practiced it twice a day were able to reduce the amount of mental stress they experienced by 19 percent.

Women who practiced progressive relaxation reduced stress by 19 percent.

It takes about 20 minutes a day for a week or so to learn PMR, but once you have it

338

Many roads lead to
relaxation.

mastered, the technique is on call for on-the-spot mind mending.

There are several different ways to do PMR, but the following is the technique preferred by psychologist Ken Lichstein, Ph.D., a professor at Memphis State University and author of *Clinical Relaxation Strategies*. Keep in mind that you should skip any muscles that are already strained or aggravated by some type of illness or injury, and check with your doctor before you begin if you have any kind of chronic disease such as high blood pressure or diabetes. PMR can actually slow the body's metabolic process so much that people who take medication for various disorders may need to adjust the dosage.

■ Relax One Group of Muscles at a Time

First, tense the muscles of your right hand and forearm by clenching your fist, suggests Dr. Lichstein. Keep it tight, feeling the strain and the tension. Hold the tension for 7 seconds and then let your muscles relax. Completely. Keep them relaxed for 45 seconds. Just give up control of the muscles and let them lie there quietly as you compare, in your mind, the feelings of tension you were experiencing just a few seconds ago to the feeling of relaxation that is now emerging. Keep in mind that the more carefully you focus your attention on the feelings of serenity and tranquillity that relaxation brings, the more those feelings will grow.

Keep your mind focused on feelings of serenity and tranquility.

Now try the large muscle in your right upper arm. Bend your arm at the elbow and flex the muscle. Tense and tighten for 7 seconds, loosen and relax for 45 seconds. Do the same sequence with your left hand and upper arm.

Now tense the muscles of your forehead by raising your eyebrows as high as they'll go and wrinkling your forehead, then relax. Tense the muscles in the middle of a your face by closing your eyes tightly and wrinkling your nose, then relax. Tense your lower face by pressing both your lips and teeth together and pressing your tongue against the roof of your mouth, then relax.

Make faces for a more tranquil mind.

Tense your neck by trying to pull it in four different directions at once. This sounds crazy, but it tenses all the neck muscles at once. People who have tried it say that your neck may shake a bit, but it never actually moves in one direction or another.

Now take five deep breaths to help deepen your feeling of relaxation, suggests Dr. Lichstein. Hold each breath for 5 seconds and softly say the word "relax" as you exhale. Mentally scan your body for any pockets of tension and consciously try to relax that particular spot.

Relax, one muscle at a time.

Pull your shoulders back as though you were trying to make one shoulder blade touch the other, then relax. Pull your shoulders in front of you and tense your stomach, then relax.

Raise your right leg about an inch off the floor and tense your thigh muscles, then relax. Point your foot and toes forward—tense this muscle for only 3 seconds, since it tends to cramp—then relax. Tense your right ankle and shin by pointing your foot and toes toward your face, then relax.

Think "relax"—and breathe deeply.

Now repeat all the leg and foot tense/relax sequences with your other leg.

340

■ *Use the 8-Minute Shortcut*

Most of us get a little impatient with doing the full 20 minutes of progressive muscle relaxation, so once we've mastered the technique—which means once we're able to detect the subtle tensions that we might have missed before learning how to relax—Dr. Lichstein has developed an abbreviated version called body focusing that we can do in less than half the time.

Body focusing gets results in half the time.

This version—which is actually a form of self-hypnosis—omits the tensing part of progressive muscle relaxation. You simply focus your attention on one part of your body at a time, then consciously let go of any tension that your mind uncovers.

Ready? Then let's begin. First, suggests Dr. Lichstein, focus your attention on your right hand and forearm. Remember how relaxed those muscles felt when you did progressive muscle relaxation. Try to feel a warmth, a heaviness flowing from these muscles as they become soft and tranquil. Let yourself explore the feeling for at least 30 seconds.

Now do the same focus/remember/feel sequence for each of the following muscles: right upper arm, left hand and forearm, left upper arm, forehead, middle face, lower face, and neck.

Then pause for a moment and take five deep breaths. Hold each breath for 5 seconds, then think of the word "relax" as you exhale. When you've completed this breathing exercise, do the focus/remember/feel sequence for the remaining muscle groups: upper back, chest and stomach, right thigh, right calf, right ankle and shin, left thigh, left calf, left ankle and shin.

The entire technique should take about 8 minutes. Dr. Lichstein recommends that you practice it at least once a day—partly to guarantee at least one instance in every day that you experience a tranquil mind, and partly so that the technique stays fresh in your mind and available for emergencies in which you really need to remain calm and focused.

You may even become proficient enough so that just taking a deep breath and repeating the word "relax" as you exhale will elicit a sense of inner calm.

Think of the word "relax" as you exhale.

The Word on Meditation

Forget the gurus searching for nirvana. Meditation is for anyone looking for a little more peace here on earth.

Meditation involves simply taking a few quiet moments to focus your attention on a specific thought, word, sound, or bodily sensation, such as breathing. The goal is not immediate relaxation, even though that is one result. Rather, meditation helps settle the mind so it can process thoughts calmly, in an organized way, throughout the day.

And the proof that it works is backed by scientific research. At the University of Arkansas, for example, researchers studied the effects of meditation on the brain waves of 25 people between the ages of 17 and 44 who practiced meditation at least some of the time. They found that during meditation, these people showed brain wave patterns indicative of a tranquil mind.

During meditation, people showed brain waves indicative of a tranquil mind.

342

■ Concentrate on Your Breathing

Find a quiet spot, sit down in a comfortable position, let your eyes gently close, and focus on your breathing for 5 minutes, suggests Jon Kabat-Zinn, Ph.D., director of the Stress Reduction Center at the University of Massachusetts Medical Center. Don't try to change your breathing or control it. Just feel it go in and out. Ride its waves. Your mind may wander, but that's okay. When it happens, just bring your thoughts back to your breathing.

Dr. Kabat-Zinn calls this technique mindfulness meditation. Its advantage over other forms of meditation is that it's effective in small doses. Take a few seconds every hour or 5 minutes periodically throughout the day to practice mindfulness. Think of it as a breath of fresh mental air. By focusing on your breathing, even if it's only for a few seconds, you can give your body subtle cues to relax that it wouldn't otherwise receive, Dr. Kabat-Zinn says. It also can give the brain a quick perk-up.

Focus on your breathing for a quick mental pick-up.

■ Let Go of Chattering Thoughts

One of the first obstacles you're likely to encounter when learning to meditate is mind drift, says Dr. Kabat-Zinn. Having your concentration broken by wandering thought is a common, but irritating, part of meditation. As you develop your meditation technique, you'll find your own way of dealing with the problem. The late philosopher Alan Watts found that he could control mind drift like this: "Listen as you would listen to music," he wrote. "Keep

Your mind will eventually become calm.

your tongue relaxed, floating easily in the lower jaw, and listen to your thoughts as if they were birds chattering outside—mere noise in the skull—and they will eventually subside of themselves, as a turbulent and muddy pool will become calm and clear if left alone."

343

Another experienced meditator suggests that you watch the rise and fall of your stomach. Think the word "rising" with each inhalation and the word "falling" with each exhalation. That should keep your mind on track.

Watching the rise and fall of your stomach can control mind drift.

■ Choose a Word for Mental Peace

The suggestion that you hang your consciousness on a couple of words is akin to the mantra used in transcendental meditation. In this type of meditation, you sit down, close your eyes, and instead of focusing your mind on your breathing, you focus on a single word or phrase.

The choice of word is up to you. If you're Jewish, you might prefer a word from the Torah. A Christian might choose a word from the Bible. Someone who practices transcendental meditation might choose (or be given) the words *eng, enga, shirim,* or *hirim.* Those who don't follow a specific faith might simply meditate on the words *peace, calm,* or *relax.* The only criterion for an effective word seems to be that it have a positive or spiritual connotation to the person who is using it.

Choose a word that has a positive connotation to you.

Mantra meditation is virtually identical to a breath meditation and produces the same results. Sit quietly, close your eyes, and repeat your mantra to yourself, letting go of all other thoughts. Allowing your mantra to fill your

344

Repeating a single word can silence your mind.

consciousness for 15 to 20 minutes can give you a full day of personal peace, say practitioners. If your mind begins to wander, just bring it gently back to your mantra. The word will drift through your consciousness, silencing the chatter of a cluttered mind.

■ Try a Gaze Meditation

Those who are more visually oriented may prefer to meditate on a *yantra,* the material version of a *mantra.* A yantra is simply any object on which you choose to focus your gaze—a lit candle, a flower, a piece of fruit, or the picture of someone who is spiritually significant in your life, perhaps a saint or a revered teacher.

Again, this form of meditation is similar to both breath and mantra meditation: Find a quiet spot and sit comfortably. Fix your mind on your yantra, and with your eyelids at half mast, gaze at it for 15 to 20 minutes.

Since your eyes are open during yantra meditation, you may want to conduct it in a special part of your home that has been set up to create a visually peaceful environment—with rugs, books, art objects, whatever you find visually relaxing. To avoid eyestrain, Dr. Lichstein says that it is particularly important that the room be dimly lit, preferably by natural light, and that your eyes be half-closed. Should your eyes become tired, he suggests closing them for a time and continuing to focus on the object in your imagination.

Interestingly, Dr. Lichstein adds, the appearance and meaning of your yantra will change in your mind and will eventually stim-

To avoid eyestrain, keep the room dimly lit.

ulate images, thoughts, and feelings that will lead to deeper states of meditation.

■ Turn Your Yard into a Meditation Garden

If you find comfort in flowers, happiness in nature, or serenity in the feel of the earth, you might also find peace of mind in a visual meditation brought to us by French explorer Madame Alexandra David-Neel. Madame David-Neel calls it a meditation garden, and she first discovered and wrote about its mind-releasing qualities while in Tibet during the 1920s. This is how it works.

Find a garden that you find visually appealing and comforting. Stand in its midst. Examine the garden in detail. Notice the flowers, their species, their petals, their vibrant colors. Notice the new blooms, how one flower complements its neighbor. Take in the majesty of the trees—the delicacy of their leaves, the weight of their branches, the wear on the bark.

Picture a beautiful garden.

Then shut your eyes and see the garden through your mind's eye. If you have difficulty holding the image in your mind, open your eyes and look again, then close your eyes and summon the image to your mind again.

Now, one by one, eliminate a piece of the garden from the picture in your mind. "Gradually," wrote Madame David-Neel, "the flowers lose their colors and their forms, they crumble into tiny pieces which fall to dust and finally vanish. The trees, also, lose their leaves, their branches shorten, and seem to be withdrawn into the trunk. The latter grows thin, becomes

Eliminate a piece of the garden, flower by flower.

a mere line, more and more flimsy till it ceases to be visible.

"Now the bare ground alone remains, and from it the novice must subtract the stones and the earth. The ground in its turn vanishes. . . ."

The goal of a meditation garden is a mind as clear and tranquil as the garden itself. It can be done in any garden at any time of the year. In fact, the ever-changing beauty is said to enhance its mindful effects.

Allow your mind to become as tranquil as a garden.

■ *Plant a Metaphor to Nature*

If you like the idea of a Tibetan garden meditation, think about planting your own. But don't think you'll be up to your elbows in peat. This garden asks more from your imagination than from your Roto-Tiller. Meditation gardens are popular in Japan. The most famous, Ryoan-ji in Kyoto, is nothing more than a rectangle of sand with 15 carefully placed stones and a little dark moss.

Meditation gardens are popular in Japan.

The idea is to sit and gaze reverently upon the garden's simple features, which become metaphors for nature. To the Japanese, for example, a rock might come to represent a towering, majestic mountain; an area of sand or gravel raked into smooth and winding patterns becomes a river meandering through a valley. However small, meditation gardens should convey a sense of expansiveness and peace.

"Purr-fect" Solutions

Imagine walking through the whirling insanity of life with a still, calm center untouched

by the constantly fluctuating barometric pressures of problems, obligations, schedules, appointments, deadlines, family, house, and job.
Does it seem impossible?

Not to people who meditate. They will tell
you that the tranquillity they achieve each day
through 15 to 20 minutes of meditation per-
meates into every facet of their daily life. It's a
wonderful benefit, but one that's not easy to
achieve. To be able to take that inner calm and
hold on to it even as you meander through a
bustling supermarket, rush to make dinner,
and pack the family off to bed takes purpose.
The following are a few more techniques designed to help foster that tranquillity.

347

The positive effects of
meditation can last all
day long.

■ *Take Your Meditation on the Road*

One way to slow down a hectic pace is to
develop a sensitivity to movement through the
motions of walking meditation. Start by taking
off your shoes and socks, says psychologist
Daniel Goleman, Ph.D., author of *The Medi-
tative Mind*. Stand up and feel the ground
against the soles of your feet. Then slowly lift
one foot, paying attention to every sensation—
lightness, suspension, tension, and motion—as
you slowly move your foot forward and then
down. Notice the sensations in your feet as
they touch the ground.

Slowly start walking, Dr. Goleman suggests, then pick up the pace. But stay at a pace
that maintains that super-sensitive awareness.
Lift your foot up, move it forward, place it on
the ground, and shift your weight onto it.
Sometimes it helps to label each movement.

Develop a sensitivity
to movement.

Concentrate on the
sensation of earth
against foot.

Think, "Up . . . forward . . . down . . . shift."
Once you have the rhythm, you'll be able to
eliminate the words and simply concentrate on
the sensation.

Once you've mastered the mechanics, you
can take your walking meditation on the road.
Meditation teacher Thich Nhat Hanh suggests
that you find a road that is not too rough or too
steep.

"Be aware of your breathing," he advises
in *A Guide to Walking Meditation*. "Walk more
slowly than you usually do, but not too slowly,
while breathing normally. Do not try to control
your breathing.

"Walk along in this way for a few minutes,
then [count] how many steps you take as your
lungs fill and how many steps you take as they
empty."

So forget honking horns, pushy pedes-
trians, and maddening crowds. With a little
practice you can walk anywhere and through
anything, aware of nothing but your own foot-
steps and breathing.

Walking can be the
antidote for a some-
times crazy world.

■ *Sit Down and Take
a Break from Reality*

Is the world moving around so fast that it's
making you dizzy? Do you have so much to do
that you don't know what to do next? Have the
things in life that were so important gotten *so*
important that you're losing all perspective?

When life feels like it's closing in on you,
it's time to sit it out for a moment.

Edward Espe Brown teaches sitting meditation at the Tassajara Zen Mountain Center

in California. In this type of meditation, you do not gaze at any particular object, you do not repeat any particular word. Nor do you move. You just sit and pay particular attention to your breathing and posture. As feelings and thoughts clutter your conscious mind, focus your attention back to your breathing and posture. The right posture, says Brown, creates the right state of mind.

A sitting meditation is as effective as it is simple. A study of 48 meditators at the University of Tokyo found that their minds dropped into tranquillity within 50 seconds of beginning the meditation. The longer you meditate, the more tranquil you can become.

Brown illustrates how a sitting meditation works through a unique approach to cooking that he teaches at workshops around the San Francisco Bay area. In the workshop he introduces a variety of vegetables—a carrot, an onion, celery, a potato, perhaps a green pepper— and prepares each vegetable four different ways: baked, blanched, steamed, and sautéed.

"Then we taste what happens," says Brown quietly. "We examine. We experience. We ask, 'How does the difference in cooking affect the flavor of the celery? The carrot? The onion?' This close attention to the details of your experience allows you to respond more accurately and reflectively to your life's circumstances."

After giving the class time to experience for themselves what the differences in taste are, Brown takes pureed tomatoes and prepares tomato sauce in a number of different ways. He passes each sauce around to workshop participants and asks, "What do chilies do?" Or,

349

Minds dropped into tranquility in 50 seconds.

Take time to experience the sensation of taste.

"What do ground nuts do?" Or, "What does minced onion do?"

In this way, says Brown, "We experience what an ingredient does rather than just assembling a grand concoction in which the taste of each individual ingredient is lost. We develop a catalog of tastes and smells from which to draw."

■ Stand on a Mountain

Yoga, a type of meditation that combines breathing and relaxation with movement, can induce a tranquil mind in two different ways, says Linda Cogozzo, managing editor of *Yoga Journal*. It improves breathing, muscle tone, and posture, all of which help combat physical stress. And it allows you to focus on yourself, then get in touch with how you're feeling, which reduces mental stress.

"When you can identify your problems," says Cogozzo, "they lose some of their hold on you. Yoga helps you do that by cultivating your ability to be aware of yourself physically and emotionally."

Yoga focuses on the physical and the emotional.

You can best try yoga by signing up for a workshop at your local Y, but to get a taste of what Cogozzo is talking about, try a yoga posture called the mountain pose: Stand up straight for several minutes with your shoulders relaxed, chest lifted, legs strong, says Cogozzo. The message of self-confidence that this pose sends to your mind will allow you the tranquillity of the strong.

Send yourself this message: self-confidence.

■ Try Yoga in a Chair

If you like the idea of yoga but don't have an inch of the flexibility it commands, you might want to try this program developed by Bija Bennett, a yoga therapist at the Maharisha Ayur-Veda Health Center in Lancaster, Massachusetts. It can be done in a chair. It combines the movement of dance with the static postures of yoga.

Chair yoga requires modest flexibility.

To begin, suggests Bennett, sit down in a chair with your hands on your knees and close your eyes. Become aware of the hardness of the chair and aware of your feet, heels, legs, the back of your calves, knees, and thighs. Allow your awareness to extend deep into your hip socket and all the way to the base of your spine.

Now take a deep breath and notice how your spine changes as soon as your breath does. Every rib is attached to a vertebra in your spine, Bennett explains, so that as you breathe, your breath moves first your ribs and then your spine. As you inhale, your chest expands, opens, widens, and you can feel your spine stretch and lengthen as a result. As you exhale, you bend back into the center of your body.

The next time you inhale, Bennett suggests, consciously fill your upper chest first, then your rib cage, and all the way down to your belly. The inhale moves like a wave from the top down. Pause for a moment, then as you exhale, first move your belly toward your spine and allow your lower back to round. The exhale moves like a wave from the bottom up. The

Feel the inhaled breath all the way to your belly.

Let your breath move
your body.

trick to achieving tranquillity as well as the unity of mind and body with these exercises, Bennett says, is to let the breath move the body. "You are linking your awareness with the movement of the spine through the breath."

Now repeat the exercise, inhaling deeply. But this time, put your palms together in front of your chest, fingers pointed upward as though you were about to say your prayers. Keep your elbows bent. As you inhale, open your arms and raise your hands—similar to what you did as a kid when a playmate told you to "stick 'em up!" Pause for a moment, then bring your palms back together as you exhale. Move slowly with the breath.

Now do the exercise again, remembering to fill the upper chest first, then your ribcage, and all the way down to your belly. Pause. Then exhale, belly to the spine, allowing your lower back to round.

A second exercise, called The Goose, builds on the first. Begin by placing your hands on your knees, dropping your chin to your chest, and allowing your lower back and shoulders to soften. Now, as you inhale, let your breath lift your chest and upper back as they expand and slide forward like a goose's. Pause, then as you exhale, let your belly move your spine so that your lower back rounds as your chin drops to your chest and your shoulders soften once again.

Lift your chest like a
goose.

Use the same basic breathing pattern as before: as you inhale, fill your upper chest first, then your ribcage all the way down to your belly. As you exhale, move your belly to your spine, allowing your lower back to round.

A third exercise developed by Bennett begins by lifting one knee and clasping your hands around it. Now, as you inhale, move the knee away from your chest and extend your spine. Pause for a moment, then as you exhale, let your knee move back toward your chest and allow your lower back to round. Use the same breathing pattern as before. Repeat the exercise, switch knees, and continue the exercise with your other knee and leg.

When you've finished with these movements, says Bennett, sit quietly and let your breathing return to normal. Open your eyes when you're ready.

353

Lift your knee and clasp your hands around it.

■ *Sense the Inner Stillness of T'ai Chi*

One technique in which your movements themselves become the focus of your mind is t'ai chi, an ancient movement meditation that is known for its gentle grace. In t'ai chi, you take several deep breaths, become aware of that warm, round center within you, and begin a series of exquisitely slow movements that allow the energy within you to flow naturally from that center throughout your body.

Any tension you feel is swept up within the flow of energy and released. Any emotion— whether anger or love—is also released. Any pain or ache or dissatisfaction is dissolved until the one thing—the only thing—left within you is a powerful, moving stillness that regenerates your very soul.

To get a sense of the inner stillness t'ai chi can bring, you might want to experiment with this simple exercise that t'ai chi master Al

T'ai chi is known for its gentle grace.

354

Huang uses in his workshops and describes in the book *Embrace Tiger, Return to Mountain*.

Stand up straight and stretch your arms over your head, clasping your hands and stretching to your fullest length. Keep stretching. You should feel all your energy flowing upward from your feet, calves, hips, chest, arms, and into your hands, says Huang. Then let your hands come apart and allow your arms to gently move out and down to your sides. You can sense how the energy moves up through your body, then down your arms and back to the earth in a circle. The length of your arm becomes the curve of a ball and your energy shoots out and down.

Now do the stretching exercise a second time, suggests Huang, but this time try to let your knees go with the downward flow of energy. Don't resist the force of gravity so firmly. Just let yourself sink, just a little, toward the floor. And let your body breathe naturally the way it wants to: draw in air as you stretch upward and exhale as you descend. Follow your own natural rhythm.

Probably the best way to get started with t'ai chi is to take a class at a local college, Y, or recreation center. Various forms of it are also taught at martial arts centers—sometimes called "dojos"—since t'ai chi is the foundation for such warrior sports as aikido, karate, kung fu, or judo.

But don't let the warrior connotations scare you away. Keep an open mind. The paths to a tranquil mind are limited only by your willingness to explore new thoughts, new feelings, new ways. And by your willingness to explore the limitless dimensions of your own mind.

Sense the movement of energy through the body.

Good t'ai chi starts with good instruction.

Some people enjoy doing puzzles so much it's like a form of meditation—deeply relaxing. For others, solving puzzles can lead to torn-out hairs. Try figuring out the one below, and you'll soon see in which group you belong.

Not Too Difficult

At the top of this illustration is a box that has been unfolded. Next to it are six folded boxes. Which of these folded boxes *cannot* be made from the unfolded box? (There may be more than one.)

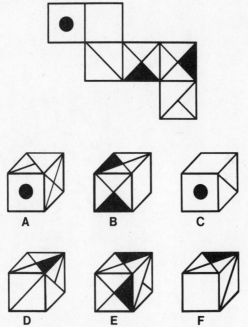

To find the answer, see Solution #12 on page 457.

Dreams

Improve Your Mind While You Sleep

As darkness and silence fall across the land and the stars flicker above, you snuggle into your warm and cozy bed. Comforted by a fluffy pillow, a cuddly blanket, and perhaps a stuffed teddy bear by your side, you close your tired, droopy eyes and fall slowly, blissfully, to sleep.

Your physical activity over the next 8 hours or so involves an occasional turn, some eyeball movement, and an intermittent snore. At least it looks that way to the outside world. To you, however, the night sparkles with magic. You sail across the desert on a carpet spun of golden angels' hair. You stop for a spot of lemon tea with your third-grade teacher (who hasn't aged in 40 years). Cary Grant pops in for a moment. You mount a pink-winged unicorn for a journey over a sea of orange marshmallow.

Welcome to the infinite universe of dreams. Some mornings you remember them clearly. Other mornings you don't recall a

Unlike the body, the brain never sleeps.

thing. But chances are you dream every night. What are these sometimes wondrous, sometimes disturbing, often bizarre and surreal images? Where do they come from? What do they mean? Can you program them? If so, maybe Cary Grant would hang around longer.

Using Dreams to Build Your Mind

What are dreams? In some cultures, dreams are interpreted as messages from the gods. Disciples of Sigmund Freud see them as windows into the unconscious mind, often reflecting our deepest desires. Some experts argue that dreams are a way for our mind to clean up the emotional "garbage" that piles up during the day.

Although the true nature of dreams may forever be up for debate, one thing remains perfectly clear: Regardless of the blank look on a sleeper's face, the brain does not turn off at night—far from it. In fact, some parts of the brain actually become *more* active, especially during one particular stage of sleep.

Some parts of the brain become *more* active.

There are different stages of sleep—very different stages. You've probably heard of "rapid eye movement" (REM) sleep, and "nonrapid eye movement" (NREM) sleep. "They are as different from one another as both are different from wakefulness," says Merrill M. Mitler, Ph.D., director of research of the Sleep Disorders Center at Scripps Clinic and Research Foundation and clinical professor of psychiatry at the University of California in San Diego.

"In fact, it could be argued that NREM sleep and wakefulness have *more* in common with each other than either has with REM sleep!" says Dr. Mitler. "During NREM sleep and wakefulness you can sweat, you can shiver, you can even walk around the room," he says. "You can't do any of those things in REM sleep."

You can't do these things in REM sleep because the body becomes immobile. Only the eye muscles and the muscles of your essential inner organs escape the paralysis of REM sleep, says Dr. Mitler. But as the *body* becomes most inactive, the *mind* soars. It's during REM sleep (generally about 2 hours a night, broken up into four or five 20- to 30-minute periods) that you're most likely to find yourself flying on magic carpets or pink-winged unicorns.

When the body becomes most inactive, the mind soars.

It's during this time of intense dreaming—and intense brain activity—that experts say you can enormously boost your brainpower by paying better attention to the meanings behind these extraordinary illusions and allusions.

Read your dreams, boost your mind power.

■ Improve Your Dream Recall

Dreams, like oxygen, can nourish your brain even when you aren't consciously aware of them. But the more you remember and study your dreams, the more you'll get out of them, says Patricia Garfield, Ph.D., well-known expert on dreams and the author of several books, including *Creative Dreaming*. Even if you have trouble remembering your dreams, worry not. It is within *anyone's* power, including yours, to master dream recall, says Dr. Garfield.

Anyone can learn to remember dreams.

What Does It Mean in a Dream When . . . ?

Have you ever dreamed that you were being chased, or that you were falling, or that you were in a car that had lost control? It would be unusual if you *haven't,* for these are among the most common dream themes, says well-known dream expert Patricia Garfield, Ph.D.

Dreams are a very personal matter, and you—the dreamer—are by far the most qualified person to interpret your own dreams, says Dr. Garfield. Certain dream themes are so common, however, that one can make some generalities about them. See if any of the following interpretations hit home for you.

You are being chased or attacked. This unpleasant scenario may be the most common dream theme of all. "I've heard of people being chased by all kinds of things . . . wild animals, robbers, sexual perverts, ghosts—one woman even told me she was being chased by a giant poached egg!" says Dr. Garfield. Regardless of whether you're being chased by ugly monsters, killer green slime, or your breakfast, the dream is probably related to a feeling of being threatened, says Dr. Garfield. Typically, animals with big teeth, like wolves or sharks, represent feelings of anger.

You are falling. "Usually this means that you're feeling insecure, that you have no support, or maybe you're feeling

Believe that your dreams have value.

The first step to improved dream recall, and perhaps the most important, requires a certain leap of faith. You must "believe that your dreams have value," says Dr. Garfield. "Even if you feel ambivalent, at least say to yourself, 'I'll pretend that my dreams have value,' and proceed from there!" she advises.

Next, you should plan to remember your dreams. As you turn out the lights, dish your-

like someone let you down," says Dr. Garfield. By the way, in case you've heard that hitting bottom in a falling dream means you will die, "that is absolutely *not* true!" says Dr. Garfield. "It is nothing but an old wives' tale—I've hit bottom *many* times," she says.

You are in a car out of control. This common theme has many variations. You may be about to crash into a truck or fly off a cliff, or you've just discovered that your brakes don't work. Whichever version you've had, "it probably relates to some form of loss of control in your waking life," says Dr. Garfield. It's important to note as many details of the dream as you can. For instance, What kind of car are you in—a Corvette or a Cadillac? "The car usually symbolizes the way we're moving through life," says Dr. Garfield.

You are taking an exam. Finding yourself in a classroom not knowing the right answers is usually symbolic of somehow feeling unprepared. Or perhaps you've been feeling like you're being tested on your job or by one of your friends, says Dr. Garfield. This dream is common for lawyers on the day before a big trial, or salespeople the day before a big presentation.

self a helping of what Dr. Garfield calls "auto-suggestion." That is, say to yourself while lying in bed, "Tonight I will remember my dreams. . . . Tonight I will remember my dreams. . . . Tonight I will remember my . . ." Z-z-z-z-z-z.

When you get up in the morning, don't spring up as if you've just discovered a bed full of lice. Lie there, calmly, with your eyes still

Don't bounce out of bed.

Recall works best
when you wake up
naturally.

closed (to avoid distractions), and let the images flow through your mind, says Dr. Garfield. Dream recall works best on mornings you allow yourself to wake naturally (for you're likely to wake up from a REM state of sleep). After you feel that your recall is complete, try rolling gently into one of your other sleeping positions. This may help you to remember even more, as dream recall comes best when you are in the position you were in at the time of the dream, says Dr. Garfield.

If nothing comes your way, one final ruse may pull your dream memories out. "Think of important people in your life," says Dr. Garfield. Your closest friends, family, and colleagues are the people most likely to star in your dreams, and if you visualize the right ones, the context in which they appeared may become clear.

Let your friends help.

■ Record Your Dreams

Once your dreams come back to you—quick!—capture them on paper. If you don't, you risk losing them. Dr. Garfield has kept a personal dream journal for nearly 40 years, and she finds it both therapeutic and fun. "It's fascinating. It's like having an encyclopedia on *you*!" she says.

Record even the minor
details.

Keep a pen and pad next to your bed. As soon as you recall a dream, write down as much of it as you can. Don't ignore what seem at the time to be minor details—jot *everything* down. If you can manage it, the best way to write your journal entries is with your eyes still shut. That way, you won't interrupt your recall. Dr. Garfield assures that it's possible to write legibly in the dark. It helps to write large, using the thumb of your nonwriting hand to help guide you down the page.

■ Find the Meaning in Your Dreams

With your dreams recorded, it's time to do some work—but enjoyable work—in trying to figure out what they're all about. Ready? Suppose you really did have that dream we talked about earlier, complete with a flying carpet, your third-grade teacher, a unicorn, and a sea of marshmallow. Where would you begin?

"You are the producer of your dreams. If you want to know what they mean, you have to ask yourself," says Gayle Delaney, Ph.D., director of the Delaney and Flowers Center for the Study of Dreams in San Francisco and author of *Living Your Dreams.* Dr. Delaney has developed a method for decoding dreams that she calls dream interviewing.

Ask yourself the right questions.

As dream symbols can mean different things to different people, she suggests you find out what a unicorn or a flying carpet means to *you.* "Describe every image in your dream as if you were describing it to someone who has no idea what such a thing is," says Dr. Delaney. In this case, ask yourself, "What is a unicorn?" Your response might be, "It is a fantasy animal . . . beautiful . . . strong . . . free." Then ask yourself what a dream about beauty, strength, and freedom may be trying to tell you. Have you perhaps been feeling unattractive and powerless lately?

Look for symbols, then interpret them.

One man had a dream in which his wife gave all of the couple's savings to the Quaker

One man used a
dream to better un-
derstand his marriage.

church, because that's what her father wanted. He used Dr. Delaney's method. "What is Quakerism?" he asked himself. (Simplicity. Clean living. Quiet lifestyle.) "What are savings?" (Vacations. Fun. Exciting life.) "What are my wife's father's expectations of her?" (To be responsible, religious, and correct.)

After examining the meanings of these symbols, the man realized that his father-in-law's expectations in the dream really represented some of his *own* expectations for his wife. He wanted her to be good, responsible, and correct, (as her father wanted in the dream). But he *also* wanted her to be fun, exciting, and fancy-free (represented by the savings in the dream). He concluded that the dream was telling him that he expected conflicting behavior from his wife.

■ Hire Your Dreams as Life Consultants

"Incubating" dreams
will get you answers
to your problems.

The man above got an answer to a question he hadn't even asked! Dreams can be still more powerful tools when you have specific goals for them, says Dr. Delaney. Getting your dreams to help resolve life's problems is easy once you learn to "incubate" them, she says. In fact, studies show that the vast majority of times, when you ask a dream a question in the right way, you'll have an answer waiting for you in the morning!

How do you incubate a dream? First, pick a night when you are not overly tired. Second, choose an issue that really matters to you and formulate a question to ask your dream. Write it down in one line, keeping it as simple as you

365

can. "Why am I afraid of heights?" "How can I solve my financial problem?" "Why do I care that Paul isn't talking to me?" Silently repeat this question over and over as you fall asleep. Every time your mind wanders, bring it back to your question.

The following morning, grab your dream journal as soon as you wake up and copy down *all* you can remember, even if your dream seems irrelevant to your question. (Remember, short dream fragments and minor details can turn out to be important.) Your answer should be there, although often it will be masked in symbols that require some interpretation, says Dr. Delaney.

Write down every-thing.

The more you work with dream incubation, the better you'll get, she says. Why does it work? There are a number of possible reasons, but "I can say with certainty that we are less defensive and more open to new ideas, larger perspectives, and new combinations of ideas while asleep than while awake," says Dr. Delaney.

Dreaming makes you more open to suggestion.

■ Look for Thought Patterns in Your Dreams

To get the most from your dreams, look for consistent, recurrent patterns, says Rosalind Cartwright, Ph.D., head of the Department of Psychology and Social Sciences at Rush University in Chicago, director of the Sleep Disorder Service and Research Center at the Rush Presbyterian/St. Luke's Medical Center, and author of *Night Life*.

Patterns signal strengths and weaknesses.

"I like to have people go through not one dream, but a number—you're looking for commonality. What are the dimensions upon which your dreams are built?" says Dr. Cartwright. "Are you always silent and everyone else is talking? Are you always weak and they're all strong?" If you find such a disturbing pattern in your dreams, you've found the road to making a positive change in your life, says Dr. Cartwright.

Simply becoming aware of your negative thought patterns helps you overcome them. "That's the ordinary function of dreaming—to adjust your mood and work out your feelings throughout the night," says Dr. Cartwright. You can help your dreams do their job better by "initiating the opposite image," she says. That is, if your dreams depict you as helpless, try to carry around images of a powerful you in your mind throughout the day. Your dreams will do the rest. Before you know it, you'll no longer be feeling so helpless!

The Wonderful World of Lucid Dreaming

Now . . . drumroll, please . . . the moment you've all been waiting for! Here's where we get to talk about how you can fly to the moon, walk through fire, hitch a ride on a unicorn, or dance the night away with Cary Grant any time you want.

A lucid dream is one in which you are fully aware that you are dreaming—*while* you are in the dream! Once you come to realize that you're dreaming within a dream, it's as if someone handed you a control switch. You can not only play with the vertical and the horizontal

Much of what dreams do is almost automatic.

Lucid dreamers are fully conscious they are dreaming.

controls on your screen, but you can make *any-thing* happen that you wish!

Was that a sigh of doubt we heard? Many are inclined to be skeptical. But many have experienced lucid dreaming, says Dr. Garfield, herself an adept lucid dreamer. She compares the experience to love. "If you have never experienced it, it is difficult to believe it can exist for you. Once love has become a reality for you, no cynic on earth can persuade you that it does not exist. Once you have been fully conscious during a dream, you *know* it can be done," she says in *Creative Dreaming*.

Stephen LaBerge, Ph.D., a researcher at Stanford University's Sleep Research Center and director of research at the Lucidity Institute, also in Stanford, is intimately familiar with lucid dreaming. "I lucid dream between once a week and four times a night," says Dr. LaBerge, author of *Lucid Dreaming* and *Exploring the World of Lucid Dreaming*.

Lucid dreaming is lots of fun, says Dr. LaBerge, but there are many other perks. "The most important benefits of lucid dreaming will depend on the person. An athlete will be able to develop skills in his sleep. A student or professional will be able to figure out study or work problems. Someone having a conflict in his life will be able to resolve it. Me, I get the most out of lucid dreaming in the area of personal understanding," says Dr. LaBerge.

To extract understanding from a lucid dream, you can actually *ask* dream characters questions you want answered. For instance, should you dream about your childhood best friend, you can ask him "What are you doing here?" Perhaps he'll tell you that you should

367

Some compare lucid dreaming to love.

An athlete can use dreaming to develop skills.

368

Lucid dreaming is
powerful medicine.

be having more fun in your life, the way you
and he used to. Or perhaps he'll tell you you're
goofing off *too* much.

Dr. Garfield says lucid dreaming is powerful medicine for dealing with nightmares and
the underlying stresses behind them. If, for instance, you're being chased in the dream, "I
suggest you turn around and face whatever is
chasing you. Remember, it's your dream. You
can do anything you want. You can be stronger
than a lion," she says. Learning to face demons
in your dreams will help you deal with your
fears in waking life.

How is this miracle of lucid dreaming per-
formed? It's not a miracle at all, say the experts. Anyone can learn to do it.

■ *Tune Your Mind to Recognize a Dream*

Practice reality
testing.

One simple exercise to do to become a lucid dreamer is to ask yourself throughout the
day "Am I dreaming?" This exercise, called
reality testing, popularized by German psychologist Paul Tholey, works best the more you
do it. The idea is to get your mind set to ask
this same question during the night. Don't
simply pop the question and quickly answer
"No." Really think about it. Look around you
to notice your surroundings. Read something.
Read it again. Has it changed? Look at your
digital watch. Is it acting as it should? Do you
see anything bizarre or extraordinary in your
surroundings?

After you've decided that you are awake,
ask yourself what things might look like if you
were dreaming. Imagine things getting dis-

torted, as in a dream. Tell yourself—and firmly resolve—that the next time you find yourself in a dream, you will recognize that you are in a dream.

■ Take Advantage of Your Awakenings

The best time to influence your mind to participate in lucid dreaming is during the night, says Dr. LaBerge. Before going to bed, tell yourself that you will wake up after each dream. When you do awaken, try to recall as many details as possible of what you were dreaming. Then, returning to sleep, concentrate on remembering that you're dreaming. Say to yourself: "Next time I'm dreaming, I want to recognize that I'm dreaming."

Imagine yourself back in the dream you just had, but this time around, you *know* it's a dream. Look for that dreamlike quality that separates dreams from waking reality. Try to stay up for at least a few minutes, repeating the above steps. The more convinced you become that you will lucid dream, the more likely you will, says Dr. LaBerge.

Imagine yourself back in your dream.

■ Spin Your Body around in Your Mind

The first time you lucid dream "you'll be tremendously excited," says Dr. LaBerge. You may get so excited that you wake yourself up. If you want to maintain a lucid dream, stay calm. If the dream starts to fade, imagine spinning your body like a top. This will help you remain in the dream state.

If dreams fade, imagine you're a top.

■ *Take Your Dreams in Stride*

If you're not one of the lucky few who lucid dream naturally, developing the ability may take time and practice. Be patient.

In the meantime, practicing your ability to recall and incubate dreams will help you get the most from your dreams and will encourage your progress toward lucidity. But don't be frustrated if dreams at first seem to be operating beyond your control and refuse to yield useful information. A good night's sleep filled with healthy dreams is an *automatic* brain booster.

You should awaken refreshed.

"If you don't wake up under a cloud of dread but wake up refreshed and in a good mood, then your dreams are doing their job," says Dr. Cartwright.

You Can Be a World-Class Sleeper

Ask an expert what the ideal amount of sleep is, and you'll likely get a question in return. "Ideal for *whom?*" he'll ask. The right amount of sleep for one may be far too much or too little for another.

Sleep is a personal matter.

If you were a goat (just suppose for a minute!), you'd need only about 2 hours of sleep a day. If, however, you were an opossum, you'd need more like *18* hours a day. For most human adults the range is generally close to 8 hours a day, and for babies, about 16 hours, says Wilse B. Webb, Ph.D., professor of psychology at the University of Florida in Gainesville and author of *Sleep: The Gentle Tyrant.*

But 8 hours of sleep for an adult is a *very* rough rule of thumb. About 60 percent of us sleep between 7 and 8 hours a day. But some healthy, energetic people get by on 5, or in rare cases, even fewer hours, says Dr. Webb. At least one case has been reported of a 70-year-old woman who consistently sleeps only *1* hour a night!

60 percent need 8
hours a night.

What is the right amount of sleep for you? If you're not getting it, you'll know. For without sleep, your brain would sputter like an engine running on fumes.

It's easy to mark someone who hasn't been sleeping well. He'll be "grim, stoic, and drag himself through the day," says Peter Hauri, Ph.D., director of the Mayo Clinic Insomnia Program and a sleep researcher for over 30 years. "It's difficult to be happy, radiant, and joyful when you lack sleep."

It's also difficult to think clearly. If brain-power doesn't get charged at night, it starts to dim during the day.

Poor sleepers, for example, lack an ability to pay attention and make good judgments. It's one reason that auto accidents are more likely to occur late at night and serious industrial accidents such as the chemical leak in Bhopal and the nuclear accidents at Chernobyl and Three Mile Island all happened in the wee hours, says Dr. Mitler.

Poor sleepers lose
mental acuity.

Studies show that after two or three days without sleep, you start to nod out involuntarily, if only for seconds at a time. These "mini-sleeps" increase in frequency and duration, until they start occurring between sentences and between steps. By day ten or so, you can no longer tell whether you're dreaming or

Why Dorothy Dreamed of Oz

Suppose you were a therapist in Kansas. The day after a particularly bad tornado passed through town, a little girl named Dorothy, accompanied by her Aunt Em, came to you troubled by a nightmare involving a wicked witch, flying monkeys, and a pair of ruby slippers. The dream, she said, occurred in a place called Oz. How might you help Dorothy to interpret her dream, and what advice might you give her?

We posed this same question to two prominent dream researchers, Particia Garfield, Ph.D., author of *Your Child's Dreams,* and Rosalind Cartwright, Ph.D., author of *Crisis Dreaming.* This is what they told us.

Dr. Garfield: "I'd suspect that Dorothy's dream had to do with growing up and becoming a woman. Symbolically, the cyclone represents change. It's something that is going to take her away to a strange new land—away from the security of the farm and the wheat fields of Kansas. I imagine that Dorothy would see this change as very frightening.

"Her friends in the dream, the Tin Man, Cowardly Lion, and Scarecrow, probably represent what Dorothy wants for herself—intelligence, courage, and a loving heart. Toto is an important element in the dream, too. Very often animals represent the dreamer's basic instinctual self. In the dream, Toto makes Dorothy's life happy and vital, but he also gets her into trouble. That would probably represent an important part of Dorothy.

"If I were working with her, I think the most important thing I'd do is point out to Dorothy that the entire time she

awake. You cease to be a well-functioning human being, says Dr. Hauri.

Few of us ever get to the point where lack of sleep leads to such a state, but a great many of us lack proper sleep. In fact, Americans to-was dreaming she had the power to do whatever she wished—for she had the ruby slippers! I'd point out that she didn't realize for the longest time that she had this power, and I'd ask her how this might relate to her waking life.

"Hopefully, she'd see that in her life too she has a great deal of power. I'd like to see her start to use it by taking on her nasty neighbor!"

Dr. Cartwright: "All teenagers go through a period of wanting to get away from home, but they're scared at the same time. I'd say Dorothy has a good, healthy dream system that is helping her to cope with these feelings and work through her fears of being independent.

"There were terrifying things in the land of Oz—the real world is full of terrifying things as well. In her dream, Dorothy activated good powerful images, what I call power givers. She had the ruby slippers to protect her. She had a strong ally in the Good Witch of the North. And she had the bucket of water with which she doused and melted the Wicked Witch of the West.

"That was exactly right! If Dorothy came to me, I'd say 'Good for you, kiddo—you're on your way!' That is, unless she wasn't sleeping well, having more nightmares. In that case, I'd like to see her for a while to encourage her to do more of the same in her dreams. I'd say something like 'Hey—another witch! Let's throw water on her too!' "

day are thought to be sleeping a full hour less than before the advent of the light bulb. Sure, that allows an extra hour for scarfing down popcorn while watching "I Love Lucy" reruns. But at what cost?

374

The benefits of good
sleep are numerous.

To turn the question around, what might better sleep do for you? The list of benefits is a very long one, but greater energy and more joyful waking hours are surely near the top.

■ *Find Your Natural Sleep Cycle*

What is the optimum number of hours of sleep for *you*? That's not hard to figure out, says Dr. Webb. Each of us has a natural, biological cycle—some call it an internal clock—that *should* dictate when, and how much, we sleep. If we'd only pay better attention to this clock, we could all be champion snoozers, he says.

You shouldn't need an alarm clock.

If you lunge every morning for the alarm clock as if you were swatting a horsefly, you're not paying attention. "Sleep has a natural end to it—you're not getting enough if you need an alarm clock," says Dr. Webb. It's all right to have a little insurance sitting next to your bed to make certain that you get to the office by 9:00 A.M., but if you know you'd otherwise sleep till noon without the alarm—and you continually bemoan the fact that you cannot—you need more sleep. Get to bed earlier, advises Dr. Webb.

Too much sleep makes you tired.

Sure, you can *live* with 7 hours of sleep even though your body craves 8, but you won't be operating at your best. "Everyone has a natural body weight," analogizes Dr. Webb. "If you're a 160 pounder, you can weigh 140—but you'll be a little hungry all of the time." Similarly, if you get less sleep than what is natural for you, you'll be a little tired all of the time.

■ Sleep When the Sun Sleeps

For countless generations we humans have evolved as *diurnal* as opposed to *nocturnal* animals. Our fellow-mammal, the rat, evolved along similar lines. "I spent three years trying to teach rats to sleep between noon and 6:00 P.M.—and that taught me how stupid I was. You can try to drive nature away with a pitchfork, but it always returns," says Dr. Webb. Some animals are *meant* to sleep at night, and that can't be changed without creating havoc.

You are what evolution made you.

If you have to stay up late—if, say, your job demands shift work—then there may not be much you can do right now to obtain optimal sleep. But realize that such a schedule will likely get tougher the older you get, says Dr. Webb. So if it looks like you'll be working the graveyard shift for the rest of your career, and the circles under your eyes are getting larger and blacker, you may want to scout out new job possibilities.

Night work gets harder to take as we get older.

■ Try to Be a Regular Kind of Guy

Regular wakers—those who arise every morning at the same hour—are usually the soundest sleepers, says Quentin Regestein, M.D., director of the sleep clinic at Brigham and Women's Hospital in Boston and author of *Sleep: Problems and Solutions.* The body likes regularity, which explains why so many of us feel like drunken sloths when the alarm starts to wail at 6:30 Monday morning. It's because

Your body craves regularity.

376

Better sleep comes with a steady schedule.

we slept till noon on Saturday and Sunday, thereby resetting our delicate internal clock.

"I suggest getting up at a very regular time seven days a week," says Dr. Regestein. "Regular sleep sets the body clock, and better sleep is the result," he says.

■ *Know the Best Time to Nap*

If the job or late-night socializing had you dragging all morning, you may want to catch up on your sleep with an afternoon siesta. If you do decide to pull the sombrero over your eyes, however, know that there's both a good way and a disruptive way to nap. The smart napper will do so without upsetting his body clock.

Nap between noon and 4 P.M.

How? The best way to nap is to sagely squeeze it in between noon and 4:00 P.M. and limit your shut-eye to less than an hour, preferably about half an hour, says Dr. Webb. Sleep more than an hour and your body clock will begin to readjust. When that happens, you'll wake up in the afternoon feeling like it's midnight, and the rest of the day you'll feel groggy. To make matters worse, you'll likely have a hard time falling asleep that night!

■ *Don't Mess with Your Body Chemistry*

All of our experts agree that poor sleep often results from poor habits. Specifically, what you eat and drink, *when* you eat and drink, and what other substances you put into your body can determine whether you sleep like a log or walk around all day in a fog.

Coffee may be an enemy in disguise.

Coffee, so much a part of American culture, *does* pep you up, but the caffeinated beverage can also slow you down by ruining your sleep, says Dr. Regestein. A jolt of caffeine stays in your system anywhere from 12 to 20 hours. If you're not getting quality sleep, coffee should be a prime suspect. Just make sure that when you cut back you do it slowly—quitting cold can bring headaches.

Other substances that can adversely affect your sleep include nicotine (just one *more* reason not to smoke), nasal decongestants and sprays, and most asthma medications. Especially troublesome is alcohol, which, although it's a depressant, can give you a hit of nervous energy 6 or 7 hours after consumption, loosen your throat muscles and make it difficult for you to breathe, and keep you running to the bathroom throughout the night. In cases of heavier drinking, alcohol can seriously disturb your sleep cycles, cutting down on both your REM sleep and NREM sleep.

You can certainly cut out alcohol and tobacco without checking with your doctor (take his permission for granted!), but check if you have any questions about a prescription medication.

As for food, "too much eating close to bedtime can disrupt your sleep," says Dr. Regestein. Your stomach produces acid to digest food, and if there's too much acid when you lie down, some of it may flow upward out of your stomach, causing late-night, sleep-wrecking heartburn.

■ Be a Sponge

Falling asleep is easiest when you're relaxed and most difficult when you're alert and tense, says Dr. Hauri. If you have relaxation

Caffeine stays in the system 12 to 20 hours.

Food and alcohol can disturb sleep.

techniques that work for you, do them in bed before going to sleep. Dr. Hauri describes such a technique in his book *No More Sleepless Nights*.

"Lie on your back, completely relaxed, and imagine you are a sponge, arms limp and away from the body, shoulders relaxed, legs apart and loose. Press your neck and back into the bed. Close your eyes, and breathe deeply through your nose. Let each part of your body relax, while thinking of your body as a sponge, limp, soaking up peace and tranquillity from the universe around you."

Release tension to sleep soundly.

■ *Refuse to Live Life as a Zombie*

Falling asleep in front of the TV is a bad sign.

"A lot of people tolerate sleep disturbances for too long without some kind of help," says Dr. Mitler. "'You shouldn't tolerate falling asleep in front of the TV at 8:00 P.M." If you're practicing everything above, you should be sleeping well at night and feeling energetic during the day. If not, see your doctor. Or, to find a sleep expert in your area, ask for a referral from the American Sleep Disorders Association located at 604 Second St., S.W., Rochester, MN 55902. ───■

The next time you can't sleep, try working on a puzzle. There's no guarantee that it'll help you fall asleep, but it's healthier than raiding the cookie jar.

Not-So-Sweet Dreams

After a heavy meal, the night watchman went to work. In the morning, he told his boss he had dreamed that a saboteur planted a bomb in the factory and that he felt it was a warning. The boss promptly fired him. Why?

Count Your Luck

While your little girl was asleep, you stealthily raided her piggy bank. You feel slightly guilty as you count the money. You have the same number of dimes and quarters, totaling exactly $2.45. When you turn honest and put it back, how many of each coin will you need to replace? (Your daughter keeps a record of how much she puts in and in what denomination, of course.)

To find the answers, see Solution #13 on page 458.

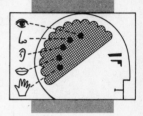

Senses

Fine-Tuning the Brain's Five Sensors

Have you ever heard the chatter of a baboon bouncing across a rain-drenched jungle in central Cameroon? Seen the sun fade into a misty pink glow from a beach in Mexico? Sniffed the intensely sweet jasmine growing freely in the alleys of Malaga, Spain?

There's a world of wonder out there. You can search for it in far-off lands—or you can discover it right outside your front door. So varied are the delights to view, sniff, taste, hear, and touch that it's utterly impossible to experience them all. But that doesn't mean you shouldn't try!

Why? Because your senses gather information with which your brain forms a picture of the world. The more information your brain has to work with, the fuller, richer, and more multidimensional this picture—*your* world—becomes. "Many of us take our

The senses help form a picture of the world.

senses for granted, but paying better attention to them is one way in which we may expand our mind—and our world!'' says Richard L. Doty, Ph.D., director of the Smell and Taste Center at the University of Pennsylvania's School of Medicine.

To feed new information through your senses, you *could* travel to Cameroon in search of a bouncing baboon. Or you could train your senses to pick up more of the world around you—wherever you are.

Perhaps you've met someone with extraordinary sensory abilities, such as a seasoned wine-taster, a professional perfume tester, or an ace private investigator. These are the virtuosos of the senses—but they weren't born that way. They were trained.

"Increasing the power of the senses is a matter of focusing and practicing—much like learning to play the piano,'' says Dr. Doty.

News from Those with Commanding Views

Seeing is more than 20/20 vision.

Eighty percent of the sensory information your brain receives comes from the eyes, says Arthur Seiderman, O.D., a Philadelphia-area optometrist and author of *20/20 Is Not Enough* and *The Athletic Eye*. Even if your eye doctor says you have "perfect" vision, that doesn't mean there isn't room for improvement, says Dr. Seiderman. "We go to gyms to work on our body, and we go to schools to improve our mind, but vision we take as a given. Anyone's vision *can* and *should* be improved!''

■ Look beyond the Obvious

It's no coincidence that another word for detective is private *eye*. "Seeing things that the layman wouldn't see is key to success in this profession," says Nathan Bernstein, president of Long Island's J & N Investigation and Claim Service, who has been a professional investigator for more than 20 years.

If Bernstein were to investigate a case for an insurance company in which someone flopped down a flight of steps, what might he look for to determine the cause? "I'd look to see if there were any cracks in any of the steps. Were any steps terribly worn? How high were the steps? Did they meet building code regulations? What time of day was the accident? Where was the closest light bulb? Was it working? What was the color of the walls, and how well do they reflect light? How close were the nearest windows? Were they clean? Were they covered with shades? Was there a handrail?"

This private eye looks where others may not.

Looking beyond the obvious is something that takes a conscious effort, but after you develop the habit, it comes more easily, says Bernstein. You can start increasing *your* awareness immediately. Notice the pictures on the walls in your friends' living rooms. Notice the books on your colleagues' shelves. Notice people's shoelaces and belts—what color are they and what are they made of? What color are your hairdresser's eyes?

Some ignore the beauty around them.

■ Freshen Up Your View

Have you ever had out-of-town guests ask you to show them your city, but you didn't have

384

We often don't see what's right under our nose.

the slightest idea what to show them? That's because we often don't see what's right up close—even if it's spectacular, says Gary L. Wells, Ph.D., chairman of the Department of Psychology at Iowa State University and an expert on eyewitness testimony.

"I was recently in Vancouver visiting a friend. There were flowers everywhere, and some of the most beautiful scenery I'd ever seen. It was breathtaking, but my friend didn't notice any of it," says Dr. Wells. If you think that you, like Dr. Wells's friend, have developed a jaded eye, it's time for remedial action.

Seek adventure.

"Expose yourself to a greater variety of scenery. Break up the habitualness in your life. Take a trip," says Dr. Wells. Not only will a trip away from home expose you to new scenery, but when you return home, you'll be likely to notice things you never have before. Not up for a voyage? "Bring new people into your environment," suggests Dr. Wells. *They* may point out some things you haven't been seeing!

■ Look at Objects from Different Perspectives

How would the Mona Lisa look hanging in the restroom of your local McDonald's? How would Michelangelo's *David* look adorning the entrance to Sal's Pizzeria? We see everything in a certain context. Change that context, and something very familiar may look quite different—perhaps fresher.

Change your point of view.

When you go to an art museum, you obviously can't lug pictures and statues from one side of a gallery to the other—but *you* can move around the room to look at the same piece of art from different perspectives. It may look quite different, says Dr. Wells.

For a revealing exercise in perspective, grab a photo of your mom (or anyone you know intimately) and turn it upside down. Study the nose, the ears, the mouth. You'll probably notice things about her that you've never noticed before. That's because you're seeing her in a new—unfamiliar—perspective (upside-down). You may also notice other characteristics that otherwise tend to get "absorbed" in an all-too-familiar face, says Dr. Wells.

Turn a photo of your mom upside down.

■ *Pay Attention to Others' Eyes*

Another virtuoso of visual awareness is Joseph Cordero, a senior inspector with the U.S. Customs Service, who works primarily at New York's J.F.K. International Airport. "Being good at this takes time," he says. "But after a while, you can just sense when someone is carrying narcotics."

How? "I look for eye contact—people will focus their eyes away from you when they're lying," says Cordero. "I notice if their hands are shaking or clenched. I look for beads of sweat on their forehead. If a couple of narcotics smugglers are traveling together and one is telling you a lie, the other will *inevitably* be looking right into his eyes, as if to say 'Wow, I can't believe how good you are!' That's a real giveaway. If you look carefully enough, people will always give you some kind of sign that they're lying," he says.

Liars always give themselves away.

Like Bernstein, Cordero says that years of practice and attention to details have given him the ability to sense when something is fishy—almost instinctively.

■ *Compare What You See to What You Know*

When it comes to seeing people, another authority is Corporal Bruce W. Danna, sketch artist for the Maryland State Police. Cpl. Danna makes drawings of crime suspects based on often-spotty descriptions. "Mainly the eyes seem to stick out in most people's minds, and anything unusual, like a scar or a limp," he says.

If you'd like to be more observant when it comes to people, if you'd like to see *more* than scars and limps, Cpl. Danna suggests a little trick. When you see somebody new, compare him to yourself. Is he taller or shorter? Tanner or paler? Slimmer or heavier? Be careful to note where you are standing when making comparisons. Again, perspective can make a difference. Someone who is 7 feet tall can appear short if you are looking at him from atop a hill!

Use yourself as the model.

■ *Strengthen Your "Corner Vision"*

"After most auto accidents, people inevitably say, 'Gee, I didn't even see the guy. It's like he came out of nowhere.' This happens because even those of us with 20/20 vision may have trouble seeing peripherally—to the sides," says Dr. Seiderman. But there is an exercise that can help you do something about it.

Practice it whenever you're walking down the street. Focus on something far off and straight ahead, like a tree. Without moving your eyes, what can you see to your sides? What can you make out, for instance, in the store windows? You also can practice this exercise when you're the passenger in a car. With your eyes focused on the road ahead, can you tell what kinds of cars are passing in other lanes?

Regularly practicing this exercise will improve your peripheral vision and may one day save you from a flying door, an errant golf ball, or a car that comes from "nowhere," says Dr. Seiderman.

Focus on something far off and straight ahead.

■ Develop Hummingbird Eyeballs

Good vision also means focusing fast and tracking moving objects. To develop the skill of eye *tracking*, read the label on a record album while it's spinning on your turntable at 33 rpm. If that's too easy, up the speed to 45 rpm. Practicing this exercise regularly should improve your tennis or basketball game by sharpening your eyes' ability to follow moving objects, says Dr. Seiderman.

Read the label of a spinning record.

To improve focusing speed, get yourself a few dozen 3-by-5-inch cards and write a number on each, starting with one or two digits. One card at a time, using a blank card as a cover, slide the top card as quickly as you can to reveal the numbers you have drawn beneath. Write down what you see. If this is too easy, increase the number of digits on the flashcards until you find reading them a challenge.

(continued on page 390)

Test Your Power of ESP

Is *all* of what we perceive picked up by our five senses—or is there more? Rita Dwyer of Vienna, Virginia, believes strongly in extrasensory perception. In fact, she says ESP once saved her life. It happened in 1959. Dwyer, then a research chemist working for a New Jersey aerospace company, got caught in a terrible laboratory explosion when working with an experimental rocket fuel. "All I could say was 'Dear God, here I come.' "

But a colleague of hers, Ed Butler, knew just what to do. He knew because he had witnessed the very same explosion several times—in his dreams. Butler pulled Dwyer out of the flames and without a moment's hesitation dragged her to the adjacent laboratory, where he was able to get her under a safety shower—just as he had in his dream. Had he hesitated, Dwyer would surely have perished.

Believing in the power of a sixth sense has made a world of difference in Dwyer's life. "I don't understand why it works, but I myself have had many telepathic and precognitive dreams," she says. An example? "One night I dreamed about lightning at the top of Mount St. Helens just as the volcano was erupting. Two weeks later it blew and lighting was seen at the crater's rim."

Very few scientists accept the existence of ESP. They cite lack of scientific proof. Stanley Krippner, Ph.D., professor of psychology at California's Saybrook Institute, has done numerous studies on ESP, but even *he* won't say for sure.

The one thing Dr. Krippner *will* say is that *if* ESP does exist, it is more likely to occur while you're dreaming than at any other time. "One can hypothesize that while we're awake, we're too preoccupied," he says. Reports such as Dwyer's of seeing the future in dreams are not all that uncommon, says Dr. Krippner.

If you'd like to set up an experiment to test *your* ESP, Dr. Krippner suggests one similar to what he says gave him positive results time and time again in laboratory settings. Here's how it works.

The basic materials you'll need are five identical envelopes and two friends. Have one friend pick four pictures from magazines. They should be vivid, emotionally striking pictures, such as a plane crashing or a volcano erupting. Have him cut the pictures out and seal each in an envelope—without showing the pictures to, or discussing them with, anyone.

A second friend will then pick one of the four envelopes. Again, without discussing it, he should concentrate on the picture, write down what he sees, even act out the picture—then put the picture into the fifth identical envelope, seal it, and go to sleep. In the morning, he should return all four envelopes to the first friend.

You, meanwhile, are paying careful attention to your dreams. You should discuss your dreams with your first friend (who doesn't know which envelope was chosen). He should take notes. At whatever point you and he feel that you've logged several significantly clear dreams (perhaps after two or three nights), the two of you should open the envelopes and look at the four pictures.

Based on your dreams (use the notes for reference), pick the picture that you believe your second friend chose. Which photograph is most closely related to your dream images? Check your answer. If you've chosen correctly, it could be a sign that your mind somehow connected with your friend's mind—and that you have experienced ESP! ————■

390

Improve your skill by adding digits. As you increase your focusing speed, you may become better at anything requiring quick reactions, such as hitting a baseball, swatting flies in the kitchen, or moving your car onto the expressway.

■ *Sign Up for an Art Course*

Art opens new visual dimensions.

If you're serious about becoming more visually aware, head for your local university, art school, or community college and sign up for a course in drawing or sculpture, says Mark Oxman, associate professor of sculpture at The American University, in Washington, D.C. He suggests you find a class that works with live models, still lifes, or landscapes.

The best way to find a good art course is to attend student shows. "If what you see looks interesting, go sign up. If all you see are lots of marks on canvas or crumpled papers, go elsewhere," says Oxman. "Take a good course with a good professor and you'll never see things again the same way. You may find that you've opened up something marvelous within you!" he says.

Secrets of the Super Sniffers

Inspectors can actually smell a crime.

You may be surprised to learn that when customs inspector Cordero is on the job, "smell is often the very first sense that comes into play," he says.

"If a suitcase has been taken apart to insert a hidden compartment, as soon as it's opened, I'll smell whatever was used to put it back together," says Cordero. The smell may be that of glue. Or it may be that of ground pepper, coffee, heavy perfume, or mothballs— all intended by the carrier to kill the smell of the glue or the hidden illegal narcotic. "Heroin has a very distinct smell," says Cordero.

Some people use their noses for a living.

Of course, what is distinct and recognizable to Cordero probably would not be recognizable to most of us. Studies have shown that the more you are exposed to a particular smell, the easier it becomes to recognize that smell and discriminate between that smell and others.

If anyone is expert at discriminating smells, it is Eleanor Fox, senior perfumer and vice-president with International Flavors and Fragrances, Inc., of New York. She is what is known in the perfume industry as a professional "nose." Fox creates new fragrances for many well-known perfume manufacturers (whose names she is not free to reveal). Generally, it takes at least ten years of training one's sense of smell to become a perfumer— and Fox has nearly four times that experience.

It takes ten years to become a professional "nose."

"Most people have a fairly good sense of smell, but they could certainly train themselves to make it better," says Fox.

■ *Set Up a Kitchen Classroom*

How can you train your sniffer? "Take an orange, a lemon, a lime, and a grapefruit, close your eyes and try to guess which is which. That may not be a simple as you think!" says Fox. If you find it too easy, the next step is to mix

Close your eyes and smell the fruit.

392

them up. "See if you can recognize the mixture. Ultimately, you can guess at percentages," she says.

The idea is to progressively make the exercise more difficult. When you've mastered citrus fruits, move on to spices. "Start with nutmeg, basil, oregano, and clove," says Fox.

■ Use Words to Describe What You Smell

You can identify and remember smells better if you describe them with words, says Fox. If you discover a new smell, like that of a flower you've never before encountered, look for comparisons to other familiar smells. But also try to relate the odor to your other senses. Something may smell "bitter," "sweet," or "sour." Something may also smell "green" (like a pepper or a field of grass), or "warm" (like toast or a spicy cologne) says Fox.

Bitter, sweet, and sour are cues.

■ Above All, Relax and Enjoy It

Most of us, when we use our sense of smell, tend to do so superficially, says Fox. Instead, the next time you pass a bed of roses or a French bakery or walk through a spring rain, "close your eyes, concentrate, use your mind as well as your nose, try to block out all else, and *smell*," says Fox.

"Enjoy your sense of smell. It's a wonderful thing. It can enhance your life so much," she says. In addition to the immediate pleasures of smell, familiar odors are powerful for bringing back or enhancing memories.

Smells can enhance memory.

"Something a year from now may remind you of the smell of that flower, and you'll say 'Aaah, I remember that—it was beautiful!' " says Fox.

■ Beware the Sniff-Robbers: Smoke, Flu, Head Bonks

While you're developing greater skills at sniffing out the world, be careful to protect what you already have. Foremost, avoid tobacco. "Don't smoke, and stay away from smokers and smoke-filled rooms," says Dr. Doty. The chemicals in tobacco smoke can wreck your sniffing abilities.

Also, avoid people with the flu who might pass you their bug. "The simple flu, particularly in people in their fifties and sixties, is the most common cause of smell loss," says Dr. Doty. The virus damages the nerve cells in the nose, forming scar tissue that blocks the passage of nerves from the nasal cavity to the brain.

Another danger to your sniffing ability is a blow to the head. "Ten to 15 percent of people who suffer serious head injury wind up either losing their ability to smell or experiencing great impairment," says Dr. Doty.

Sensitive noses don't appreciate tobacco.

Viruses damage nerve cells in the nose.

Tips from the Tasters of Life

Without smell, your sense of taste would be like a fine radio stripped of its antenna. Without smell, your tongue can pick up only the basic tastes—salt, sour, sweet, and bitter.

Taste and smell work in harmony.

394

Smell is 50 percent of taste.

The thousands of nuances that make up the menu of life—differentiating broccoli from chili and chicken soup from Cracker Jacks—are dependent on your sense of smell as well as taste, says Dr. Doty. "You can test this by eating a chocolate bar with your nose closed—you won't recognize the flavor," he says.

But taken together, your mouth and your nose form a powerful pair, especially if they've been given the opportunity to taste some of the finer things in life. Few of us have had as much experience in this as Phyllis Richman, food critic at the *Washington Post* for over 15 years. "The best way to train your palate is to do tastings," she says.

■ Become Your Own Private Food Critic

Critics can identify the cook by the taste of the food.

"Eat similar things, or different versions of the same thing, to alert yourself to the distinctions," says Richman. "Once I went to three French restaurants for rabbit with mustard sauce. That way, I learned about three chefs by eating the same dish in succession."

You can do the same with olive oils, butters, or anything you eat, says Richman. Appreciating subtleties becomes easier after you've sampled various delights back to back, as is done in wine tastings.

■ Break Up Your Courses

Gourmets often espouse breaking up the courses in a large meal with a small spoonful of sherbet (or *sorbet,* as they say in French) to refresh the palate. This isn't a bad idea, says

Richman, but there's nothing magic about sherbet—even when it's called sorbet! "A lot of things will serve the same purpose. You can also sip a small cup of consommé," she says.

The point is to rinse your palate with something liquid and light. If you do choose sherbet, make sure it's the right kind. "Raspberry is too heavy, it intrudes with its own flavor. Much better is lemon or lime," says Richman.

Cleansing the palate makes perfect sense.

■ Have Fun with Seasonings

If you were making tomato sauce, would it matter whether you added the basil before or after you cooked it? You bet it would. "Yesterday, I was in Louisville and had grits. They didn't use salt in making them. I sprinkled some on top, but it wasn't the same," says Richman.

Which spices you add to a dish is important. *How* is important, too! Richman suggests that you play around with the possibilities. "In some sophisticated restaurants, they're bringing the aroma of herbs into play in a very interesting way—not by adding them to the food at all, but by sprinkling them on the sides of the plate!" says Richman.

The secret is *when* to spice.

As an experiment, "try tomato sauce with basil cooked in. Second, try sprinkling some basil on top. Third, try sprinkling it on the sides of the plate. See if you can tell the difference," says Richman. She also points out that seasonings sometimes take time to "unfold," which is why soups and stews often taste so much better the day after they're made.

Wake Up and Smell the Opportunity

If you have a nose for sniffing out opportunity, take a whiff at this: You can increase your thinking ability and on-the-job performance and even enhance your health by turning on the right fragrance at the right time.

Research tells us that smells can influence our behavior and health. In Japan, for example, executives can awaken to an alarm clock that, 10 minutes before sounding, sprays a scented mist that they claim makes the mind more alert. They work in offices where lemon- or lavender-scented perfume wafts through the ventilation system in order to boost productivity. And Oriental perfumes, abroad and stateside, have long been doctored with the slightest scent of baby powder to subconsciously remind those wearing it of good childhood memories.

The reason: Certain scents can trigger certain emotions. And these in turn can trigger certain ways of thinking.

"We know so much about vision, hearing, and the other senses, but we're just beginning to touch the tip of the iceberg with the sense of smell," says Alan Hirsch, M.D., a psychiatrist and neurologist who heads the Smell & Taste Treatment and Research Foundation in Chicago. "Although all of this research is still new, we've already discovered that the sense of smell is vastly underrated in its importance. We found that we can change brain wave frequencies with smells."

Lavender, for instance, induces a more relaxed state—making you *feel* more relaxed so you can *think* more relaxed. Jasmine has the ability to excite—even in concentrations so low you wouldn't know it exists. This results in boosting thinking ability. And we have long known that certain odors—like baby powder—can trigger good memories of childhood, bringing forth feelings of happiness and security.

Other odors have similar impact, depending on where you were brought up. "Research has shown us that, generally, people from the East Coast have good childhood memories from the smell of flowers. In the South, it's fresh air; in the Midwest, farm animals; and in the West, the smell of barbecuing meat," Dr. Hirsch says.

Besides lavender, soothing smells that seem to significantly reduce anxiety, blood pressure, and even panic attacks include those of desserts (particularly spiced apples) and the seashore. The theory is that pleasant smells invoke pleasant memories.

At the University of Cincinnati, researchers discovered that floral scents—like those of freshly cut flowers—in an office significantly boost productivity among computer operators. Japanese researchers earlier discovered that air scented with a lemon spray decreased errors among workers by 54 percent, with jasmine by 33 percent, and with lavender by 20 percent. Meanwhile, researchers at the Monell Chemical Senses Center in Philadelphia recently discovered that customers stay at store counters longer—increasing sales potential—when there's an aroma of fresh flowers.

On the flip side, Dr. Hirsch says certain smells can have a negative effect on mood. Regular exposure to the smells of urine and feces—like those experienced by employees at hospitals, nursing homes, and animal shelters—leads to a higher incidence of depression.

"I think, like other animals, man relies on smell to establish a rapport based on some primitive or subconscious level," he says. "I believe that 'love at first sight' is often a result of 'sniff at first sight' because smell may play a more vital role in making a first impression than sight or hearing."

This research, which Dr. Hirsch predicts will come into full bloom in coming years, has enormous potential—particularly in the field of mental health and productivity. Besides being a valuable psychotherapy tool, aroma research "may someday eliminate the need for sleeping pills. Instead, you'll just smell an odor to promote relaxation," he says. "I'm sure the Japanese are already working on that!"

Hints from the Herculean Hearers

Dave Simpson is a Philadelphia musician and data processor who has never known the gift of sight. But, as Simpson points out, there's more than one way to perceive the world. Even those of us who have vision can tend to overuse it—at the expense of the other senses, particularly hearing.

The blind can hear what the sighted can't.

Simpson has the ability to hear what often goes unnoticed by sighted people. "Actually, I don't think my sense of hearing is better than anybody else's," he says. "But sometimes I can pick out a friend's voice on a crowded subway platform before they see me." Part of the reason for his skill, of course, is that he is more dependent on his hearing than most of us. But beyond the necessity, Simpson has had a chance to sharpen his hearing, much like the food critic sharpens her palate.

Simpson doesn't knock vision. "There's no need for able-bodied people to minimize their ability to enjoy their sight. It's a real boon to be able to see. But once in a while you might want to change to another station to 'see' what's on it," he says.

■ *Slow Down and Tune In*

"People in our rushed, sometimes crazy world feel swamped with the amount of information there is to absorb. So they go into survival mode, picking up information in quick bits," says Simpson. Quick bits means speed reading, glancing around rooms, and watching television news—all of which use primarily the eyes. Hearing is the far slower sense. "A sentence can only be heard over time," says Simpson.

In olden days people would listen more, says Simpson. In ancient Greece, for instance, citizens would sit for hours and listen to a poet recite the *Iliad.* Only a few decades ago, families would sit before the fire and listen to long tales on the radio. You can still capture these joys of yesteryear—but you'll need to make a little effort.

"Figure out where you can cut back on being inundated. Say no to the visual manipulation of TV and billboards. Say no to absorbing excess information. Then start to delight in the world," says Simpson. "Go out into the woods. Listen to the birds. Make a list of all the sounds you hear," he says. "When talking to someone, do *nothing* else. Treat the conversation as an exciting new 'vista' on the world."

The TV generation listens less.

Thomas K. Arnold, a pop music critic for the *Los Angeles Times,* says that listening to music can be tremendously more enjoyable if you shut out everything else. "I suggest you take your favorite record, and instead of listening to it while reading or entertaining friends, just lie in bed, close your eyes, and *really* listen," he says.

Close your eyes and listen to the music.

■ *Take Your Ears on Your Next Vacation*

"In Cairo, you hear a lot of the same sounds you would in any American city, but there are many differences. For instance, there's the sound of the call to prayer coming

Cultures even differ in
sound.

from the mosques. You hear donkey carts rat-
tling along. Bicycle bells. People speaking Arabic. Arabic music. The cars sound different—
they're smaller and their horns are whiney.
Even the flow of traffic sounds different, because there are no traffic rules in Cairo," says
Steve Coryell, travel editor for radio station
KRLD in Dallas/Fort Worth.

Traveling to a new city or country is a *dou-
bly* fascinating experience if you *listen* as well
as watch, promises Coryell.

■ *Fine-Tune Your Musical Ear*

Single out one instru-
ment during a concert.

In addition to shutting out distractions
while listening to your favorite album, music
critic Arnold suggests that you may increase
your enjoyment by playing a little game. "If you
single out one instrument at a time, you'll
really have fun. I did that recently at a Moody
Blues concert. I singled out the keyboards, then
the drums," says Arnold. "By putting certain
aspects under a microscope, you'll have a better understanding and appreciation of the
whole," he says.

■ *Go a Little Wild*

Play an imaginary
guitar.

For those of you who appreciated Tom
Cruise in the movie *Risky Business,* Arnold has
another suggestion: "Move from acute observer
to acute participant," he says. "Close the door
and shut the curtains so you won't be embar-
rassed, pick up your air (that is, your imaginary) guitar, jump up and down, and jam with

the music! Really get into it! It's much more of an enjoyment that way—*great* therapeutic value!" says Arnold.

If playing air guitar along with Bob Seger isn't your style, there's nothing wrong with playing a little . . . dah dah dah DUM . . . "air piano" along with Beethoven!

Tidings from the Talented at Touch

Touch is the sense from which we derive the most pleasure and the most pain. Touch is our sensual sense. Our intimate sense. A light touch on the back of the neck can make us weak at the knees. A jab to the stomach can make us keel over. Touch is the snuggly, cuddly, squeezy, nuzzly, goosebumps sense. It also has a practical side.

Touch is the sensual sense.

■ Feel for the Usual

"I definitely use my sense of feel on the job—a lot," says customs official Cordero. "When a suitcase is being used to conceal something illegal, I can often feel the false bottom, top, or sides," he says. "If you do five Samsonite suitcases a day, you get to develop a feel for it. I can tell when one weighs more than it should. I know how it should feel when it drops."

Similarly, private investigator Bernstein uses his sense of feel when on the job. In the case of the man who fell down the stairs, "I'd feel the banister to see if it were solid or shaky.

Decisions can be made by feel.

I'd knock on the step to see if it were solid or rotting." If investigating an auto accident, "I'd press my foot on the brakes to feel for the tension to see if they were working. I'd feel along the body of the car for imperfections—the car will give in areas where there was prior damage and repair—important in determining the value of the car and the cost of damage from the most recent accident," says Bernstein.

Next time you go out to buy a used car, do more than admire the shine on the hood. Press the brakes. Knock the fenders. Go for a ride— does the car feel stable? *Feel* for excess vibration in the steering wheel. If you're repairing a wall or building a cabinet, your fingertips can test for smoothness better than your eye. Use them!

Both Bernstein and Cordero say that touch, like your other senses, becomes more sensitive the more you use it. After years of feeling for false bottoms in suitcases, Cordero now does it automatically, almost unconsciously, he says.

If you think about it, you've been handling money for years and you don't *really* need to look in your hand to tell a penny from a quarter from a dime—do you? With practice, your touch can become just as sensitive to many more things!

Your sense of touch can be handy in the marketplace.

Here is a puzzle to test your sense of vision.

Opposites Detract

Two of the four boxes *cannot* be made from the unfolded cube shown below. Which ones are they?

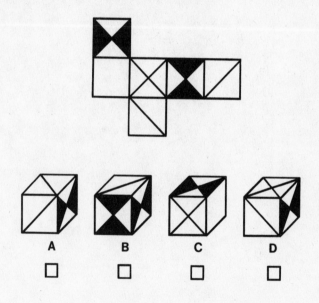

A ☐ B ☐ C ☐ D ☐

To find the answer, see Solution #14 on page 458.

Mind/Body Healing

Power Your Thoughts against Disease

She was recently married, with plans for a child. For Debby Franke Ogg, it should have been the best of times. Instead, it was the worst.

In September of 1984, she was diagnosed as having a nodular lymphoma, a cancer thought incurable. At age 42, she was told by her doctors (all three of them) that she had only a few years to live. "Every day when I went to sleep and every day when I woke up, I felt terror."

Today the terror is a thing of the past. Debby Franke Ogg is alive and remarkably well. The tumor has shrunk almost to oblivion. She is now the mother of a little girl and an active member of her community in upstate New York.

Was it a new medical miracle that saved her? Was it some experimental serum from a high-tech laboratory at a top-notch university? Or an advanced surgical procedure involving lasers?

No, it wasn't any of the above. Nor was it a mistaken diagnosis. Nor, according to Ogg, was it luck. She will tell you without a moment's hesitation that she was healed by the same thing that made her ill in the first place: her thoughts.

She used her mind to cure her cancer.

An Old Science Renewed

The notion that our thoughts can either make us ill or heal us did not originate with Ogg. It is a connection that has been recognized since the beginning of recorded history, says Jeanne Achterberg-Lawlis, Ph.D., author of *Imagery in Healing: Shamanism and Modern Medicine.*

Mind/body healing goes back to the beginning of time.

Socrates said, "There is no illness of the body apart from the mind." But what may have been recognized by healers 2,400 years ago was generally *not* recognized by most healers of 10 or 20 years ago. For back around the turn of this century, allopathic medicine (based on vaccines and pills) came to so strongly dominate the scene in America that all other medical theories were summarily dismissed.

The allopathic approach emphasized that for every disease there was one germ and there was (or soon would be) one drug that could be administered to kill it. Legislation was enacted to outlaw many traditional healing practices, including those that suggested a patient's thinking might affect his health, says Dr. Achterberg-Lawlis.

In the early 1980s, she and her husband, G. Frank Lawlis, Ph.D., conducted studies at the University of Texas Health Science Center, showing that the life expectancies of terminal cancer patients could be accurately predicted by looking at each patient's attitude. "But nobody wanted to hear about it," she says. "We found it very difficult to get published in medical journals."

People's attitudes predicted their survival rate.

Today, however, the attitude is different. In the past several years those same journals have exploded with articles about the power of the mind to heal. In one study, for example, grief-stricken widows and widowers were found to have fewer white blood cells, which defend the body against foreign invaders. In another study, researchers at the State University of New York at Stony Brook found a definite correlation between good moods and high amounts of another germ-fighter in the saliva. Conversely, people who reported feeling down on the day of the test showed lower-than-normal amounts of the same health defender.

The grieving had few white blood cells.

Researchers at the Ohio State University College of Medicine who took blood samples from 38 married and 38 separated or divorced women came up with similar conclusions. Married women with marriage problems were generally depressed in both spirit and immune function. Women suffering through the first year of separation from their husband had "significantly poorer" immune defenses.

Divorced women showed depressed immune defenses.

New research has even given us important clues about the specific ways we may modify

408

our thinking patterns to achieve unsurpassed health.

Mental Profile of a Survivor

"I would rather know what sort of a person has a disease than what sort of disease a person has," said Hippocrates many centuries ago. What sort of a person is Debby Franke Ogg? What might she have had in her favor going into the steep uphill battle against an "incurable" cancer? In what ways might her mind have fortified her body—ways that no known medical treatment could?

First, it should be said that the connection between *bad* thoughts and *bad* health has been much more accepted by doctors than has the connection between *good* thoughts and *good* health. Few doctors would deny, for instance, that stress can undermine good health. Nevertheless, the latest research has looked at some mental profiles of the healthy. Here are the factors that seem to make a difference.

Bad thoughts breed bad health.

■ Build Strong Relationships

"I felt there were some things in my life that weren't right—and I set out to change them with the help of my husband, who was just wonderful, and my very dear friends," says Ogg.

A large number of studies have shown that no man (or woman) should be an island. "We have clear, indisputable evidence that social relationships are a predictor of health and

Modern studies prove ancient wisdom.

Bad Day Today, Sick Tomorrow

Today is just one of those days when you can't do anything right. You spilled coffee all over your desk. You put the paper in the copy machine backward. You told the president of your company that his latest idea stinks. If you create one more problem for yourself, you're going to have a nervous breakdown by 5:00 P.M.

Well, maybe not a nervous breakdown. But you probably *will* start feeling a little ill: a sore throat, headache, backache, or flulike symptoms are most likely.

At least that's the conclusion of research from the University of Illinois at Urbana-Champaign, the University of California at Berkeley, and the University of California at San Francisco. They studied the way normal, everyday stress affected the health of 75 married couples over a six-month period.

Using questionnaires that balanced the good, the bad, and the ugly during the couples' day, the researchers were actually able to determine how much stress the couples experienced. Then they compared the results of the questionnaires with a log the couples kept of any symptoms or illnesses.

The result? The researchers found that even normal, everyday hassles involving such things as meeting deadlines, paying bills, and taking care of the car actually determined whether or not the couples would get sick.

And it wasn't just a case of the straw that broke the camel's back. People got sick whether they had just a few hassles piled on top of many or a lot of hassles piled on top of even more. Even people who had very little stress in their lives on a normal basis were affected by minor hassles.

Only two things seemed to block the effects of stress, the researchers reported: Lots of friends and a good shot of self-esteem. ———■

mortality," says James S. House, Ph.D., professor in the Sociology Department and program director at the Survey Research Center of the Institute for Social Research at the University of Michigan.

Just how important is it to your health to have friends and loved ones in your life? Referring to dozens of studies that show that people with more social relationships live both longer and healthier lives, Dr. House says that social relationships are as important as "the health effects of smoking or not smoking."

All the same, when presented with the evidence, people often say, " 'Well, that's good—but there's nothing I can do about it,' " notes Dr. House. "But that's not true," he asserts. "We have direction over our relationships just like we do over whether we smoke or exercise."

Dr. House maintains that we certainly don't need people around us all the time to be healthy, but we should make sure that we have a healthy amount of contact with other folks, whether it be family, friends, neighbors, or colleagues.

People involved in friendships live longer.

■ Look on the Sunny Side

"I provided an environment where my mind, my body, and my spirit could thrive—and I knew they would," says Ogg.

If you tend to look at the world as a positive place, you'll not only be more fun to be around, you'll likely have better health for it. Such was the conclusion of a 35-year-long study that looked at 99 graduates of Harvard University's classes of 1942 through 1944.

Harvard's optimists fared better than the pessimists.

As 25-year-olds, the graduates were asked a series of questions to determine whether or not they looked at the world through rose-colored or mud-smeared glasses. When these same graduates were given physical exams 20 and 30 years later, the optimists were in much better shape than the pessimists (that is, the pessimists who were still alive).

411

Optimism is healthy.

■ Learn How to Fight

"When my doctors were telling me when I'd be dead, well, we just didn't agree on that. I really didn't believe that I was going to die. . . . There were days I felt nothing but rage," says Ogg.

Sure enough (although some physicians are undoubtedly loath to admit it), being a skeptical patient, not treating your doctor's prognosis as God's final word, refusing to accept anything as inevitable, and freely expressing anger about your condition seem to be critical personality traits among survivors of formidable diseases.

One woman refused to accept her death sentence—and lived.

■ Have Something to Look Forward To

"I was diagnosed in September. By December, the nodes were starting to go down. By January, I was pregnant with Jenny. I had her on October 7, 1985—13 months after I was diagnosed with lymphoma," says Ogg.

Is it possible that looking forward to giving birth helped Ogg deal with her illness? It's more than possible, it's probable. Studies show that major upcoming events in people's lives

(continued on page 414)

Endorphins: Opiates for the Mind

Some call them "the body's natural painkillers." Others have linked them to "runner's high," the great feeling many get during exercise.

Endorphins, discovered by brain researchers in the late 1970s, are the subject of a burgeoning field of research so young that new theories pop up every day.

The first evidence of their existence came with the discovery that certain brain cells have opioid receptor molecules into which the opiate morphine seems to naturally fit, like a plug into a socket. Could it be, some researchers surmised, that the human brain produces an opioid substance very similar to opium?

Yes, it could. And endorphins seem to be one of them.

"Beta-endorphin slows the heart rate and respiration and lowers blood pressure," says Lee Berk, doctor of health science, assistant research professor of pathology and laboratory medicine at Loma Linda University, in California, who has been studying endorphins for a decade. "It is a euphoric substance, contributing to feelings of well-being."

Beta-endorphin also seems to play an important part in relieving pain, possibly by blocking the transmission of a pain-carrying brain chemical called substance P. Studies have found that endorphin levels rise among pregnant women—nature's way, perhaps, of providing pain relief during delivery. On the flip side, people who suffer from chronic headaches and premenstrual syndrome may actually be suffering from low endorphin levels, some researchers theorize. Insufficient endorphins—which might result from a genetically weak endorphin system—might even cause psychological depression.

Overall, human beings need endorphins to lead an energetic, productive life, says Murray Allen, M.D., a researcher and consultant at the School of Kinesiology of Simon Fraser University in Canada.

"Endorphins help people thrive," he says. "Following physical activity, they have a major calming effect on the central nervous system, muscles, arteries, and a host of hormonal glands. They influence the body heat mechanisms so you can be active in a wide range of external temperatures. And they give you a sense of calm and fearlessness in the face of risks, enabling you to accomplish more, giving you a sense of achievement."

Endorphins may also account for the pleasantly mellow, satisfied feeling we get at the sight of a beautiful sunset or the sound of music. Researchers at Stanford University found that people who were given an endorphin-blocking drug before listening to their favorite music were unable to experience their usual euphoria.

But all is not positive in the world of endorphins. Some types may impair learning or memory. Others may suppress the immune system: Studies show that one type, alpha-endorphin, along with some others, may reduce the effectiveness of the T-lymphocytes and natural killer cells the body needs to fight infection.

For the most part, though, it seems the goal is to have more endorphins working for you, not less. And researchers know that certain situations can prompt the body's production of these chemicals. Physical pain and stress top the list. One such stress is moderate exercise.

Acupuncture—the ancient oriental medical system in which needles are inserted at certain points of the body—can also stimulate endorphin production, some studies have shown. So can chiropractic adjustments. And although no one

(continued)

Endorphins: Opiates for the Mind—*Continued*

is advising it, binge eating or eating lots of sweets may boost endorphin levels, possibly to chemically counteract feelings of depression.

A good laugh seems to stimulate endorphins, too, says Dr. Berk, whose most recent research examines the hormones' links to humor. Blood samples taken from people chuckling through funny movies showed significant changes in the ratio of endorphins to other stress-related hormones, he says, although he adds, "I don't think anyone can say quite yet that endorphins increase with humor." But we certainly won't laugh if he discovers that they do. ——■

often foster a will to live that bolsters the body through rough times.

History gives us this striking example: Former presidents Thomas Jefferson and John Adams both passed away on July 4, 1826—seemingly postponing their death long enough to witness the 50th anniversary of the signing of the Declaration of Independence.

A study by researchers at the University of California, San Diego, has shown that the death rate among Jewish-American men is significantly lower just before Passover (the most frequently observed of all Jewish holidays) than immediately afterward.

Jewish deaths were lower before Passover.

414

■ Put Laughter into Your Life

Are there any serious medical studies that show that laughter is good medicine? "I have a bibliography of thousands," says Patch Adams, M.D., director of the Gesundheit Institute in Arlington, Virginia. "But I laugh at all these studies on laughter—why do we need studies about something that is *so* obvious?"

Dr. Adams does not wear a white jacket as most of his fellow physicians do. He tends to his patients dressed as a gorilla, a Viking, a court jester, a Renaissance frog, a medieval knight, Louis the XIV, Santa Claus, or "something just as goofy," he says. Not only does he find such "goofiness" helpful to his patients, but "it's healthy for me, too," says the ponytailed doctor through his handlebar moustache.

One doctor tends to his patients dressed as a gorilla.

What actually happens inside the body when laughter and other positive feelings are used as healing tools? According to Alison Crane, founder of the American Association for Therapeutic Humor, researchers have found that a good chuckle stimulates the heart and respiratory system, decreases muscular tension, and tends to lower blood pressure.

Laughter stimulates the heart.

The late Norman Cousins, a writer and magazine editor stricken with ankylosing spondylitis, was perhaps the first to bring the laughter connection to the public eye. He said that reruns of "Candid Camera" and old Marx Brothers films were instrumental in his recovery from the rare disease.

Cousins commented, "It is possible that laughter serves as a blocking agent. Like a bulletproof vest, it may help protect you against the ravages of negative emotion."

416

Laughter is like a bulletproof vest.

How can *you* bulletproof your health? "I act silly every minute I can," says Dr. Adams. He quotes Mary Poppins: "In every job that must be done/There is an element of fun/And every job you undertake/becomes a piece of cake." Dr. Adams suggests that if your life is not filled with wonder, curiosity, and *fun,* you should make it so.

■ *Destress Your Life*

You can exercise for hours every day, eat only raw vegetables and whole wheat toast, drink only pure spring water, and *still* be unhealthy. Studies suggest, for instance, that the so-called Type-A behavior found in individuals who are always racing the clock is just as likely to lead to coronary artery disease as is high blood pressure, a cholesterol-packed diet, or heavy smoking.

There's little disagreement among doctors that stress (whether it's physical or one of the more subtle psychological varieties such as anger, anxiety, fear, and frustration) is responsible for, or contributes greatly to, many modern maladies.

Nuns have lower blood pressure than the rest of us.

Nuns who live in relatively stress-free environments, for instance, have lower blood pressure than the rest of us. And doctors know that recurring heartburn and other digestive disorders are often due to stress-triggered biochemical reactions that result in excess stomach acid. Stress can also depress the functioning of your immune system, making you more susceptible to infectious diseases.

What can be done about stress? Well, you could quit your job, sell your house, and move

What You See Affects the Way You Feel—and Heal

A Room with a View is more than a movie title. It's also an aid to recovering after surgery. So say researchers from the University of Delaware who looked at patients recovering from gallbladder operations. They found that those who were assigned to rooms with windows looking out on nature did considerably better than those who had to stare at nothing but a brick wall during their days of recovery.

The patients with the pretty views had shorter hospital stays and fewer negative evaluations from nurses, required fewer doses of painkillers, and had slightly fewer postsurgical complications. One of the researchers speculates that a hospital window view could influence a patient's emotional state, and this might affect his recovery.

Although the patients in Delaware looked mainly at trees, it's suspected that any kind of natural vegetation will do—and a water view might be even better.

to the mountains of Nepal to tend goats. Or you could find a patch of deserted beach somewhere in the South Pacific and live on coconuts.

Or you can take the advice of experts who say you can beat stress right on its own turf. One researcher studied corporate executives, high-powered lawyers, and others who face more than their share of stress every day. He's found that it's not the *amount* of stress in our lives that matters—it's how we choose to deal with it.

How well we deal with stress depends on our hardiness, or more specifically, "three sets

How you deal with stress is more important than the amount of stress.

You need commitment, control, and challenge.

of beliefs about ourselves and the world," says Salvatore Maddi, Ph.D., professor of social ecology at the University of California, Irvine, and president of the Hardiness Institute. He calls these sets the three C's—commitment, control, and challenge. If you've got the three C's, chances are you are going to be a lot healthier than someone who doesn't, he says—regardless of whether you work on Wall Street or Sesame Street.

Commitment, according to Dr. Maddi, refers to the ability to find something to provoke your interest and curiosity in whatever you're doing. People with commitment are good at getting involved, and they find their activities interesting. People who lack commitment are alienated and bored. They hang back and say, "I don't want to get involved."

Control, says Dr. Maddi, is a gut feeling that your life's course is determined by you—not by your boss, your spouse, or anyone else. People who lack this sense of control often feel like victims of circumstance.

See everything in life as a learning experience.

Challenge rests on the belief that human life is all about growth through learning. If events are painful, a challenge-oriented person will see them as opportunities to grow despite the pain. People who shun challenge see the world as a threatening place. They say, "Comfort and security is what it's all about."

■ *Keep Your Life Out of the Fast Lane*

Those in the fast lane need to remind themselves to take it slow on a regular basis, according to Meyer Friedman, M.D., a San Francisco cardiologist and an expert on Type-A personalities. Announce to your spouse and friends that you intend to turn over a new leaf and whip your Type-A behavior patterns. To help adjust your attitude, Dr. Friedman suggests you practice smiling at other people and laughing at yourself. Also, play to lose, at least some of the time.

When something angers you, immediately make a note of it. Review the list at the end of each week and decide objectively which items truly merited your level of anger.

419

Smile at others, laugh at yourself.

Keep tabs on what gets your goat.

■ Go Dig a Hole

Sun Bear is medicine chief of the Bear Tribe Medicine Society, a frequent lecturer on traditional North American Indian healing, and the author of several books, including *Sun Bear: The Path of Power*. When people ask him how to heal the spirit, he often suggests digging a hole.

"Go out into the land and dig a hole in the ground. Speak into the hole, say everything you feel bad about in life—all the things your ex-husband, or boyfriend, or father and mother did to you. Everything. Then fill the hole with dirt and say good-bye to those things forever. Before you do, however, throw in a pinecone or an acorn, so that some good grows out of it. Your bad feelings will serve as fertilizer, compost for the Earth Mother."

Literally bury your troubles.

Lourdes: Cures Medicine Can't Explain

It all began more than 130 years ago when a young French peasant girl reported that a "lady from heaven" appeared before her in the foothills of the Great Pyrenees just outside the town of Lourdes. Reports of their conversation, and an investigation by the Catholic church, led many to believe that the child, Bernadette Soubirous, had met the Mother of Christ.

Though the child said no words were ever spoken about healing the sick, people started flocking to the site of the visitation to pray in the grotto and bathe in the water in the hope that their thoughts would be heard and a cure would be bestowed from the Lady of Lourdes. Stories of miracles and cures raged for years, stories so intriguing that both the medical community and the church eventually stepped in to examine the claims.

Is it possible, they pondered and probed, that thoughts and desires of hope for a hopeless cause could be so powerful that they could result in a miracle?

It just may be possible—especially when you consider a report in the *Journal of the Royal Society of Medicine* detailing the exhaustive trial and scrutiny that went into examining each claim. Of more than 1,300 claims of miraculous cures since 1947, a tribunal of medical officials has decreed that 27 of them cannot be explained by medical science. Since 1858, some 6,000 people have claimed cures, and the Catholic Church has recognized 64 of them as miraculous. While the medical tribunal will not go so far as to call them miracles, they do say they are "medically inexplicable."

"The declaration by the International Medical Committee of Lourdes that it considers a cure to be medically inexplicable does not make it a miracle, because that is a matter for the Church, not doctors," reports the journal.

What makes a cure medically inexplicable? Today, to uphold the claim, a person must be examined before and after a visit to the Grotto. The committee, which is made up of 25 medical officials, must conclude that the disease was serious and beyond a state in which it could respond to any treatment before a visit to Lourdes, and that all traces of the disease were completely gone for at least three years after the visit. The examination must pass 18 stages of investigation before the cure can be proclaimed medically unexplainable.

According to the journal, few claims survive the exhaustive scrutiny of these doctors. Just one missing document can make a claim invalid. Since 1954, 17 cures have been declared unexplainable by the medical tribunal. Of these, 13 have been declared miracles by the Catholic Church.

According to the medical journal, the most recent miracle took place in 1976 and involved a gravely ill 12-year-old Sicilian girl with a malignant bone tumor that necessitated amputating her leg. The people in her town collected money to send her to Lourdes, where she spent four days in August praying at the Grotto and bathing in the water. She returned home deathly ill and was confined to bed. She grew worse and her mother prepared for her funeral. "Nonetheless, the villagers continued to pray to Our Lady of Lourdes for her cure, and her mother regularly gave her Lourdes water," reports the journal. "Shortly before Christmas she suddenly said that she wanted to get up and go out." Later X-rays revealed the bone had returned to normal. Four years later, the child was strong and disease-free, and the cure was declared "scientifically inexplicable."

Each year, some 65,000 sick and dying people are among the four million who make the pilgrimage to Lourdes. A 1,500-bed hospital was erected near the site to care for the most needy. ■

422

Pictures of Health

"I saw my lymphoma as gray puddles, and the sun would come up and dry up the puddles," says Debby Franke Ogg, in describing how she used mental imagery to overcome her lymphoma. "Or, as I became more enraged with it all, I would see myself with an axe, chopping the lymphoma to bits and pieces."

The theater of the mind can indeed be a real savior of the body—at least in certain instances, say the growing number of doctors who use imagery as a tool to fight everything from headaches to cancer.

Imagery is a successful disease fighter.

One such doctor is Errol R. Korn, M.D., a San Diego County, California, practitioner who counsels many of his patients in imagery techniques. "I think imagery is the most important thing for determining health," he says. "If you know what a person's images are, you know whether a person is healthy."

Imagery, say some doctors, can work wonders in both relaxing us and giving us the positive attitudes necessary for good health. And imagery has also been shown to change body chemistry and control bodily functions that we normally think of as being beyond our control.

Imagery can change body chemistry.

There are certain symptoms and illnesses that seem to be more responsive to imagery than others, notes Martin L. Rossman, M.D., author of *Healing Yourself*. These include headaches, neck and back pain, "nervous stomach," spastic colon, allergies, palpitations, dizziness, fatigue, and anxiety.

Other generally more serious health problems such as cancer, heart disease, arthritis,

423

and neurological illness "are often complicated by or themselves cause stress, anxiety, and depression. The emotional aspects of any illness can often be helped through imagery, and relieving the emotional distress may in turn encourage physical healing," says Dr. Rossman. He emphasizes, however, that good medical care for serious health problems is essential and "perfectly compatible with imagery."

But, notes Dr. Korn, imagery is not a technique you should use only when you're sick. "The time to learn imagery techniques is not once you're sick or dying," he says. "The time is now."

Use imagery to stop disease.

■ *Get in Touch with Your Senses*

Dr. Korn explains that imagery is visualization (seeing something in your mind's eye), but it also may, and in fact *should*, involve feeling, tasting, hearing, and smelling—using all the senses of imagination. "Which type of imagery would be most successful? That depends on the person using it. Some people find it impossible to visualize something, but they can hear or taste it," he says.

Imagery should use *all* of your senses.

Try, for example, the following lemon trick.

Involve the senses for better "vision."

Imagine picking up a big, fresh lemon. Imagine slicing it in half and squeezing the juice into a glass. Visualize a few bits of pulp falling into the yellowish juice. Imagine the smell of the juice as you raise the glass to your lips. Now take a mouthful and let it swish around in your mouth.

424

Are you salivating? If so, you now see how imagery can work.

■ Form a Picture in Your Mind

Patrick Fanning, author of *Visualization for Change,* suggests you begin to practice imagery by lying down, closing your eyes, and relaxing. The next steps call for using all your senses to see what you want to see. If you want to see an apple, for example, you should also imagine its feel, its taste, and the sound it makes as you bite into it.

Gaining the ability to make images appear real will take time and patience, says Fanning. But with practice, you can perfect it to an art form. In his book, he gives many examples of the kinds of imagery that might prove helpful for various conditions.

Form your own healing image.

If you have heartburn caused by acid reflux, imagine a strong, industrial-strength valve at the top of your stomach. Imagine yourself shutting off the valve firmly to keep the burning juices down where they belong. Visualize other little valves that dispense acid into your stomach. Close them all off tightly.

Watch your heartburn go away.

If you suffer from hemorrhoids, visualize the blue, bulging veins shrinking back to normal size. See the blood flowing smoothly and evenly.

If you have a skin condition, such as dermatitis, eczema, or acne, picture sores drying up like mud puddles. Watch your skin change from red to a healthy, normal color.

Books and tapes on imagery can be useful in developing a visualization program. But Dr.

Korn stresses that personal, one-on-one instruction by an expert is most likely to produce the exact healing image that's right for you.

The Hypnotic Zone

Hypnosis is a mysterious mind game where strange and wonderful things can happen—if you let them. Under hypnosis, you may be able to visit your dentist and, without a drop of novocaine, feel not the slightest twinge of discomfort while he drills away. If you suffer from allergies, hypnosis might help you relieve them. The same goes for migraines, high blood pressure, ulcers, and the myriad symptoms of stress. You might even be able to give your immune system a boost in fighting off infections like colds and the flu.

Hypnosis can relieve pain.

Under hypnosis, you might finally be able to rise above your fear of heights, quit smoking, lose 10 pounds or 100. Or perhaps you'd like delving into your psyche, reliving childhood experiences in vivid detail, or gleaning lessons from your dreams. You might even use it to improve your self-esteem and motivation, learn new things more effectively, and cultivate your creativity.

"The hypnotic state is a natural state of mind that we enter and exit a hundred times a day," says California hypnotherapist Josie Hadley, coauthor of the book *Hypnosis for Change*. "You enter a light trance state, for example, every time you drive down a highway. Your mind wanders. The part of your mind

You enter into a hypnotic state 100 times a day.

(continued on page 429)

Quantum Healing: Ancient Practice Renewed

A rabbit noses its way through the tall summer grasses lining the path to the lake, its fur sparkling with a thousand drops of early morning moisture. The sound of a paddle dipped into the water and muffled by mist merits a twitch of ears. And so do the slow, graceful movements of the 50 or so men and women who are silently performing t'ai chi—an ancient Chinese movement meditation—at the water's edge.

Halfway up a hillside overlooking the lake and its surrounding woods, endocrinologist Deepak Chopra, M.D., stands sipping a cup of herb tea in the morning sun. As one of a new generation of doctors who has resurrected the ancient study of mind/body healing, Dr. Chopra has come to this retreat in upstate New York to spend a weekend teaching some of the techniques to the men and women now at the lake.

In just a few hours, he will explain, as he already has in seminars throughout the United States and in a series of books (*Return of the Rishi, Quantum Healing,* and *Perfect Health*) how the twentieth-century Western discovery of neuropeptides—naturally occurring chemical messengers found in the brain—supports the practices of healers in India that go back 5,000 years.

He will explain that, triggered by something as simple as your own thoughts and emotions, neuropeptides can carry messages from the brain to immune system warriors throughout the body—warriors that will then attack bacteria, obliterate viruses, and even massacre cancers.

He will explain that the immune system can make the very same chemical messengers and send them right back to the brain with battlefield reports that will give the brain an opportunity to evaluate the situation and fight back.

And he will explain that this "conversation" between brain and immune system is not held on a private line. The glands of the endocrine system can listen in on the conversation and send messengers of their own—disease-fighting hormones—into the battle.

But, he'll also explain, none of the action will occur on its own. These warriors have to await orders to charge—orders that come from *you*. Or, more specifically, from your mind.

He calls it quantum healing. At the quantum (submolecular) level, your body is not a frozen sculpture of flesh and bone, explains Dr. Chopra. It's actually a dynamic flow of energy that changes from minute to minute. "Your stomach lining is replaced every five days. Your skin is new once a month. You make a new liver every six weeks." Actually, he adds, "You replace 98 percent of yourself once a year."

This constant replication of molecules, cells, and organs is the reason that many scientists now look at the body as a collection of ongoing individual processes rather than as a solid lump of cells.

Dr. Chopra's method of getting the body and mind in touch with each other is through the senses. He explains that the senses provide natural paths—through touch and smell, for example—that your mind can use to kick neuropeptides into action.

Massaging your skin, for example, stimulates and releases a flood of hormones and immune system warriors—including the cancer-fighting interferons and interleukins—that then travel throughout the body to areas that may require healing.

Certain sounds are also able to make the "connections"
(continued)

427

Quantum Healing: Ancient Practice Renewed—*Continued*

by the way they resonate in specific parts of your body. Vibrations can both maintain the health of an organ or, if there's a problem, heal it, says Dr. Chopra.

Dr. Chopra also uses smell—or more specifically, certain scents akin to certain mind/body types—to heal. He explains that any odor you smell goes directly to your brain, where it plugs into smell receptors in the hypothalamus, a small group of cells that are involved in memory, emotion, temperature, appetite, and sexual responsiveness. Scientists aren't quite sure how the odor actually activates these cells, but they do know that the hypothalamus can launch a wide variety of neuropeptides and send them to receptors throughout the body. When these neuropeptides get to their destination, whether in the skin or even the heart, they literally bury themselves in cell walls and attract immune system warriors to the spot.

How successful are such techniques at restoring health? Dr. Chopra is reluctant to quote statistics. Instead, in his seminars and books, he points to individuals in whom he has seen these techniques work: the antenna repairman in Seattle who grew new muscle after his leg was burned by an electrical shock, or the mother of three in California who was able to halt the spread of deadly bone cancer. But restoring health is really only part of the mind/body healing story. The real power of mind over body, says Dr. Chopra, is its ability to *prevent* disease from ever starting.

doing the driving is your subconscious rather than your conscious mind."

Your subconscious mind is home to your habits and patterns, freeing you from having to constantly think about everything you do, Hadley explains. This subconscious state also happens to be extremely responsive to suggestions for change. Hypnosis, then, takes a shortcut to your subconscious and opens the door to healthier ways of being.

■ Gain a Hold on Your Weaknesses

Just how powerful hypnosis may be is a subject of long-standing interest to David Spiegel, M.D., a researcher and associate professor of psychiatry and behavioral sciences at Stanford University Medical Center. Hypnosis appears to affect the brain's processing of information, says Dr. Spiegel, who measured the brain waves of hypnotized subjects who were told that a cardboard box blocked a bright light flashing in front of them. (There actually was no such box.) He discovered suppressed brain wave activity in the occipital cortex, the part of the brain that processes most visual signals, strongly suggesting that the brain was not registering the light. Hypnosis, Dr. Spiegel concludes, has an unusual ability to alter perception, including the perception of pain.

Hypnosis affects how the brain processes information.

Most people experience hypnosis as a kind of intense attention, says psychologist Julie Linden, Ph.D., past president of the Greater Philadelphia Society of Clinical Hypnosis. You can direct this attention toward specific goals, she says—for example, away from your den-

You can feel relaxed in a tense situation.

tist's drill and onto "a very pleasant visual scene in which you're out on a boat in the middle of a lake, enjoying your surroundings and feeling very relaxed."

■ *Desire Must Come from the Heart*

"Motivation is crucial," says psychologist Richard Malter, Ph.D., clinical director of MIND (Malter Institute for Natural Development) in Schaumburg, Illinois. Dr. Malter helps smokers kick the habit in a group hypnosis class. As much as you might say you want to change a habit, he says, deep down you really may not.

"People have psychological blocks that can interfere," he notes, especially when it comes to addictive behaviors like smoking. (But even so, using hypnosis in a private psychotherapy session may get to the root of such blocks, he says.) And for those who truly are motivated, hypnosis exercises like learning to imagine and then turn off the neon sign in your brain that screams "cigarettes!" have helped countless people quit. What's more, Dr. Malter says, many of his students have transferred the benefits of self-mastery to other areas of their lives, from learning to relax during stressful periods to improving their bowling scores.

Beating bad habits is like weeding—you want to go for the roots.

Some have improved their bowling scores.

■ *Know the Score before You Begin*

Everyone responds to hypnosis differently, says Hadley, and it doesn't work for everyone. The effects grow on you and are most dramatic after three to six hour-long sessions, she says. If you feel no different after your first couple of sessions, "then hypnosis is not for you." You may also find that the techniques are great for, say, improving your efficiency on your job but useless when it comes to losing weight—or vice versa. This type of variation is perfectly normal, Hadley says.

Also, choose a hypnotist with care, advises Hadley. During an initial appointment, ask where he was trained, whether he belongs to a professional association, how many years he has practiced, and whether he has treated the problem you're there for. Finally, Hadley says, ask yourself how you feel about the person, because "90 percent of the process is how well you connect."

Hypnosis is not for everybody.

■ *You Can Learn to Hypnotize Yourself*

Slowly now: Ten—your eyelids are growing heavy. Nine—your eyes are closing. Eight—your breathing is slow and deep. Seven—your heartbeat is calm and regular. Six—imagine a bundle of warm, relaxing energy slowly pouring through your head, your arms, your chest. Five—feel the energy pour through your stomach and legs and feet. Four—see yourself standing at the top of a long staircase. Three—you are now descending the staircase, step by step. Two—you are aproaching the bottom of the staircase, feeling more and more relaxed. And . . . One—you step off the staircase and come to a comfortable place, a special place, the most peaceful place in the world.

432

Start with a relaxation exercise.

Repeat a suggestion over and over.

Hypnosis is a skill that just about anyone can learn, says Dr. Linden. Start with a relaxation exercise, such as the one we just described, stated in a soothing voice. (You might want to consider recording your own personal tape.) Then add "suggestions" designed to guide your imagination to make the changes you desire. Suggestions should be concise, positive, and believable, says Hadley. Repeat them for maximum effectiveness.

One suggestion for weight loss, for example, might be: "You are enjoying a healthy meal of fresh, delicious vegetables and fruits. You eat modest portions and then stop, and feel fine. You are totally satisfied, totally satisfied."

A suggestion to help improve your self-esteem could state: "Imagine yourself talking to your co-workers. See yourself as confident, capable, and talented. You are kind to yourself, and you no longer have time for negative thoughts or feelings. You fill your mind with positive ideas and productive goals. You look at life as an adventure."

Conclude your session by slowly counting from one to ten while interjecting that when you awaken, you will feel as if you have had a long rest. At "ten," open your eyes.

Something that may surprise and perhaps even relieve those new to hypnosis: You will be aware of everything that happens throughout the process (and be able to remember it afterward). "At the very same time that you are the participant, you are also observing the process," says Dr. Linden. "You find yourself following the suggestions but not in a willful, conscious way."

You can also choose at any point to follow

It's a well-known fact that married men live longer than bachelors. In celebration of whatever it is about marriage that makes it good for our health, the first puzzle below asks you to find nine terms related to weddings. The second one is just for fun.

Here Comes the Bride

Each of the following three sets of letters has been made up of the names of three items relating to weddings. You don't see them because the letters have been dropped in haphazardly. Unscramble the letters to find the three words or phrases in each of the three sets. All the letters are used in their proper order.

B B O R U V I Q D U E E E S T M A I I D L

G R H I O R N N E O G Y O M O M O N

M F L O W E T D H O E W R E D I I N N R G L G M A A I W R R C L H

Simple Math

Okay, math buffs, this one's for you. Rearrange these matchsticks, by moving only *two,* to make a correct equation. (There may be several solutions.)

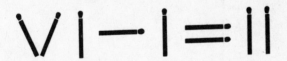

To find the answers, see Solution #15 on page 458.

434

or ignore suggestions, a factor that makes two things clear: You're ultimately in charge, and hypnosis is no magical solution to all your problems.

What hypnosis should do for you is make you feel relaxed and refreshed—and on the way to changing your life. ────■

CHAPTER

17

Maturity

Ideas for Lifelong Wisdom

You know maturity when you see it, but explaining it—that's tough. Even those who have given the matter years of thought have a hard time squeezing a definition into a few words.

"Maturity is the most important thing we try to assess in deciding whether a certain individual should be hired or promoted," says Lester L. Tobias, Ph.D., a management and consulting psychologist in Westborough, Massachusetts, and author of *Psychological Consulting to Management*. But what is it? A mature person, at the least, "possesses a strong sense of independence, a healthy dose of self-respect, and an ability to deal with life's obstacles," says Dr. Tobias.

The Reverend Mark W. Sahady, pastor of the Antiochian Orthodox Church of St. Mary in Wilkes-Barre, Pennsylvania, is known to his 300 parishioners as a man of insight and clarity. He says mental maturity is built on one's virtues. Among these is

435

436

Maturity is difficult to define.

respect for others, a willingness to give of ourselves, an ability to temper our emotions and desires, and a trusting and loving heart.

Yet another definition comes from David Klimek, Ph.D., a clinical psychologist in private practice in Ann Arbor, Michigan, and the author of several books on life and love, including *Beneath Mate Selection and Marriage*. Maturity, he says, "is becoming all you were meant to be." And what might that be? Dr. Klimek starts his list with clear-thinking, intuitive, creative, intelligent, and peaceful.

Sound familiar? Dr. Klimek's list very closely matches the topics explored in this book! So what better way to conclude than with a discussion of how to tie together all these aspects of brainpower—and hopefully send you on the road to greater mental maturity!

Life Is for Living

One person who has actively combed the globe in search of the true meaning of maturity is Christie W. Kiefer, Ph.D., an associate professor of anthropology in the Human Development and Aging Program at the University of California in San Francisco and author of *The Mantle of Maturity: A History of Ideas about Character Development*. He found the definitions are broad at best. "But if you look at the great world religions and philosophies, they all tend to agree on certain qualities of maturity," he says.

Involvement in life is the number one quality.

What's the first quality on the list? "Involvement in life," says Dr. Kiefer. "Maturity represents a centered person who accepts the world as it is and participates in it fully."

■ Never Cease to Seek Out New Experiences

One person who understands the importance of this credo is Virginia A. Geraci, who at age 50 reentered the 9-to-5 world. She is now a data processor for the Nassau County government in Long Island. It had been 25 years since she worked outside the home—raising *nine* children kept her more than busy! Was it frightening returning to the office at an age when most are looking to retire? "I was terrified," she says. But now she realizes that breaking through that fear was part of maturing.

One woman found the courage to widen her world.

"I was always extremely shy, all through my life," says Geraci. "But going back to work brought out another personality. It was a real turning point in my life! It gave me a whole new outlook!" Geraci says that raising nine children was unquestionably a maturing process, but when the youngest one had grown, it was time for *new* experiences.

■ Don't Pass the Buck

Master Sergeant Michael Branski, a former drill instructor at the U.S. Marine Corps Recruit Depot at Parris Island, South Carolina (now with the Corps public affairs office), says that a primary goal of a Marine's basic training is to instill maturity. How? "We make them

Hup, two, three, four...Y'all aren't kids anymore.

responsible for whatever they've done—good or bad," he says. "A person who possesses maturity realizes that what he does is of his own choosing. He lives with his decisions and doesn't defer blame onto something or someone else. The mature person accepts responsibility."

Maturity means taking responsibility.

■ Do What You Gotta Do

The mature person is also a doer, says M.Sgt. Branski. "If one possesses maturity, one has the ability to do what one is supposed to do, when one is supposed to do it—regardless of circumstances. Being an adult is not always convenient," he says.

Yes, maturity means having the tenacity to do what needs doing—but *not* going about it pig-headedly, adds Dr. Tobias, a partner with the management and consulting group Nordli, Wilson Associates. The mature person "doesn't avoid obstacles or bash his head into them. He deals constructively with them, without over-persisting." In other words, try and try again— then find an alternative!

Deal with obstacles constructively.

■ Edit Your Life Script

One aspect of maturity is having control over your own life, says Dr. Tobias. To have control, you must learn from your past mistakes, he says. "The immature person remains locked into 'unconscious scripts,' doomed to repeat the mistakes of the past, chalking them off to the faults of others or 'bad luck.' The mature person doesn't continue playing the same losing games over and over. He learns what works in life, and what doesn't. He knows that he can 'edit his own life script,' " says Dr. Tobias.

Know what works and what doesn't.

People Needing People

Jim Noble, a 54-year-old country singer from Independence, Missouri, learned about maturity through the school of hard knocks. To him, maturity is "dealing well in relationships. I think that's the basis for everything—that's maturity—you have to get along with people," he says.

Understand the value of relationships.

It's difficult to believe that such "noble" words come from a person who once accosted a man in the hallway of an apartment building, held a knife to his neck, and attempted to steal his wallet. But he did just that, 30 years ago. Instead of the money, however, he got a sentence in the Buchanan County, Missouri, jail.

It wasn't the food, the squeaky bed, or even the lack of freedom that got to Noble. "By far the most painful thing was missing my wife and three sons," he says. He still plays the song he wrote in jail describing that pain. He calls it *A Letter to Daddy.*

Dear Daddy, won't you come home tonight?
I hear Momma crying, but she says she's all
    right
But I know there's something wrong
For she cries all night till dawn
Dear Daddy, won't you come home tonight?

Those words haunt my every dream
Till I feel I could scream
I'm sorry darling, Daddy can't come home
  tonight
For I'm locked here in this cell
I've made my own living hell
I'm sorry darling, Daddy can't come home
  tonight

Find a benefit in a bad experience.

Jim Noble isn't at all happy that he broke the law and went to jail, but he did benefit from the experience. Above all, "I came to realize that I don't walk this world alone," says Noble in a warm and friendly voice. That realization made a big difference not only in the way Noble thinks but also in the way he acts. "Now I treat people with respect. I treat them how *I* want to be treated—gently and quietly," he says.

According to psychologists such as Dr. Klimek, Noble has the right idea when it comes to understanding maturity.

■ *Experience the Meaning of Humility*

Mature people, says Dr. Klimek, tend to be "warm, natural, and accepting. They come across as almost humble, not trying to impress anybody, not critical of other people or of themselves. They have a nice capacity to consider the thoughts and feelings of others. They are easygoing and fun to be with."

Help others.

Mature people also tend to go out of their way to help others, says Father Sahady. Many get involved in programs to feed the hungry, house the homeless, heal the sick, teach the illiterate, or in some other way lend a helping hand to their communities.

■ Be Accepting and Trusting

From the vantage point of someone born almost a century ago, Anna Rothberg says that maturity is a process of learning to accept. "Let me tell you, I've seen a lot of change in my life. But I accept everything that happens. I don't say to younger persons—'How come you do that? *We* never did those things!' No, I don't do that. I listen. I accept," says the 93-year-old children's book writer from Siesta Key, Florida.

Dr. Klimek also talks of acceptance as a mark of maturity. "The pains and hurts from the past have been resolved and integrated in mature people in such a way that they do not harbor resentment toward others. There's a comfort, a peacefulness that they bring to every situation. They don't get rocked very easily by external events," he says.

> Acceptance is a mark of maturity.

But we should point out that mature people, while calm and accepting, are no pushovers. They "definitely are not wimps" says Dr. Klimek. "If you stomp on them, you're going to get hit right back!"

> True adults don't get knocked around.

"Most mature people are not particularly paranoid," says Dr. Klimek. "There's a realistic adjustment to the world. They know that some people can be vicious, but others are not." Mature people, he says, "don't carry around the attitude 'everybody is out to get me.'"

■ Put Humanity on a Pedestal

Regardless of anything else in life, always remember that you are significant. "Accept yourself—warts and all. That's the mature

> Accept yourself— warts and all.

(continued on page 444)

Books That Foster Mature Minds

Thomas Jefferson, scientist, philosopher, architect, inventor, geographer, and third President of the United States, once said, "I cannot live without books."

Books are gateways to the wisdom of the ages, and wisdom is surely a large part of maturity. But whereas all men are created equal (Jefferson actually said it first), all *books* certainly are not. Of the masses of books you have to choose from, which should you read? If maturity is your goal, we have a few suggestions from Tom Adams, Ph.D., a program officer at the National Endowment for the Humanities.

Somewhere on your reading list you might want to include a few selections about youth coming of age. There's a large selection in this genre, but among the best is certainly Mark Twain's *The Adventures of Huckleberry Finn.* You'll find humor, morality, and a strong flavor for mid-America in the days of steam engines and paddleboats as you follow Huck and Jim on a raft down the mighty Mississippi.

For a tale of a boy growing up in another America—the backwood mountains of Virginia during the Great Depression—turn to Russell Baker's *Growing Up.* This Pulitzer prize-winning autobiography by the well-known *New York Times* columnist is easy reading and emotionally appealing.

A book of a much different kind is Thomas Mann's *The Magic Mountain.* It tells of a young man visiting his cousin in a sanitarium high in the Swiss Alps who stays on when the doctor finds a spot on his lung. He and the other patients share their thoughts and feelings inspired by illness and death. It's heavy reading, but it offers a hefty serving of food for thought. Not quite as grave, Virginia Woolf's *To the Lighthouse* "is a great classic, a book that talks about the perspective people have on their lives over many years and how that perspective can change," says Dr. Adams.

Other books look at the stages of life with the eyes of mature experience. *The Memory of Old Jack* by Wendell Berry follows the reflections of a 92-year-old Kentucky farmer on the last day of his life. Travel back in time as he recalls a lifetime of friendships, enemies, courtships, failures, and successes. "It's a lovely, poetic book dealing with a world of changing values," says Dr. Adams. Another lyrical and moving novel is Zora Neale Hurston's *Their Eyes Were Watching God,* a tribute to the priceless quality of life choices freely made.

Also in the category of books that will expand your mind, *Democracy in America,* by Alexis de Tocqueville, examines the fabric of American society. Written in the 1830s, it endures as "a great book for reflecting about our country," says Dr. Adams. For a different look at society, turn to *Twenty Years at Hull-House* by Jane Addams. It's a fascinating account of social conditions in turn-of-the-century Chicago.

This list is but a drop in an ever-expanding ocean of literature. Where should you go from here? Consider the classics—Homer, Shakespeare, Dickens—there's a reason they're classics! As well, "read in as many areas as you can," says Dr. Adams. "History is very important because in a way it introduces you to everything else." But so too should your lifelong reading list include selections from philosophy, religion, politics, literature, poetry, and the natural sciences.

What, you may wonder, was the kind of book that Thomas Jefferson "could not live without"? According to several of his biographers, among the president's favorites was Laurence Sterne's *Tristram Shandy,* a satiric novel that poked fun at the establishment of the day. ━━■

attitude," says Bernard Kligfeld, rabbi to congregations in New York and Arizona for four decades, and currently with Temple Beth Shalom in Sun City, Arizona. "God created every human being as a unique individual," he says. And that includes *you!* A mature person appreciates himself—even when he's failed to get a promotion, can't figure out how to set up the VCR, or flunks his driver's test.

Remembering you are human means acting human—at *all* times—"*even* when others are acting inhuman," says Rabbi Kligfeld. A prime example of this kind of maturity was displayed by those who risked their lives to save others from Hitler's persecution, says Rabbi Kligfeld. "Raoul Wallenberg [the Swedish diplomat who risked his life to save thousands of Hungarian Jews], and those in Holland who sheltered Anne Frank and her family—these are examples of mature people," says the Rabbi.

Be humane in the treatment of others.

■ *Respect the Gifts of Nature*

Mature people not only exhibit respect for other human beings, they show a sensitivity toward all things, says Dr. Tobias. They live in harmony not only with people around them, "but with their ancestors and descendants, as well." Part of maturity, says Dr. Tobias, "is being concerned about the environment that you leave to your children."

Learn to live in harmony with nature.

Father Sahady agrees. "We were given dominion over the earth—but that doesn't mean we have a right to destroy it." The priest tells of a time he was walking in the woods and stooped down to pick up a rock to throw into a creek. A friend asked "Did you ever think that that stone was meant to be where it was?" That's an extreme example, says Father Sahady, "but people and things have a right to be as they are," he says.

Rabbi Kligfeld says that when it comes to worldly problems such as the quality of the environment, the mature person accepts that he alone cannot save the planet, but understands that his role is nonetheless important. "I'm careful about how I use materials, what I do with my waste, and how much freon I release into the atmosphere," says the Rabbi. The mature person "doesn't ignore responsibility just because he can't do the whole thing himself," he says.

Make a contribution to the planet.

Signposts on the Road to Maturity

Just as psychologists and theologians differ in their definitions of maturity, so too does the guy or gal on the street.

If maturity means anything, it's "zest, and your love for people and learning," says author Anna Rothberg.

"The Fishin' Hole" TV host Jerry McKinnis, 53, known to his viewers as something of a wise philosopher in fisherman's khakis, sees maturity as "being cool—having patience."

And Susie Thomas, a six-year-old first grader in Las Vegas, Nevada, who is known to her teachers and neighbors as a "pretty precocious kid," doesn't have a clue what the word

Mature people know how to sit still.

To children, maturity is being grown-up.

maturity means. But she does know the difference between being a child and being a grown-up: "Mommy tells me when to go to bed and what to do and I can't tell her what to do," says Susie.

But from this assortment of opinions about maturity come a few clear directions.

■ Question the Meaning of Life

Jim Noble did more than write songs in jail. He also had time to reflect. Reflection is to maturity what fertilizer is to a garden, says Dr. Tobias. "Sit down, take stock, and genuinely reflect. Most people don't do that. There's always something else to distract you or fill the mind. But to know yourself, it's *essential!*" he says. "If you don't know yourself, then you don't know what's in your best interest—so how can you possibly make mature decisions?"

Know the person you want to be.

Dr. Klimek encourages spending at least one hour a week in quiet time and reflection. Ask yourself " 'What's it all about?' 'What am I working for?' 'What kind of person am I and who do I want to be?' 'What are my goals?' " In short, "take a detailed personal inventory," he says.

■ Keep Your Antennae Up

Ask for feedback.

It's not only of yourself that you must ask questions. Often others can see in us what we cannot see in ourselves. That's why, in order to grow, "we must openly and honestly ask for feedback," says Dr. Tobias. More important, we must take it once we get it! "Accept the feed-back you get as real, or at least as someone's perception. Deal with it—don't just dismiss it."

Who can you ask to tell you about your-self? "Your spouse, parents, siblings, children, teachers, colleagues, friends . . . anyone who knows you," says Dr. Tobias. Aside from what others *tell* you about yourself, pay attention to nonverbal feedback—grimaces, glances, bored looks, and other signals, he says. Also notice the positive gestures people send you, such as feelings of love and concern.

Pay attention to what others tell you.

■ *Set a Pace for Others to Follow*

The difference between maturity and im-maturity is often reflected in one's pace of life, says McKinnis, a director for ESPN television when he's not hosting his fishing show. "When I was in my teens, twenties, early thirties, I was on fire all of the time—physically and mentally. The older I got, the more I started thinking things through, looking more at the whole pic-ture of life," he says.

"Now, I take things in stride. At ESPN it's often a beehive, very stressful, lots of tension, always a deadline. Twenty years ago I would have gotten jumpy. Today, when someone comes barreling at me with something that has to be done yesterday, I simply say 'We can get this going by doing such and such,' and I figure out how it can be done," says McKinnis. "I've found out that everything a person does can be done better if you slow down and do it."

Yes, but what if all around you people are acting like bees in a fire? "In most cases,

Be cool when the heat's turned on you.

How's a Kid to Know He's Grown-Up?

Pity the poor American teenager. Unlike his counterparts in many traditional cultures—where elaborate rites of passage clearly mark the end of childhood and the beginning of adulthood—the American teenager is forced to spend years in pubescent limbo, neither boy nor man, neither girl nor woman.

"Being an adolescent in our society is one of the most confusing phases in life! No wonder we have so much trouble with teenagers. All they're trying to do is establish some sort of identity for themselves," says Melford Weiss, Ph.D., professor of anthropology at California State University in Sacramento and an expert on both ritual processes and adolescence.

In many African and Native American tribes, for instance, older boys are traditionally taken out into the wilderness, where they must prove their manhood with acts of skill and courage. Among the East African Samburu tribe, for example, a boy cannot become a man until he has sacrificed an ox. Following these rites of passage, boys are transformed into men—and their societies then give them all the rights and responsibilities that come with being a man.

But what is the equivalent of sacrificing an ox to a kid growing up in Dallas, Boston, or Philadelphia? "Is it turning 18 and having the right to vote? Does that really make you feel like an adult?" asks Dr. Weiss. "Is it serving in the armed services? Being old enough to consume alcohol? Paying one's own bills?" Or is it graduating from high school, college, or making X-amount of dollars a year?

people will follow your lead. If I'm acting crazy and immature, so will everybody else. If I'm calm and mature, they'll act that way," says McKinnis.

A rite of passage, as exists among the Samburu and other traditional cultures, "solidifies *who* you are, *when* you are, so you know what you have to do and how you are supposed to act," says Dr. Weiss. In contrast, in America and most other industrial societies, "we give children different privileges of adulthood at different ages."

Perhaps the closest thing we have to a ceremonial passing into adulthood is getting a driver's license, says Dr. Weiss. "Most kids recognize this as the transition from dependent child to independent almost-adult. With a car, you can go where you want and do what you want." But even air-conditioned mobility doesn't make for full adulthood in America.

Is there a prescription for the problem of teenage alienation due to years spent in juvenile oblivion? "No," says Dr. Weiss."Our rites of passage into adulthood are connected to too many institutions within our society. When you mess with the definition of adult, you mess with all kinds of related things. You couldn't change the system without a bloody revolution."

So what does Dr. Weiss do to ease the anxiety of *his* adolescent daughters? "I tell them it's tough being a teenager. If it helps, try to remember that a good part of the cacophony and confusion is a product of our culture's lengthy adolescent period, without clear-cut markers to identify the entrance into adulthood. Perhaps you can create your personal marker. In the meantime, just hang loose, be flexible, and adjust to the craziness."

Mature people learn to slow down, but they don't fritter away their lives, adds Rabbi Kligfeld. "A mature person doesn't waste time; he knows that time is precious, so he spends it

Life is more than a game.

450

doing significant, meaningful, and rewarding things."

The Joy of Maturity

Happiness is part of maturity.

There is one aspect of maturity we have not yet mentioned. It is one on which all of our experts and nonexperts agree. We're talking about happiness.

"I don't mean happy-go-lucky or laughing-one's-head-off happiness. But mature people have a peaceful happiness in their soul," says Father Sahady. Dr. Klimek says that mature people, by age 50 or so, "almost always will say, 'Life is better than I ever thought it would be!'" And Dr. Tobias says maturity brings with it "a belief that the world is filled with opportunity."

So, you may ask, does happiness come before maturity, or maturity before happiness? It appears they come together.

■ Develop the Power to Love

Discover the secret of enduring relationships.

In Sun City, where Rabbi Kligfeld lives, residents are on the elderly side. "I often see couples who have been married for 40 or 50 years walking hand in hand," says the Rabbi. Not all of these loving couples are necessarily happy or mature. But developing comfortable loving relationships is part of both, he says.

No (mature) man is an island.

What's the secret to enduring relationships? It's discovering "the power to love," says the Rabbi. "I'm convinced that that's what we're *really* looking for throughout life—even though most of us *think* what we want is to be loved," he says. "The mature person reaches a point where he is in control of himself, and finds that power."

Once you have the power to love others, you can find happiness in love—without the anxiety that often accompanies young love. You needn't wait for others to validate you with their love before you can express your love, says Rabbi Kligfeld.

■ Find What Makes You Thrive

Maturing is "noticing what makes you thrive, and what makes you unhappy, jittery, and nervous—and pursuing those things that make you thrive," says Dr. Kiefer. This may sound like something any sane person would already do, but it's not so. "It takes a tremendous amount of courage to live for yourself and stop living for others' expectations," says Dr. Kiefer. Often we become wrapped up in what others and society in general expect of us.

Live up to your own expectations.

■ Find Someone to Look Up To

Following the road to maturity is a little easier if you have someone to lead the way—a role model, a mentor. "Mentors play a very important role, bringing out the qualities that are valuable, and demonstrating what some of the ideals can be," says Dr. Tobias. An ideal mentor will also provide admiration and faith and will egg you on to be everything you were meant to be.

A mentor will help you achieve your goal.

You may find a mentor at work, in school, in your church, or in your neighborhood. Of course, mentoring is a two-way street. "You can't just pick a mentor and expect to be mentored," says Dr. Tobias. On the other hand, "usually people are willing to be mentors. People want to give back," he says. Keep in mind that a mentor doesn't have to be a person you know. John F. Kennedy is still a mentor to many who never met him.

■ Put Your Money Where It Counts

Society's expectations often lead us to chase material wealth and prestige, sometimes at the expense of things that *really* matter, like family, friends, good health, and making the world a better place, says Dr. Kiefer.

In America, "the most immature and disturbed people are often the most conspicuous," says Dr. Klimek. But the mature person—even the wealthy mature person—tends to be unconcerned with material possessions. This doesn't mean you should go so far as to quit your job to live in a grass shack on some South Pacific island—but you should learn to balance your life. The mature person, says Dr. Klimek, realizes "you only go through this world once."

So make the most of it. ————————■

Mature people are not concerned about material things.

PUZZLE POWER

By now, if you've done the other puzzles throughout this book, your puzzle-solving skills have probably matured. Want to try just a few more? Here are a few quickies.

Time Flies!

Joe said to his friend, "It's really surprising. Yesterday I was 20, but next year I'll be 22." How could Joe make such a statement without lying?

Don't Count on It

Your aged grandmother tells you she was born on February 29, 1900. How old is she as of the date you are doing this puzzle?

Think Fast!

How many common English words can you make from the letters D R I B A? Use all the letters each time.

To find the answers, see Solution #16 on page 458.

Puzzle Power Answers

Solution #1

Solution #2

Mix and Match
CHEESE, FRUIT, and MEAT
APPLES, PEARS, and PLUMS

Say "Cheese"
CHEDDAR, ROQUEFORT, and LIMBURGER

Solution #3
Total Recall

Solution #4
"Plane" Numbers

```
   757
   757
 +  45
 ────
  1559
```

Three Spring Chicks

April is 6, May is 9, and June is 20.

Solution #5
The Right Direction

If you have good geographical knowledge, you found the word "CORRECT" after crossing out letters.

Race Pace

Jim was last. Just set up a chart of the runners.

"Buy" the Letter

A mango costs 15 cents. The logic is 3 cents per letter.

Solution #6
Fail, Pass
FAIL
PAIL
PALL
PALS
PASS
There are several variations of this pattern.
Brainteaser
BRAIN

Solution #7
The Straight and Arrow

The idea here is to go out of the square's boundaries. Most people don't think to do so, even though staying within the square was not mentioned as part of the restrictions of the puzzle.

Find the Key Clue

A key *is* the clue. Many people view the problem as one of reach, but it is actually a problem of getting the strings together. If you tie a key ring or other object to one string and set it swinging, you can grab it while still holding the other string.

Solution #8
The Missing Link
Z is the missing letter; the words are (clockwise from the top) WOOZY, GLAZE, LAZED, HAZEL, BRAZE, RAZES, DOZEN, and ZONED.

Solution #9
A Stone's Throw
People who live in grass houses shouldn't stow thrones.
Help Wanted
"Needs" and "dense" are the missing words.

Solution #10
Wise to the Word
She said, "No." Furthermore, you know she is a liar and her companion is a truthteller. If they were both liars, both truthtellers, or she was a truthteller and her companion a liar, she would have answered, "Yes"—and you wouldn't have known whether she was lying.
Match Points

Solution #11
Don't Surrender
ATTACK AT DAWN MONDAY. (The lieutenant read the first letter of each word.)
Pile of Money
There were half a dozen different ways to make this move. The most common was
POOR
POOL
POLL
POLE
PILE
RILE
RICE
RICH

Solution #12
Not Too Difficult
Two boxes—A and D—cannot be made from the unfolded boxes.

Solution #13
Not-So-Sweet Dreams
The watchman had been sleeping on the job. Otherwise, he wouldn't have been dreaming.
Count Your Luck
Seven of each coin.

Solution #14
Opposites Detract
Cubes A and C cannot be made. This is a good test of your structural visualization skills.

Solution #15
Here Comes the Bride
BOUQUET, BRIDESMAID, and VEIL
GROOM, RING, and HONEYMOON
MOTHER-IN-LAW, FLOWER GIRL, and
WEDDING MARCH
Simple Math

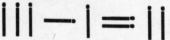

Solution #16
Time Flies!
Joe was speaking on December 31, his birthday. He was 20 on December 30, turned 21 on December 31, and will be 22 next year on December 31. This puzzle was tested on a 90-year-old woman neighbor, who saw it immediately.
Don't Count on It
Your aged grandmother is pulling your leg. Nineteen hundred was not a leap year under the Gregorian calendar, since it was not divisible by 400. But the year 2000 will be.
Think Fast!
BRAID and RABID are the only two commonly accepted anagrams.

Index

Note: Page references in *italic* indicate boxes. **Boldface** references indicate tables.

A